outrageous fortune

outrageous fortune

the life
and times
of the new
american
play

todd london
with **ben pesner**
and zannie giraud voss

Published by Theatre Development Fund
520 8th Avenue
Suite 801
New York, NY 10018

Design by Victor Mingovits

ISBN-13: 978-098431090-6
ISBN-10: 098431090-8

10 9 8 7 6 5

When Theatre Development Fund was founded in 1968, the serious new play on Broadway was in jeopardy. John Booth, one of TDF's founders and its first president, said that a primary motivation for the Fund was the realization that rising costs had caused producers to become risk-averse, stating in the announcement article: "We cannot permit the worthy play to become extinct." That conviction has been in the organization's DNA from that point on.

John Booth's passion for the American play and playwright never dimmed. He stayed an active trustee at TDF from 1968 until his move to New Mexico in 2003. As the twentieth century drew to a close, he challenged TDF to undertake a study of the American playwright to determine how TDF and others could "be most helpful in facilitating and encouraging the work of promising playwrights and the performance of their works." You are holding the result of that challenge. His early memos about the project were written in 1999. A decade later, the project is finished. We hope he would be pleased.

CONTENTS

ACKNOWLEDGMENTS

PROJECT TEAM:
Todd London, Project Director and Writer
Ben Pesner, Writer
Zannie Giraud Voss, Research Director
Victoria Abrash, Roundtable Coordinator

THEATRE DEVELOPMENT FUND
PLAYWRIGHTS PROJECT COMMITTEE
(committee dates of service indicated)
John Booth, Chair: 2001–2008
Gene Gill: 2002-2009, Chair: 2007–2009
William Baumol: 2001–2009
T. Edward Hambleton: 2001–2005
William Riordan: 2001–2009
Geraldine Stutz: 2002–2005
Edwin Wilson: 2001–2009

SPECIAL THANKS TO:
Gigi Bolt, John Breglio, Liz Engelman, Teresa Eyring, Susan Feder,
David Holbrook, Marc Masterson, Diane Ragsdale, Emily Ruddock,
James Still, Stephen Tepper, Katie Turick, Tamsen Wolff, Celia Wren

AND TO OUR HOSTS AROUND THE COUNTRY:
League of Chicago Theatres, Chicago
New Dramatists, New York
Sundance Institute Theatre Program, Los Angeles
Theatre Bay Area, San Francisco
The Playwrights' Center, Minneapolis

Introduction

BY VICTORIA BAILEY,
Executive Director, Theatre Development Fund

I am a lucky person. I have been able to earn a living working in the theatre, something I decided I wanted while a teenager. Having come of age in the theatre in the mid-seventies, I witnessed the growth and maturation of the not-for-profit theatre. The field was still young when I started; theatres were blossoming and the possibilities seemed infinite, at least to me. I spent twenty years at the Manhattan Theatre Club; we produced over 150 new American plays while I was there. I met hundreds of artists and other professionals. Because I was in New York, I also learned all about the commercial theatre, and came to respect those who stake their own personal resources on a project in the hope that it will provide a long and lucrative opportunity for its artists.

In 2001 I came to Theatre Development Fund, an organization whose belief that theatre has to be nurtured and that strengthening audiences is a large part of how to do that resonated with me. I was released from the pressures attendant to producing plays day in and day out. I stopped having to worry about next week's audience and next year's subscribers and got to think about how to build audiences, how to get a casual theatregoer to become a more regular attendee. I thought that I would be leaving the world of new plays, and discovered that one of the first things waiting for me was the yet-to-be-formed Playwrights Project, that is, *this* project.

What I have seen and learned through the process of this study is complex, revelatory and, in many cases, disturbing TDF is rooted in research and this study is no different. It flows from careful research, both quantitative and qualitative. The work was exhaustive, occasionally exhausting, and comprehensive. We surveyed and analyzed; we held conversations in communities across the country. We spoke with writers and artistic directors and new-play "mavens." Of course, it was important to us that we talk to as many players as possible.

As we talked and traveled, it was clear to us that the new play does appear on stages all over the country. But it was also clear that the ecosystem in which the new play is produced is not healthy. Playwrights cannot make a living from their plays. Artistic directors are deeply troubled as they work to navigate the marketing and funding pressures facing their theatres. The lines of demarcation between the not-for-profit and commercial theatre are increasingly blurred.

Much in this report may be painful to read; none of us— playwrights, artistic directors, managing directors, trustees, funders, producers, and observers—come away scot free. Please don't embrace or reject any one part of it; read it all, and then respond. A guiding principle to this work was that it be comprehensive and look at the whole ecology of new-play production. There is no executive summary; the study blends together the statistical analysis, the reporting, the interviews, and the conversations from the field.

One of the clearest messages I've received throughout the course of this study is that language is failing us. Writers and those who produce their plays are not talking honestly with each other. Nor are they speaking honestly with their audiences or with funders. None of us are listening to the entire story, but rather only the piece we like, the part that confirms what we already believe.

We must learn to speak together and to listen. This experiment, the not-for-profit theatre in America, is not yet a success. Despite our best efforts, audiences are declining. The phrases "theatre" and "culturally irrelevant" can be used in the same sentence. We think many of the reasons for that—and some of the antidotes for it—lie in this study. Read and then let's talk.

How This Study Was Conducted

BY ZANNIE GIRAUD VOSS

The quantitative analyses reported on in this book are the result of several data collection efforts launched by Theatre Development Fund (TDF). There were two waves of surveys to theatres. The first was sent to a random sample of Theatre Communications Group members in 2003, and the second, launched in 2005, was administered to a selection of theatres that regularly produce new works. In total, we received ninety-four usable theatre surveys. Playwrights were identified through a variety of connections aimed at identifying working professional playwrights at all stages of their careers. As the theatre sampling tilts toward theatres dedicated to new-play production, so the playwright sampling favors playwrights who have successfully gained entrée to the field. These include graduates of college- or university-based playwriting programs; members of writers' collectives and labs; fellowship and grant recipients; writers featured in new work festivals, competitions, and commissioning programs; playwrights whose scripts have been produced; and prize and award recipients. In total, 340 playwright surveys were sent and 250 usable surveys were returned, for a 73.5 percent response rate. In the case of both theatre and playwright surveys, not every respondent provided an answer to every question.

Unless indicated otherwise, the reported average is the statistical mean of the responses. When there is mention made of a mean response by some subset of participants that is "significantly different" than that of others, it shows that statistical tests of significance indicate that we can be 99 percent sure that the differences did not occur simply by chance. Some sections of the report reference various factors (e.g., age) increasing the likelihood of certain results or phenomena (e.g., academic training as a playwright). In this case, we employed standard regression analysis.

To flesh out and garner insights into the survey findings, TDF organized a series of roundtables with playwrights and theatre leaders. In total, thirty-one playwrights provided insights during four gatherings in three cities; six groups involving forty-one artistic leaders met to exchange ideas in four cities; eight new-play development mavens and three playwright educators contributed reactions and advice in New York. In addition to the group discussions, fifteen leading professional producers, agents, playwrights, educators, and artistic directors gave in-depth interviews that enriched our understanding of the findings and their resonance in the field. Discussions were free-flowing, using statistical findings as a jumping-off point. These conversations were moderated by project director Todd London, who posed general questions raised by both the data and previous groups. In this way, field discussions elaborated each other, covering similar ground and tackling different aspects of the study. Interviews lasted approximately 1.5 hours; focus groups averaged 3.5 hours. They were recorded and transcribed to ensure accuracy and facilitate interpretation.

ONE

Dialogue in the Dark:
Playwrights & Theatres

THINK ABOUT the relationship between playwrights and
theatres, and images will spring to mind: Chekhov, surrounded
by the actors of the Moscow Art Theatre, reads his play to them.
Molière, starring in his own work, gets carried from stage to
deathbed by his company—his literal and figurative family—for
whom he writes and with whom he brings his comedies to life.
A wharf in Provincetown, fog sifting in and water lapping at the
floorboards—Eugene O'Neill's first sea play is being performed
by the band of passionate amateurs who discovered him. Or
think about Brecht directing his own play with the Berliner
Ensemble; Caryl Churchill discovering hers through research
and improvisation with the Joint Stock Theatre; or August
Wilson traversing a country and a century in step with not one
theatre, but many, partners in ambition, vision, song. And then
there's Shakespeare, looming over all of them, a player among
players on the banks of the Thames, at home in his Globe.

In the United States today, it's hard to find examples like
these: Theatres defined by the voice and vision of a particular
playwright or group of playwrights. Except in relatively small
ensemble-based theatres, playwrights are no longer embraced by
companies the way, for example, the Group Theatre embraced
Clifford Odets. Moreover, as our professional theatres have
expanded and created sustainable institutions, the playwriting life
(and living) has remained unsustainable. This is what playwrights

see: Houses for the art, bigger and more beautiful than before, but few homes for artists. There are more and more stages, but, despite the organizational energy that goes into building them, playwrights will tell you that, when it comes to filling them, a bland sameness covers the land.

The artistic leaders of these theatres *have a different* outlook, a different set of concerns. They worry about aging and shrinking audiences, a cultural and critical climate that is unwelcoming, if not hostile, to new plays and artistic ambition. Many claim to be hungry for new work of quality, while arguing that there's a dearth of it. Some profess a commitment to writers and decry a lack of commitment by writers to the theatres. Again and again, the heads of theatres fault playwrights for a lack of interest in, or knowledge of, the audience.

This study describes a collaboration in crisis. Our report locates that crisis not in individual writers, artistic directors, or producers, but in a *system of theatrical production* that has become increasingly alienating to individual artists and inhospitable to the cultivation of new work for the stage, despite an apparent dedication to it. In a field defined by collaboration, the conversation between theatres and playwrights has grown discordant, inauthentic. Playwrights and artistic directors, viewing the same picture from opposing angles, ultimately don't see the same picture at all.

Of all the findings in this study, the divide between playwrights and theatres is the most profound and troubling of all. This divide serves as the background for the rest of the report. It is our hope that, by recording this divided scene, we can help bridge it.

This report is an attempt to document and understand the ecosystem of new-play production nationwide—through surveys, statistical findings, national conversations, and individual interviews. It's a snapshot of the field. It is intended to encourage the excited growth and production of new plays. Its urgency derives from a fear that the channels by which plays of quality get to the stage have become increasingly blocked, and that talented playwrights might be leaving the theatre in large numbers. It is rooted in the belief that works of merit don't emerge without a cultivation of the field in general—that more plays, more productions, and more attempts cut paths for better plays, better productions, and more ambitions and fruitful attempts. There are numerous ways to create work for the stage—director-led, ensemble-created, improvised, etc.—but this study is frankly playwright-centered. We look at plays that are written and how they do or don't get produced. In the final chapter, we identify creative solutions and novel ideas already being tried to improve the current climate. We hope that these practices will point the way to others.

The World According to Playwrights

THE ARTIST AND THE INSTITUTION

For playwrights, the not-for-profit theatre *is* the theatre. Over the past three decades, the nonprofits have become the generating center of new-play development and production. Broadway, the traditional center has, as we'll discuss shortly, ceded that ground. Among artists known for their isolation and individualism, it is surprising to find something close to unanimity in how playwrights view their collaboration with the nonprofit theatre. This is how they describe it: The playwright-producer relationship, by nature an intimate, invested, idiosyncratic partnership, has become, in most cases, a mechanistic process driven less by creative collusion and mutual artistic excitement than by such institutional concerns as marketing, box office, and fundraising. Where playwrights believe risk should be a guiding principle, risk-aversion rules the day. Where lasting relationships between theatres or producers and playwrights were once seen as key to success, such loyalty now seems rare, unprized. Bodies of work go unsupported, while theatres vie for a handful of plays that have already proven themselves in New York or at other prominent theatres.

Almost without exception, playwrights describe today's not-for-profit theatre as "corporate." Playwrights use the word to highlight numerous systemic diseases. The first of these is a kind of passionless group decision-making. They suspect that too few artistic directors are choosing plays from personal vision and passion, as they claim to do (artistic directors speak of falling in love with a play). Most playwrights think that theatre suffers from what one writer calls "the corporatization of decision making."

> In theatres, people are afraid to be the one to say, "This play is worthy and we're going to do it," and "I'm going to put my neck on the line for this play, and if it bombs at the box office, then I'm going to be the one who's responsible for its bombing." When a theatre decides to do the hot play by the hot new playwright, no one is responsible because that person has been anointed. But if somebody decides to do a new play by someone who's not the hot new playwright, the person who really pushes for that, it's their ass on the line. If it fails, they're going to be the one who takes it from the board, or from the rest of the artistic staff.

Regardless of mission or not-for-profit status, theatres—according to playwrights—practice bottom-line thinking. A prominent musical librettist tells the story of being produced at a large New York nonprofit, where creative teams make regular visits to Board meetings:

> They were asking about what the production is like. The last comment came from a woman who is quite an adventurous supporter of the theatre. She said, "We certainly hope it's gonna be a hit." And there was laughter all around the table. And I thought, whatever they will tell you, their first obligation is to the bottom line. Whatever the mission statement is of the theatre, the first obligation

is to make money, and if you're making money, then
everything's okay.

Surely, this comment was intended as a joke, but, as the
playwright indicates, it was a revealing one. This complaint
echoes throughout meetings with playwrights; many see no
solution. "You can't have an artistic system be corporate, because
all the corporation is about is making money. The current
system neither makes money nor produces good art, so we're in
a terrible bind. I don't see the way out of it."

Truly, something that has been creeping in for a long
time—nonprofit artistic directors, like Arena Stage's eloquent
founder Zelda Fichandler, began questioning the deleterious
effect of institutionalization on art as far back as the 1960s—has
taken firm hold. The corporate has become pervasive, until the
theatre as it is hardly resembles the theatre playwrights imagine
for themselves. "Institutions have gotten so top-heavy," says one
writer with a string of awards for work on and off Broadway.
"They're like movie studios now. There are all these people
who have to justify their salaries. The money's not going into
production." Another playwright frames it differently, but comes
to the same conclusion: "'Where are all the good new plays?' is
something one hears all the time. That question is coming from
a theatre that needs to fill seats at between thirty and fifty dollars
a pop, which demands a certain kind of play. It's a theatre that
has a very large budget for that play, which demands a certain
kind of return. It's entirely analogous to Hollywood."

When the *New York Times* ran an "Arts and Leisure"
feature in March 2008 celebrating the new building boom
among theatres in Minneapolis, Philadelphia, Washington,
D.C., and elsewhere, it was without comment from playwrights,
for whom such a boom has, historically, led to artistic bust, as
theatres with growing overhead have been, in their eyes, forced
to play it safe to meet their capital expenses. Indeed, for many,
real estate often turns artistic organizations into corporate ones.
"What we're seeing is not a problem with people's appetite for

theatre," says one such writer. "It's a problem with real estate-based theatre. The solution is a matter of funding the people or the artists, rather than sustaining the structures."

The terminology of this overarching criticism from writers remains the same, regardless of where they live. It is applied by playwrights at every level of career, from the earliest aspirants to the most established and recognized writers in the field. In several private interviews, the artistic directors themselves even employed it. For example, the artistic director of a major New York City theatre, an acknowledged leader in the development of new plays, pointed to these structures as the prohibitive factor in the growth and aesthetic breadth of the field:

> We have a fantastic crop of people who are interested in writing new theatre. You've got a theatre world where John Guare has been continuously writing since he was a young man in the 1960s, and that's one side of the spectrum, and at the same time you have writers in their twenties who are really exciting. That part of it is in great shape. The negative part is in a way the corporate, which is the institutionalized and systematized structures for new plays, which in some cases are strangling the range of those plays.

What does this mean for the growth of the field as a whole? How hospitable is this theatre for the new? And without a healthy environment for new plays and voices how will our theatre grow and thrive?

WHERE HAVE ALL THE LEADERS GONE?

> *These artistic directors, and we know most of them, they are brave, bold, funny people, and they are doing boring, dementedly old-fashioned things.* —PLAYWRIGHT

To hear playwrights talk, there is currently a profound lack of leadership in the American theatre. Where vision is required, there is conservatism; where there should be boldness, there is cautious pragmatism; where there could be adventurous engagement with new kinds of writing, there is timid protection of the status quo. Some writers, as we've seen, blame the system, and many blame the people at the helms of the theatres themselves. "Very few artistic directors are great producers," suggests a playwright who has worked at major theatres across the country. "They usually are directors who basically want to direct. I'm talking about artistic directors with vision. I don't know where they are, and I wish there was something to help that."

In fact, the subtext of most playwrights' critique of the artistic leadership of nonprofit theatres holds that "artistic director" is, more often than not, a misnomer, that the theatres' leaders have stopped functioning as artists at all. "Taking the flying leap, which is what we do as artists, is what I expect from artistic directors, and don't get very often."

With a vision vacuum at the top, theatres have become mechanized, writers generally believe, bringing a one-size-fits-all attitude to the work of production. As a result, the special and personal engagement between producers and plays is becoming a thing of the past. Plays, these writers contend, are unique creatures. Each requires its own kind of development, design process, and rehearsal process; each has its own audience. "People don't know how to produce," one playwright, also an artistic director, asserts. "A lot of institutional theatres have no idea how. Nothing is special to them, so therefore, everything is the same, everything is produced the same way, which it can't be."

JOSEPH PAPP

When asked about positive examples of artistic leadership, playwrights turn with great regularity to the past. One man towers over all such conversations, as well as being consistently singled out as a champion by playwrights of color: Joseph Papp. Papp founded the New York Shakespeare Festival/Public Theater in the 1950s and led it until his death in 1991. He still embodies for many the brave, devotional, idiosyncrasy required of the creative producer.

Despite—or perhaps because of—his charismatic but chaotic approach to new work, Papp looms large in the memory of many writers and theatre leaders. "Aesthetically, Papp had an incredibly wide range of interests, and many artists came into his focus—sometimes briefly and sometimes for a longer time," says Lincoln Center Theater's Anne Cattaneo. "When he met you, his enthusiasm was instantaneous, and he often kept his promises: to produce an unwritten play by an actor, to find a large grant for a fledgling translator. Papp's commitment could lift an artist from obscurity into the public eye." Next came a long-term commitment to producing a writer's work. "When I began writing my plays," recalls Tina Howe, "Joe Papp read the first one and said, 'I want to do it, and after that I'll do anything you write.'" Papp similarly told the then-twenty-three-year-old playwright David Henry Hwang, "I'll do anything that you write," Hwang says. He produced five of Hwang's plays in the next three years.

Writers claim that Papp's style of institutional leadership and loyalty to individual writers has all but disappeared from the theatrical movement he helped create, having been replaced by a more corporate management ethos. "Joe Papp wanted to do something, he did it," playwright/performer Laurie Carlos says. "He didn't ask twenty-five people, 'Is this okay, do you like this person?...' He didn't even have to know you. He didn't have to approve of you. If he saw something and it sparked, he'd do it. Period."

Moreover, something of Papp's style flew in the face of today's chilly professionalism and the tendency toward the corporate. Unlike most theatre managers, Papp was willing to "take the leap into something that didn't necessarily make sense," says Hwang.

There was a wonderful un-professionalism that is sometimes really useful to stimulating a creative atmosphere. Things have gotten so professional now, both in terms of the financial structure of the theatre in New York, the top-down pressure that the success of the commercial theatre has imposed on other New York theatres, and also in terms of play development and the sort of growth of the dramaturgical industry. There was something slapdash about the whole process, which created a lot of bad work, and also allowed for a lot of good work. I miss that.

He also shepherded plays directly into production. "There was no reading or workshopping," explain Howe. "It was just bang, you went into rehearsal, and in rehearsal and previews you figured out what the problems were."

Papp's approach had its pitfalls. "This honeymoon proved to be short lived," Howe continues. "He turned down my biggest commercial hit, *Painting Churches*, with a succinct, 'I just don't get it.'" Papp didn't read scripts, or read them closely, more than one writer recalls. By way of example, Hwang reveals that Papp gave him notes on his first play, *F.O.B.* With the arrogance of youth, Hwang resubmitted the same draft six weeks later, without having changed a word. Papp called and said, "The script is great now, we're going to produce it."

Even outside the relatively small group of his anointed writers, playwrights felt welcome into Papp's artistic family, as Eduardo Machado recounts. "Mr. Papp made it very clear he was never going to produce me, but I could go and make Xeroxes at the Public, I could sit on the oriental rug and bitch and moan." He continues, "You could walk in there and nobody was afraid." The theatre was a home. "You were a part of something, a community."

Papp's Public Theater became a vibrant hothouse for theatrical experimentation. Theatrical lawyer and producer John

Breglio invoked Papp when analyzing the changes brought about by the recent flood of enhancement money from commercial producers, which, he argues, limits risk-taking on the part of the not-for-profit theatres and has the potential to muddy their missions. By contrast, he described the purity of Papp's vision for the Public as follows: "We do things that nobody else would produce. We don't do the things that Broadway does."

The body of work produced by Papp is unequalled in the history of the American theatre. The Public's buoyant atmosphere gave artists the oxygen they needed to grow and experiment, whatever the result. Producer Elizabeth McCann remembers the chaotic, fertile, energetic community Papp oversaw at the Public, and feeling the "vibrant sense than anything could happen in this place."

WHEN BOARDS SPEAK

Though many playwrights believe that the theatres' artistic leaders have led them off course, still others see the increasingly corporate culture of the art as "just the way it is." A large group of writers lay the responsibility for the changed theatrical culture at the feet of nonprofit boards of directors, whom they see as holding sway, practically or implicitly, over artistic agendas. This shift in power has its roots in the theatres' evolution beyond their founding artists. "This whole business of the leadership changing in the regional theatres, this move from the founders to the next generation. At that point the board is choosing, essentially, the leaders. At a lot of theatres, the boards have been together longer than the artistic director. The board hired the artistic director, and they have more longevity than thirty years ago."

Because the orientation of trustees is often corporate, their increased power translates, playwrights believe, into a cultural shift, changed conversations, changed priorities. "Most of them come from for-profit organizations," notes a writer with a long tenure on staff at one of the country's largest theatres.

They say, "I don't get it; why are you always in the red? I
know, let me look at the chart. Ah—new plays, new play,
new play, new play. Why do them? Why don't we get a star,
get a play that we know?" We already have the complication
between artistic staff and the playwright, but we have another
layer where they have to answer to the board.

The heightened influence of boards, many playwrights
believe, also adds to insularity within the artistic selection
process. A Pulitzer and Tony Award–winning playwright flags
this tendency, adding the press to the equation:

> The artistic directors are talking to the newspapers and their
> boards. They're in this closed loop of conversation. It's like
> we can't get the newspapers to cover this, so we need to think
> of something they'll cover and that will make our board
> happy, because they read the paper.

Possibly, as one of the field's senior dramaturgs suggests,
the playwright's alienation results from the way those theatres
have grown up.

> Theatres used to be run by writers. You think about David
> Mamet or Circle Repertory. The writers were in residence,
> they were on salary, they were in charge, they were part of
> the core group. Then, as the theatres got bigger and staffs
> got more established, writers got shoved out. They're not as
> social as everybody else, and boards didn't approve budgets,
> and so they're gone. They're on the outside.

The board's heavy hand, playwrights argue, stifles the
energy needed for new work to thrive. It fosters safe-thinking,
unadventurous programming, and sameness. Playwrights seem to
be saying the cultivation of the new in the theatre demands risk;
the prevalent system of nonprofit theatre squelches its leaders'

tolerance for risk.* As one playwright, a winner of multiple Obie Awards, puts it: "No board goes to an artistic director and says, 'Can't you be a little riskier?'"

A QUESTION OF FORM

Most theatre leaders present their companies as artist-centered, determined to serve the playwright's vision. Playwrights don't view them that way. Theatres, they say, usually focus their greatest energy and attention on ticket buyers. Playwrights attribute the theatres' conservatism to their over-concern about audience. They blame artistic directors for avoiding work that is unconventional in form, for a lack of bravery and imagination about the new. A young playwright in Minneapolis articulated a sentiment that found almost universal agreement among writers nationwide:

> Looking at theatre mission statements and seeing who is selling themselves to their audiences as being a leader in cutting-edge, experimental, daring, bold new work, and all those catch phrases ... I feel that the regional theatres that advertise [themselves] as that often do the same new plays that the Roundabout or Manhattan Theatre Club are doing in New York. [There is a] disparity between what theatres consider bold and daring, and what a group of playwrights would consider bold and daring, which is work that probably isn't being done in regional theatre anywhere in America. You [would] consider those plays to be very, very solid and more formally conventional.

---

* The irony that the not-for-profits, created to assume risks that the commercial sector can't tolerate, have become so risk-averse, has been noted by playwrights and commercial producers alike. There may even be a growing sense that the commercial model, without boards and funders, offers independence and freedom not found often in the nonprofit world.

The intensity of the belief among writers that theatres program to the tastes of the audience—known or imagined—is a flash point for their differences of opinion with theatre artistic leaders, who perceive possible audience reception as only a small influence in programming.

> **FINDING:** More than 82 percent of the writers agree or strongly agree that "Expectations about audience reception and interest" are a prohibitive obstacle to production, making this by far the single-most daunting hurdle for the new play. In stark contrast, only slightly more than 31 percent of the theatres agree or strongly agree that this is a prohibitive obstacle.

This deep disparity—eight out of ten playwrights seeing this as a major barrier while less than a third of the theatres see it that way—brings audience to the foreground of any question about fostering new-play production (see Chapter V).

> **FINDING:** Fifty-five percent of the writers claim that the unconventional style of their plays can block their way to production.

Formal novelty or difficulty is, many writers believe, the contemporary theatre's bugbear, even more than tough subject matter. Theatres, many playwrights believe, manifest their conservatism by shunning work that is unusual, nonrealistic, or that plays with form in ways that complicate the narrative. This widespread belief adds dimension to the portrait of theatres as corporate. It paints them as aesthetically reactionary as well, resistant to formal and, possibly, generational changes in the art itself.

Playwrights tend to locate that barrier in the artistic directors themselves. These artistic directors, the logic goes, at the helm of increasingly corporate structures, have others reading for them. They read fewer and fewer plays and, therefore, read less and less well. Their tastes, therefore, fail to evolve or keep up with changes wrought on the form by new writers. (Additionally, formally new plays, meanwhile, may be the hardest to "get on the page.") This playwright's sentiment echoes throughout the profession:

> There's so much good work that is out there that isn't being produced, or that has been produced at small theatres that have never made the leap to mid-sized or regional theatres. It does make me wonder if people don't know how to read a play anymore. They aren't able to look at it on the page and envision what it's getting at.

On this side of the divide, playwriting appears to move forward, while the curators of new work, by standing still or moving very slowly, grow more conservative, a kind of artistic Doppler effect.

The state of playwriting is healthy, most writers agree, but there's a failure of imagination on the part of theatres, an inability to make sense of emerging voices and new work. Theatres, this common critique goes, lack the vision to realize those voices in production, and woefully underestimate their audiences' ability to appreciate challenging material. At the same time, they fail to educate these audiences about unconventional dramatic forms. Through the eyes of the playwright, the obstacle of unconventionality is symptomatic of a widespread failure of imagination:

> Reading writers like Sarah Ruhl and Sheila Callahan, if you can't read a stage direction that says, "Five people pop out of Samantha's head" and have some idea that it can take place

in your theatre, no matter what your theatre, then there's a problem. We need to get to everyone to that point. It's a new kind of writing.

Or, as one well-established playwright and multidisciplinary artist asked, "Are theatres coming to a place where they don't even understand what the craft is?"

THE AUTHENTIC CONVERSATION: A PARALLEL STUDY

Simultaneous with the TDF study, the Andrew W. Mellon Foundation provided a grant to David Dower, a San Francisco–based director and founding artistic director of The Z Space Studio, a developmental lab and company of theatre artists in the Bay Area, to conduct a related investigation in the "new works sector" of the American theatre, including playwrights, producing theatres, presenters, ensembles who devise work, and so forth. From January to August 2006, he surveyed the field in order for the Mellon Foundation to better understand what Dower calls "the infrastructure for new works and new voices in the American theatre." (During the course of his intensive exploration, Dower moved to Arena Stage in Washington, D.C., where he currently serves as associate artistic director and oversees the new NEA/Arena Stage New Play Development Program.) Dower visited fifteen communities, and spoke with hundreds of artists and artistic administrators engaged in making, producing, and presenting new work.

Asked what his most salient discovery was, Dower answered without hesitation: the lack of authenticity in the conversation between individual artists and institutions. He had expected dissatisfaction among emerging artists, but was surprised that artists who are successfully making their way through what he calls the "gates of opportunity" also find the ecology of the field unhealthy. "Particularly among playwrights," he recalls, "there was this feeling that the institutional interest was not aligned with the needs of the writers. When you talk to the artists they feel most at home, in a setting like New Dramatists.* They don't feel comfortable even with the language of the institution."

Dower heard the same critique of theatres that we did, and encountered the same disjunction between the perception of playwrights and that of artistic leaders from institutional theatres. He goes on to explain that in institutional theatres, "The priority is the institutional survival. The institutions that do the work of producing plays have a whole bunch of other people to serve first."

Dower's insights about the imprecision of terminology—"the language of the institution"—with regard to work on new plays, are particularly helpful when trying to understand the playwrights' complaint that theatres don't deliver on their artistic promises. "There is a glut of buzzwords," he notes, "largely invoked as a way of demonstrating value to the funding community, it seems." For example, "everyone wants to be perceived, to a greater or lesser extent, as an 'artist-focused home for the development of new works by emerging voices.' They design 'workshops' and 'residencies.' They fund activities purported to 'develop' plays. But what they are actually doing, and why they are doing it, swings wildly in every instance. And it's bewildering to artists. The words have no actual agreed-upon meanings."

Dower worries out one term in particular: "artist-focused," with which many, if not most, theatres describe themselves. If they

* Full disclosure: Todd London, the project director of this study and one of its authors, also serves as artistic director of New Dramatists, a sixty-year-old center for the support and development of playwrights, located in New York City. Because this study centers around new-play production and because New Dramatists does not produce, the issues of new-play and playwright laboratories such as this one seemed, from the outset, connected, but mostly outside the scope of this report. It would, though, be as false to leave out references to that organization as it would be to avoid acknowledgment of London's role there.

are truly artist-focused, he asks, then "why are the artists so uniform in their experience of being isolated, marginalized, or 'in the way' at many of these organizations? He differentiates this focus from other kinds, more apt when discussing theatres: "audience-focused," "product-focused," and "community-focused."

The distinction is a helpful one. Product-focused organizations rely on ticket sales or funding based on a quantifiable audience to sustain its operations. Regardless of their real and professed concern for the artist, their institutional viability is not dependent on their valuation by these artists. As a result of this product focus, the playwright's work comes to be viewed as a product, and the institution's investment becomes attached to that product—through credit, the assignment of future rights and royalties, as well as control over its future life, including when and where it will be produced.

Audience-focused organizations, according to Dower, curate around the notion of service to their audiences; their principal goal is to create a dialogue with their audience, to provide "opportunities to experience the art." They channel new work to their audiences via subscription, open runs, and other programming, including new-play-development events, including readings, workshop productions, and talk-backs, during which theatregoers get to give the playwright "feedback" on the work. Usually presented and funded as artistic development activities, the events are almost universally derided by writers as unhelpful. As such, they are. As audience-development tools they may be key, though in the long run, to "bringing audiences to the new."

Community-focused theatres are committed to the development of artists from within a specific underserved community. They play a valuable role, both socially and as a point of access to the field. Again, the confusion of language and purpose creates the rift. For artist-focused organizations, by contrast, readings and workshops enable artists to measure their own progress, complete a process, develop their own, rather than a random audience's, evaluation. Here process creates its own ends, so artist participation, satisfaction, and creative outcome become essential to the ongoing institutional life and the chief measures of its accomplishment.

These theoretical categories are not exclusive, and we assume that the practices and true aims of every organization place it somewhere on a continuum. Moreover, Dower is quick to point out that the artist-centered developmental organizations he considers successful—The Playwrights' Center of Minneapolis, Sundance Theatre Lab (L.A. and Utah), New Dramatists, and Z Space, notably—are not inherently more valuable than major producing theatres. His point seems to be, rather, that their purpose is clearer, less divided. They do what they say they do, and the artists they serve know it.

Different kinds of organizations serve different ends, Dower stresses, and all are important to the ecology of the field. Their variety is essential, as is the way they complement each other. At the end of his very personal journey through the field of new work, Dower concludes that the problems don't stem from one set of aims or another, but from the lack of clarity about these aims, the blurring of purpose. If artists and theatres are to collaborate authentically and effectively, they must say what they mean and do what they say.

The Theatre's-Eye View: Nonprofits

Leaders of American not-for-profit theatres see the state of playwriting and new-play production in a different light. While, privately, some will complain of a lack of imagination among their peers and a sameness to the seasons of theatres across the country, in groups the diagnosis is more likely to spotlight other issues. They worry about losing audiences, especially to other media. They rail at the current critical climate and the marginalization of theatre within the culture as a whole. Most share a sense that new work is financially riskier and harder to fund, with some exception for world premieres, than work on classics, musicals, and familiar titles with bankable stars. They agree with the playwrights that usual methods of new-play development have dead-ended.

Artistic directors and their associates are much more muted, more polite, in their criticism of playwrights than the other way around. That said, some believe there aren't enough good, let alone great, new plays to go around. A passionate minority implies that dramatists aren't doing their jobs—that is, grappling with the issues of the day and speaking clearly to audiences. In point of fact, many fault playwrights for not writing with actual audiences (their theatres' audiences) in mind. Some claim that too many playwrights are writing unproducible plays, without regard to the realities of the stage. Others complain that writers submit work that isn't ready for production, isn't finished, isn't good enough. They worry about writers abandoning the field for film and TV, and on occasion criticize them for abandoning it or, more regularly, for writing plays that feel like TV.

Although artistic directors may disagree with playwrights about the reasons behind the troubled climate for new plays, they agree that the winds are rough.

> **FINDING:** Two-thirds of the theatres surveyed believe that it has become harder (58 percent) or much harder (9 percent) to develop new plays in the past decade. What has shifted? Seventy-five percent of this group attributes the increased difficulty to financial constraints—too-high expenses and not enough funding.

A founder of the National New Play Network, an alliance of twenty-six, mostly small and mid-sized nonprofit theatres, that "champions the development, production, and continued life of new plays for the American theatre," observes that "in the last two years, and we've seen it across the Network, things have gotten a lot harder very quickly. We're choosing smaller plays, and so forth. I don't think it's any harder on new plays in particular, it's everything."

The head of one of the nation's oldest theatres thinks the trouble starts with the audience. "The main problem has to do with the audience's fear of what's new. And, because there's a fear of what's new, because it starts to grind onto box office," theatres look at new plays and ask themselves, "'How can we do this because it's not going to sell as well as whatever else everybody thinks will sell well?'"

For many, this difficulty, and the tendency toward contraction, is specific to the new, unknown, and unproven. "Every time we do a new play," a Minneapolis-based playwright and literary manager explains:

> the theatre loses money, and that's just the way it is.
> Brand-new plays we play at fifty-percent capacity. A known,
> "knighted" person's plays will probably play quite a bit
> higher, but in general a good average for a play that's new
> and extremely good would be a seventy percent or above. If
> it's an established play it's over the moon, eighty or ninety
> percent, standing-room-only kind of stuff.

This kind of financial drain becomes hard to justify to a board of directors, according to the head of a twenty-five-year-old theatre, which established, and then shut down its new works festival after its major funder pulled out.

> We weren't making any money on the New Work Festival.
> We were charging five dollars a show. We hoped to push

it into a place where we could make money so we could point to it and say, "It is bringing in income, so let's keep supporting it." But at the time, it wasn't. We couldn't say it was income-generating. We could point to the new plays that came out of it and say, "This play started here, and it brought in some money." But basically they were still seeing that the money this was costing wasn't really showing up.

Even at the largest theatres in the country, money to give new plays the time and attention they need to get ready for production is in short supply. "Play development is not in our budget, so it's on a cash-flow basis," the associate director of one such theatre explains. "I'm always chasing the cash." Another artistic director describes the triage that takes place when the money crunch begins.

> If they're having marketing problems, one of the first things to go is money that was spent on play development. I don't think it's harder to produce a play you're dying to produce. What gets caught is the stuff that, maybe there's something there but you just don't have the money to do it right now. Money solves a lot of problems in play development.

Even before the economic downturn in the fall of 2008, times were hard for nonprofit theatres. But is it especially harder to produce new plays now than it was a decade ago? Or are the difficulties attributed to new-play production the result of a different kind of lack of imagination in budget, marketing, and fundraising? Is the squeeze real or perceptual? Are there other ways to look at the same picture?

One artistic director insists that the thinking behind the caution is out of date.

> There's a lie out there in the resident not-for-profit theatres that you're taking a bigger risk if you put on a new play.

We are selling more for new plays than we are with the recognizable class of works. It's all word of mouth. Our new work has blown people away, and so they're coming. The managing directors are all going, "You can't do another new play." That's the old thinking. It's not necessarily true.

Do the leaders of theatres agree that their companies have grown too corporate and market-driven and just refuse to acknowledge it publicly? In discussion, intense critiques of institutional theatres by artistic directors are rare. Certainly, the group nature of our national conversations mitigate against them. By design, our study assembled artistic directors chosen from among effective, even exemplary producers of new work.

Artistic directors are artists first, as well as lovers and defenders of the art. Does their responsibility as the public face of their institutions ever put them at odds with themselves— promoting the art while fronting for operating practices that, having evolved over time to benefit the life of the institution, don't always feed the work's creative fires? Do they weigh the strengths of a system that successfully supported, for example, Tony Kushner, August Wilson, and Wendy Wasserstein, more heavily than its flaws? Or does their investment in serving their audiences (even when those audiences are conservative in taste) lead them to value a kind of institutional context that writers disparage?

Two artistic leaders, who have in recent years moved to large institutional theatres from smaller organizations built around resident and ensemble artists, admitted to being derailed by such pressures, and, in stories told "off the record," specifically confirmed the kinds of critiques heard from artists, agents, playwright advocates, and others. Are these stories exceptional or do they prove the rule? To be sure, artistic directors struggle against the pressures of our corporate culture. They fight to maintain support for artists. And like independent artists, many artistic directors wrestle with the pressures of making a living while making art, which become more intense as the economic and cultural environment grows more hostile. One such artistic director states it simply: "The more institutionalized you get, the harder it is to say, 'I like it and that's it,' because there are all of these other factors."

THE WORLD OF NEW PLAYS

The most dramatic thing that's happened with major playwrights is the ironic realization that Broadway is still the end-all for many of them, but has never been less accommodating. Douglas Carter Beane was hurt in some respect by that production of The Little Dog Laughed, *because this very fine play twenty years ago would have moved to the Theatre de Lys or to someplace else and run for two years, like* Wit. *There were plays that ran for two, two and a half years, Off Broadway. What is the alternative now? Instead, they put this fine play up on Broadway and it's considered a huge commercial failure. It lost all its money, and who got to see it?* —COMMERCIAL PRODUCER

The center of new-play development and production long ago moved out of Times Square and into the theatres of Off and Off Off Broadway and numerous other urban centers of the country. This shift of the center began with the explosion of new-play activity in regional/resident theatres in the 1970s and '80s—often dated from the commercial transfers of Howard Sackler's *The Great White Hope* and Arthur Kopit's *Indians* from Arena Stage in D.C. in 1967 and '69, the dedication of the Mark Taper Forum's founding artistic director, Gordon Davidson, to the cultivation of new work, and the national success of the Humana Festival at the Actors Theatre of Louisville, Kentucky, begun in 1976.

That explosion coincided with a decades-long decline of Broadway as a home or generating base for new plays—as opposed to musicals, revivals, or proven classics. From a peak of 188 new plays produced in 1926–27 (49 new musicals and 26 revivals were produced that year), Broadway has declined in the production of new plays consistently ever since, as can be seen below:

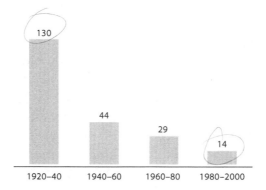

1.1 AVERAGE NUMBER OF NEW PLAYS ON BROADWAY PER YEAR

To put it more starkly, in the 1920s, a new play opened on Broadway at a rate of around one every other night; in the new millennium, the rate is closer to one every two months. The 2007–08 season saw the opening of seven new plays, two were premieres from the Royal National Theatre of Great Britain, one as a transfer from a regional nonprofit theatre (Steppenwolf), and three were produced for Broadway, plays by name writers: David Mamet, Aaron Sorkin (creator of TV's *The West Wing*), and Mark Twain, who, having died a century ago, was not interviewed for this study. The nonprofit Manhattan Theatre Club, which operates a Broadway house, also produced a new play there that season.

On top of that, commercial opportunities for plays Off Broadway have dried up in the past decade. Despite a boom in commercial Off-Broadway in the late '90s, and a spreading sense that new venues would add to a boom for new-play production, this promise quickly collapsed. Off Broadway was originally an alternative theatre, with relatively low ticket prices; now even mid-sized nonprofit theatres Off Broadway routinely charge fifty to seventy-five dollars per ticket. "Now I'm asked for $75 to see a play in a basement," one producer marvels. Gone, too, are the not-so-distant days when a play like Terrence McNally's *Frankie and Johnny in the Clair de Lune* or Alfred Uhry's *Driving Miss Daisy* could settle into a commercial Off-Broadway run for two or three years, command a movie deal, and make its playwright a nice living.

Beginning in the late 1990s, the larger Off-Broadway houses began to close. The Lucille Lortel Theatre (formerly Theatre de Lys), began to rent strictly to nonprofits. Variety Arts and the Promenade closed. Westside Theatre began a run of *I Love You, You're Perfect, Now Change*, which kept its upstairs theatre locked up for nearly twelve years. The literal or virtual loss of these theatres, along with that of some other venues, including the destruction of the John Houseman Theater on Manhattan's Theatre Row, changed not only the dramatic landscape of New York City, but also the economic landscape for new plays and playwrights. While a number of new theatres, including several Off-Broadway multiplexes have been added during this time, more than one of those has already closed.

The actual toll of this instability dramatizes the shrinkage. Approximately thirty-seven theatres still operate as commercial Off-Broadway houses, some large, some small, some frequently renting to nonprofits, some tied up with long-running shows. Half as many (eighteen) have been demolished in recent years, including, as we've seen, some key, larger theatres. Add to that the roughly twelve theatres that are now being used for nontheatrical purposes—including a movie theatre, drugstore, and Scientology center—plus twenty-six or so that now exclusively house or rent to nonprofit companies, and you see that commercial Off Broadway has kept fewer than half as many spaces as it has lost, an erosion that by any other name does not smell sweet.

Where can a new play, considered unsuitable for Broadway (as most plays are now, due to the transformed nature of that street), go for a long run, a long commercial life? The answer is discouraging: Almost nowhere. With the larger theatres tied up by long-running megamusicals and more intimate musicals settling in at traditional playhouses, few Broadway spaces are available for nonmusical works.

In contrast to Broadway and commercial Off Broadway, the ninety-four producing nonprofits we surveyed across the country claim to mount, on average, nearly three new plays each season (almost nine every three seasons). Despite any variance in how these organizations define "new play," and regardless of whether these numbers are replicated among the other nearly 1,900 professional theatres operating in the United States*, the tallies prove two points, long and widely held: 1) the center of new-play activity has completely shifted to the decentralized, nonprofit theatre; and 2) there is no longer any life or living for playwrights in the commercial theatre on or off Broadway.

PLAYS OF QUALITY & MERIT

There's a surfeit of new plays of varying qualities and speaking to various styles and issues and content. It's actually remarkably healthy in many respects. —ARTISTIC DIRECTOR

We live in a boom-time for playwriting. Few dispute it. Professionally accomplished playwrights are, apparently, writing more plays than our theatre has seen before. Has all this activity led to a similar boom in quality? Are the plays being written any good? Artistic directors are split here. On one side there are those who feel that there's a surfeit of good plays; on the other, there are those who see a dearth. "I am reading plays now that I am really

* Based on the number of IRS 2005 Form 990 filers with budgets higher than $75,000, according to the National Center for Charitable Statistics at the Urban Institute.

excited about. The quality of plays is so much better than ten years ago. There's so much more relevance, there's so much vitality," the head of a small experimental company enthuses. The artistic director of a larger regional theatre seconds his emotion. "I have far more plays that I love than I can produce. I have many works that I think, 'God I want to put this play on, even though it's a messy, not-perfect play.'"

Two California-based artistic directors add their voices. "There are definitely more writers that I'd love to be able to commission to work with than I have slots to do. There are an awful lot of great writers writing really good work that's not getting produced. I'm certainly reading good plays," says the artistic director of a community-based ensemble. The second, from a company with a long track record of promoting new writing, agrees. "We are, in fact, generating more artists with a greater sense of craft than we have been for a long time; more regional theatres are producing new works than certainly was ever in my consciousness."

Other artistic directors throw cold water on the notion that there are more good plays wanting productions than places for them: "We're in a trough now," observes one, from the vantage point of thirty years at a leading new-play theatre. A colleague backs up his assessment. "It's cyclical…. Looking at it from the perspective of twenty-five to thirty years, there are times when there are a lot, and times when there are not too many. We're in a little bit of a valley." A veteran of new-play development shares their sentiment. "I don't find the work, even in the development stage, that I feel is exciting. I'm not looking for bull's-eye work. I'd rather find a play that's a big old mess. That turns me on much more than the well-made play. If I can find three or four of those, I feel really lucky."

For others, the problem is less about merit or quality than about finish. One artistic director, who is also a playwright, lays the blame at the playwrights' feet. "Writers should not be sending their first drafts…to theatres to evaluate, and then boohoo when they don't get produced. I'm sick and tired of reading first drafts.

They now expect that the staff of the theatre is going to help them finish their play. A writer should write his or her own play."

An associate artistic director elaborates, arguing that this allegedly willful lack of finish goes hand in hand with defensiveness, a resistance to the necessary development to ready work for production. "Everybody wants a production, and it's a difficult conversation to have, because many of the plays have merit, but are not ready for production. Then the playwright thinks they're ready for production, so you go through that haggle."

AESTHETIC DIFFERENCES

Are the plays being submitted unfinished or flawed, or are they the wrong kind of plays? Again, artistic directors and playwrights assess the state of the art so differently. Is there a gap in the kind of writing they value?

"I have noticed in developing and producing new plays there are two categories," one longtime leader of a small Midwestern theatre posits. "There are writers and plays of the moment about a really specific personal or social issue that can just take off; and then there are the writers with a very serious kind of aesthetic that you can't put your arms around in terms of 'how do I sell this?'" The head of a large New York theatre faults contemporary playwrights for the narrowness of their concerns:

> There've been very, very few plays that have been willing to tackle the big issues of the time. And the unfortunate thing is that you keep reading all of these plays about big issues by bad writers and all these plays by good writers about nothing. That's a result of how we train writers. Our most talented writers may get taught the idea that the uniqueness of their vision is more important than the size of it....
> The big danger, as reflected in the American theatre for playwrights, is the privatization of playwriting. Many, many plays are beautifully written that are just taking such a small, small scale of interest.

This statement hangs in the air with the contrary view of many writers—that artistic directors don't "get" what they're saying in their plays, that the development of new aesthetic approaches blinds result-oriented producers from the larger meanings, from the politics of their work, and that the leaders of the theatres favor "issue" plays because they can sum them up and sell them. They can thus convince themselves that they are doing important work, even if the plays they program are conventional in form and at heart. This conventionality reinforces the nearly universal sense among writers that our theatres have grown more conservative.

Even many artistic directors share this appraisal. The head of a large regional theatre attributes the increased conservatism among theatres to financial calculation: "I have sensed from a number of theatres around the country a desire to do material that is more box office–proof. And for many people that means plays that already have a track record—even if it's a contemporary play that has a track record." Even the novelty-hungry New York City theatre has turned more conservative, an Off-Broadway associate artistic director reflects, "In the twenty-plus years I've been in New York the market has shifted. You used to be able to see really cool stuff, writers who were experimenting with form, really pushing the boundaries. I don't find that anymore in New York."

Several artistic directors confirm the theory that form, rather than content, is a major barrier for much new work, a limitation they blame on audiences. A regional theatre artistic director offers a blunt example:

> It would be easier for me to do a play like *Quills* in which Jesus comes out of the grave with three erect penises and fucks Mary on the floor than it would to do *No Man's Land* by Harold Pinter. A play that is abstract in the storytelling—I'd do it, but that would be more controversial than content. It's the form, not being able to understand the story, that's the most difficult for an audience, as opposed to graphic content.

And this example—a thirty-five-year-old play by a Nobel laure-
ate—isn't even new.

Small, experimental theatres, committed to unconventional
storytelling, regularly butt up against audience expectations
when it comes to form. "Many audiences are uncomfortable
with narrative innovation," says the head of a theatre that excels
in just such innovation. "They're made uncomfortable by lack of
resolution."

HOW PLAYWRIGHTS GROW

An environment of precipitous economic decline may only
reinforce the sense of financial risk associated with producing
new plays. How then, coming out of years of creeping
conservatism and entering a time of widespread fiscal peril, can
theatres help plays and playwrights grow? A literary manager
associated with two culturally-specific theatres—one a venerable
pioneer and the other young and scrappy—turns the analysis
back to opportunity and the need of theatres to sustain writers
over time, to encourage the growth that only happens through
experience: "The really good plays are rare rather than common.
But how do writers get good? It's not like most of them spring
fully formed. They need years to write those plays and ask those
questions about how to make them better. Where exactly they're
getting that is not clear."

The terms of quality may slip and slide—good plays, great
plays, good writers, great writers, common or rare—one solution
remains steady. How do writers get good? How do good writers
write better, even great, plays? The most common answer is the
most obvious one: by seeing their work in production. "I know
a lot of good plays and not a whole lot of great plays," a literary
manager admits.

> In the current climate, a play really has to be a great play in
> order for it to cross the threshold of being produced. What
> that does to the environment and the culture is leave out a
> lot of good plays by writers who might be great if their good

plays got produced. What kind of bar are we setting, and what criteria are we using when we're talking about plays of merit? If the majority of theatres in the country are talking about producing one new play in their four-show season, how good does that play have to be in order to crack that? The result is a lack of production for plays from writers, who, five years from now, might write a great play if their plays are being produced.

Where will playwrights get the years they need to write those plays and learn to make them better? That may be the most urgent question of all, and the one to which the American theatre has yet to find an answer.

RICHARD NELSON ON NEW-PLAY FIXES

The notion of helping playwrights has recently come under fire in playwriting circles, and several writers referred to a 2007 speech given by American playwright Richard Nelson, then-chairman of the playwriting program at the Yale School of Drama, to the Alliance of Resident Theatres/NY annual meeting. Nelson claims that theatres have created a culture out of the assumption that plays are things to be fixed and that they must help the writers do just that.

Nelson contends, "The profession of playwright, the role of the playwright in today's American theatre, I believe, is under serious attack," arguing that "perhaps the greatest threat to the playwright in today's theatre comes not from those greedy and ignorant, but rather from those who want to 'help.'"

"Playwrights are in need of help." This is now almost a maxim in our theatre today. Unquestioned. A given. But where does this mindset—for that is what it is—a mindset, come from? Of course playwrights need things—money, productions, support, encouragement.

So do actors, directors, designers, artistic directors. But THIS mindset is different, because what is meant here is: "Playwrights are in need of help—to write their plays. They are in need of help—to do their work." They can't do their work themselves.

What is really being said to the playwright by all the help? From the playwright's perspective it is this: that the given now in the American theatre is that what a playwright writes, no matter how much he or she works on it, rewrites it at his or her desk, the play will ALWAYS not be right. Will ALWAYS need "help." In other words, writing a play is too big of a job for just the playwright to achieve. This, I believe, is now a prevalent attitude in the American theatre. And this mindset is devastating.

Nelson cites McCarter Theatre Center artistic director Emily Mann, who told him that the greatest change she's seen in her seventeen years as artistic director of the McCarter is the tendency of playwrights to submit unfinished plays. He remarks on young playwrights who confess to leaving "chunks of their plays purposely badly written—hoping that the "help" they receive will concentrate on these areas and not on others that they care about. Tricks, games that many a screenwriter has learned over time, but now finding their way into the writing of plays." Nelson proposes a different approach:

> Now a culture of "help" breeds a culture of dependence, and this is what, I believe, we now have in the American theatre: the culture of readings and workshops, one unimaginable when I was a young playwright thirty years ago. A culture of "development." And this culture, more than being an activity, a process—is a mindset. Having spent a great deal of time in classical theatre, I have watched actors and directors approach classical plays

that have massive contradictions, and address those plays not as works to be fixed, but rather to be solved. So I am arguing for a theatre where the mindset is not to fix new plays, but to solve them.

Again, the divide. Are playwrights creating the conditions for this help by refusing to do the work necessary to complete their plays or are they responding to an institutional culture that infantilizes them, insisting that all plays are broken until the theatres say they're not? Do writers fail to see the limits of what they've written or do theatres miss the integrity and viability of the work? Has the collaboration between writers and theatres grown so inauthentic that playwrights will knowingly submit flawed drafts to make the theatres' literary and artistic staffers feel like they've made their stamp on the work? (Some have claimed to hold finished drafts in a drawer to be revealed after theatres prescribe inevitable changes.) Is it true, as one playwright claims, that no one, "unless they're really cynical or clever, submits anything that they know is flawed to a theatre?"

Other Voices Weigh In

THE DISAPPEARING PRODUCER: NONPROFITS

When it comes to new plays, many agree that both nonprofits and the commercial theatre are suffering, each in their own ways, from the decline of the profession of the producer. For nonprofits, the issue boils down to one of focus and scale. While traditional producers gave their intense all to one play or, at most, a handful of plays at a time, the artistic leaders of not-for-profit theatres are, along with their management partners, builders of seasons and institutions. All producers fundraise, but in an America without significant government subsidy for the arts, only nonprofit producers fundraise for so much other than production: seasons of plays, buildings, educational programs, endowments, the process of new-play development, audience development, and more, each of which requires not only money but time, attention, organizational thought, infrastructure, board and community engagement. Physical plant and staffing costs are, inevitably, the fastest growing budget items for most theatres. The days of producers and playwrights sitting together while they hammer out the details of a play headed for production are long gone, buried under decades of institutional growth and necessity.

The season model developed through the support and encouragement of the Ford Foundation and the National Endowment for the Arts in the 1960s. One playwright, who has worked extensively in both commercial and nonprofit spheres, encapsulates the situation:

> This model—where all these theatres are going to get buildings, and then buildings are going to have seasons, and that's the way you should run a theatre—has some drawbacks. There is a certain beauty in the commercial system, though it doesn't happen much anymore with straight plays. A producer only does what he or she is passionate about, and works on that show and tries to get that show in. The commercial producer is the person who has the clout to do the show. That's the person who's raising the money. Yes, commercial producers generally have a number of projects, but they commit to the projects because those are the ones they're passionate about. As opposed to, "I have eight slots to fill."
>
> The need to fill these slots can be counterproductive because people do things not just out of passion, but just because they've got to put something in there. You happen to fit into the slot in the season, and now you're trying to get access to somebody who's making the decisions about how much money to spend on it or whether we can hire another actor from out of town. And that person...maybe wasn't really that excited about your play, but just thought it was okay.

This critique combines elements of a more global evaluation of the nonprofits, heard from playwrights, agents, and, ironically, Broadway producers themselves, one echoed earlier in the testimonials to Joe Papp. Among these elements:

- The growth of institutions separates artistic directors from the playwrights themselves, with literary departments often standing as institutional buffers;
- Plays are chosen with input from so many "departments" that the passionate connection between producer and playwright is short-circuited;
- With most artistic directors drawn from the ranks of directors, more energy and resources surround the projects that they direct themselves, while producing functions are spread out among managers, dramaturgs, associate directors and others, serving, movie-style, as "line producers," further separating the people who choose the plays from those who write them, and watering down this core collaboration;
- Unlike traditional producers, the artistic curators in institutional theatres—i.e. artistic directors—don't control the purse strings, marketing, or fundraising, and, therefore, often have to compromise with those who do.

The issue is one of focus and risk: How can nonprofit producers give their all to each current project when they're constantly projecting ahead to the next and the next? Additionally, some argue that because the heads of nonprofits draw regular salaries and benefits, they enjoy more security than their commercial counterparts or independent artists. This relative security diminishes risk, which, in turn, diminishes the ambition for and passionate investment in individual projects that fuels theatrical achievement. Security, this line of thinking goes, reinforces timidity, protection against loss. One commercial producer recounts a conversation with a nonprofit manager who has served in the same theatre for thirty years: "Do you know what that means that you've had a weekly paycheck for thirty years? How many producers and/or managers in this business can make that statement?" Ultimately the producer concluded: "That security that he had under him made him afraid of challenge. Security doesn't reinforce you to the extent that, listen, I'm secure so I can afford to lose. No, it makes you afraid that you will lose. And I think, probably that happens with artistic directors."

A good deal of the playwrights' criticism of institutional theatres is echoed in other corners of the field, specifically from agents (all of whom represent directors and designers, as well as playwrights) and producers, general managers, and lawyers, who straddle the commercial and nonprofit worlds. Though they often sympathize with the struggles of the nonprofits, they particularly fault them for losing their way *as* nonprofits, for aping the commercial theatre they began as an alternative to. An agent worries the point made by many others:

> Every time you're trying to get a play or a musical on
> now, it's always being judged by: "Could this become
> commercial?" It's not just about let's do good work. It ties
> into my old feeling about not-for-profits—don't forget
> you're not-for-profit. Every play you do in a season does not
> have to be the play that's going to move and become *Proof*
> and *Doubt*. Everything is judged by the future life, based on
> money coming back to the theatre over the life of the play.
> That's where you get into dangerous territory, especially
> with new writers, because not everyone's gonna write plays
> that are going to be commercial. You can't learn how to be
> a playwright unless you're being produced—you can't. And
> that's nothing new. But every play should not be chosen on
> whether or not it can have a commercial run.

Another agent misses vision and courage in artistic producers. Here, too, Joseph Papp is the model, a man with a mission keeping his theatre *on* mission, creating a "purposeful dialogue" with the audience. Now, "everyone is looking for their safety."

There is, some believe, "a failure of imagination across the board. It's the elephant in the room: What is the theatre today? What is the culture?" From this perspective, theatres are behaving like factories, cranking out work with little attention to the most basic questions: "Why do we do it? Why do people go?"

THE DISAPPEARING PRODUCER: BROADWAY

The situation is different, but no better, in the commercial theatre, specifically on Broadway, where the high cost of production has transformed the profession from one of singular expert producers to one of parades of investors, most of whom have little experience with producing. As one producer observes, "There is nobody who makes their living as a producer of commercial plays anymore."

"One of the tragedies here," a Broadway insider laments, "is the disappearance of the truly knowledgeable, experienced, passionate producer of material. What you have are tons and tons of investors." The more producers a play has, the less authority any one has. Another producer implicates himself in the problem, illustrating that the very thing that has long distinguished commercial new-play production—the working intimacy between producer and playwright—has, in fact, broken down now that plays begin their lives elsewhere and Broadway has proven almost terminally inhospitable to growing new work: "I have good relationships with playwrights, but I don't sit around with them and go through drafts. Most people who put on plays have different relationships with their writers now than writers did with their producers twenty years ago." This same producer sums up a sentiment prevalent around Broadway:

> We're packagers now. There's a play that's on in a major
> regional theatre now that a number of us are trying to
> compete for. And what we're all doing is then going out and
> whatever producer gets it, trying to put people together and
> package it.

As "packagers," commercial producers say they have a hard time competing with nonprofits. To hear them tell it, when nonprofit theatres, specifically the Roundabout Theatre Company and Manhattan Theatre Club in New York, began producing on Broadway and, thereby, became Tony-eligible, they created a situation where a television or film star, looking for the kind of acting credibility Broadway confers, could be eligible for a Tony by doing a ten-week run. This packaging-as-producing approach, with its emphasis on stars instead of plays, was scorned by several in New York, including one agent who tagged it "crack cocaine for audiences," and a producer who compared the approach to MGM in the studio days of movies. Commercial producers are hard-pressed to recoup their investment in such a short run, and a playwright's shot at a long run becomes subject to and limited by the schedules of stars. Stars, seeking great roles, may favor proven works over untried ones. All this, coupled with what an agent calls, the "slavish Anglophilia" of the commercial theatre, further erodes the traditional partnership of producers and writers and stacks the decks against new plays and American playwrights.

Agents tend to be critical of, but somewhat sympathetic to, the institutional theatres, at least to the extent that they attempt to produce new work. They are much less forgiving of the commercial theatre. One faults the nonprofits with taking fewer chances with writers than they once did, while expressing quite low expectations of Broadway, which risks even less and provides little sustenance for writers. Another takes the comparison to Hollywood that playwrights made of institutional theatre even further, calling most commercial producers "dilettantes." "Hollywood is creeping in in so many ways," the agent claims. As in the movie industry, plays go into "turn-around," where workshops serve to encumber rather than move them forward. Auteur directors, he argues, are on the rise, with producers making their closest relationships with the director, rather than with the writer. For another agent, the metaphor is starker: "New York is Las Vegas."

THE PRODUCER-PLAYWRIGHT PARTNERSHIP

The most eloquent statement we heard on the impact of the current theatrical climate on playwrights came, perhaps surprisingly, from a commercial producer, Elizabeth I. McCann, a multiple Tony Award–winning producer of plays for Broadway, currently associated with numerous productions, and with the renaissance of Edward Albee's career since his *Three Tall Women* premiered in 1994 (McCann produced its commercial Off-Broadway run). In addition to her defense of playwrights, McCann encapsulates the traditional—and powerful—partnership between the producer and playwright, a collaboration that, prior to the explosion of nonprofit theatre in the 1960s and '70s, defined the American dramatic theatre for decades.

> You cannot put limitations on a writer. He must be able, when he sits down at that machine, to write without any restriction. If Tony Kushner needs forty-nine actors and someone flying in from the ceiling, he can't sit down to write that play being told, don't write it for more than five actors and don't have any difficult scenic effects, because it's restricting his imagination and his vision— and that's happening. It's happening in the not-for-profits and it's happening in television. But the writer must have a limitless opportunity to express his imagination.
>
> Just about every playwright writes to a small cast, because they figure, "How am I gonna get this on, given the resources of these not-for-profit theatres, I can only get it on if I have a small cast." And that's death for a playwright.
>
> I got involved in a production of *The Cherry Orchard* in London, so I ended up watching it a lot. And those Chekhovian plays, which have large casts, the fascinating thing about it is his ability to take a small scene and put two servants on stage and the scene lasts a page and a

half and it just registers. You get the whole sense of that community from the strength of writing a page and a half between two servants.

Our poor playwrights wouldn't dare write that scene, because everyone would be down on them. "You can cut that scene with the two servants." And so, they are restricted very much by the economics of the theatre today. Only so many actors. And they start thinking that way; they start writing that way. When they get down at the typewriter, they figure, well, I'd better write this play for three people before I send it out. And that is a tremendous restriction on the playwright.

How you turn that around, I don't know. How you try and have any meaningful conversation with Actors' Equity, and you say, "Look, you know, why can't we create a kind of situation in which if a play needs ten actors, we can get a 20-percent cut in scale, or something? To compensate for the playwright's need." But, of course that argument would get you nowhere.

A playwright should not have any limitations when he sits at that typewriter, and a producer should have no other interest except what he wants to see on stage. The dominant thing is: Never produce a play you're not prepared to see more than once, because, if it's a hit, you're going to see it. And the producer has to have that sort of insane belief, too.

I believe in keeping everybody's focus on what they're doing. Frequently in [the nonprofit new-play-development] process, casts get changed. You're not dealing with the people who will finally put that play on. You do a play in La Jolla and then three months later you do it on Kansas City, and in the meantime you've written a screenplay for Disney. And then you've gotta get your head back into the play.

You have to give deep pause as to whether or not there

will be another great American play. There'll be good plays, but will there be another great one? Because all the circumstances work against the playwright and work against the producer. And, although they may disagree, the producer and the playwright have to be *joined*.

Bridging the Divide: Relationship, Continuity, Home

So many people long for a home. I don't feel like one specific theatre is my home. People are your home, because they move around. That's how it works now. I know very few people who go, "This theatre will do pretty much everything I write." It used to be that way. I have a fantasy of having a theatre home. If I had the right theatre home I wouldn't go anywhere else. Are we loyal to theatres? I would love the opportunity to be loyal to a theatre. I would take it very seriously. In TV and film they are loyal. That's why people get first-look deals. —PLAYWRIGHT

Elizabeth I. McCann's words cut to the heart of the work ahead: "The playwright and the producer have to be joined." In light of the divisions that have grown between playwrights and institutional theatres, as well as the decline of the producer-playwright collaboration, one thing is clear: The relationship between writer and theatre, specifically the theatre's artistic leadership, is the bridge that needs repair.

"Relationship" is a word that crops up throughout discussions about the state of the art. In artist-centered organizations, to draw on David Dower's earlier distinctions, "development"—that is, growth over time—belongs to the playwright, as much as to any given play. Playwrights grow bodies of work. They collaborate over time with producers, directors, actors. Their work matures as they mature and, also, as their knowledge of an artistic company and its community deepens.

Think about the examples with which we began—Chekhov, Molière, Shakespeare, O'Neill. History suggests that the success of playwrights and plays, more often than not, is fed by the continuity of artistic relationships. Continuity is an ideal, shared by *numerous* playwrights. "Home"—artistic home, creative home, producing home—is the name they give that ideal. Theatres often profess to sharing that ideal; few claim to have created it.

Among playwrights, the search for home in the theatre now has a nostalgic quality, since hardly any hold out hope of finding one within the current climate. One playwright captures this common feeling of looking back while longing forward:

> In the old days, playwrights were associated with theatres and there was real loyalty. Playwrights would go to Manhattan Theatre Club over and over again, or [...] Joseph Papp, or Second Stage. Now there is no loyalty, and you see that Terrence McNally and [A.R.] Pete Gurney, [Jon Robin] Robby Baitz, their plays go to all these different theatres. That feeling that we have our writers and we want to develop our writers has collapsed on the theatre side. All playwrights want is a home. What writers need more than anything is a place to develop their work, a place to grow. They need to expand. I was delirious to be at [a theatre] with 108 seats. That was a heaven to me. Wendy Wasserstein was really special. André Bishop [Lincoln Center Theater artistic director] has produced eight of her nine plays, and that's huge. Her home was a little bigger than the home a lot of us may have had for a few minutes here or there.

Another established writer echoes this sentiment, mapping a series of three homes he has had over the course of his career, each of which said, "We'll do all your plays." "The thing that is missing is continuity inside some kind of an artistic community," he explains. "Without this, every time you go into a theatre you're auditioning."

The feeling of home doesn't always derive from the relationship between playwright and artistic director, as one writer, who describes himself as the "king of residencies," explains.

> I'm not hanging out with the artistic director, because he's hardly ever there. It's not just the artistic director that I want. It's the producing people, the audience-development person, the casting lady that's going to be really important for me later. I want to meet everybody *not* in artistic, because those people are really interesting. They're going to have a huge impact in how I do my work later.

For most writers, though, this sense of home is so rare that the very notion of theatres adopting playwrights and just doing their plays seems, in the words of one, "really radical." "Theatres don't think that way," he argues.

They think, "Who is this person who's in our space?" The playwright can do so much more—an artist in the theatre as a liaison to the community, the community owning the theatre, owning the playwright. That conversation excites new work, brings new projects. The playwright may also bring in other writers, so the theatre can grow.

Even a fleeting experience of almost familial support can inspire a writer.

> Sometimes I go into theatres, and I just love the staff because they've read all the plays. They're excited about everything, even though it may be a failed production. They believe in it. That's a whole different environment compared to, "You're slot three; I'm already working on slot four." The hokey notion of the family is so important.

This continuity, a lasting mutual knowledge, has its practical, as well as spiritual, side. "One of the best things about writing for a theatre where you have a good chance that you're going to get produced, is that you're actually writing for a space," a New York City–based playwright elaborates.

> Thinking about the play from the beginning, you're thinking about the room it's going to be in, which is enormous. That's something that playwrights for the last 3,000 years have always known. I know what the theatre at Epidaurus looks like, what Drury Lane and the Comédie-Française look like. When we write a play, generally, we have no idea where or how or who, which has a huge impact on actually how we write.

Many artistic directors see the benefits of making homes for playwrights. As the head of one of the nation's "flagship" theatres muses,

> I think it works well when playwrights feel that they have a home with an organization, when they have commissions, when they have deadlines, when they know that they're writing for a theatre, when they know that someone is listening. And when they have an ability to be able to work on their play outside of commercial pressures before the play is put on.

There are, throughout the country, theatres that, in one way or another, build upon this priority. They build bridges with writers through ongoing, deepening relationships. Some create formal or informal residencies for playwrights. "We have a fifteen-year relationship with our resident playwright," explains the artistic director of a mid-sized theatre, devoted to new work.

> We produced his plays, but other than one commission, we never paid him a dime in between, except for once. Yet he is absolutely as much a part of our success as we are part of his. He comes to every opening, he comes to our fundraisers;

he's a part of the theatre. There's a no-lose situation. If every single theatre in the country that does any new work at all had a resident playwright with the only commitment being that if we like your play we'll produce it, but we'll help it along in the meantime…you would have ninety-six playwrights who would be a lot happier.

Sometimes this enduring relationship grows out of the ensemble nature of the theatre. Steppenwolf Theatre Company in Chicago is celebrated for its long-lived company of actors, but among the company are playwrights as well. A reason that theatre is successful with writers like Bruce Norris and Tracy Letts, a colleague reasons, "is that the mission of the theatre has to do with ensemble. The principle is you're better working a second, third, fourth, and fifth time together than you are the first. That's very much a core value of the company. It's part of the culture…"

Moreover, enduring relationships don't require the absolute commitment to produce everything a playwright writes. Rather, playwrights require honesty and clarity, true collaboration. "In the relationships that we have been able to sustain," a director of new-play development explains:

it has had to be OK with both sides being able to say "no." When I think about the people that we have done multiple projects with, there are probably an equal if not more number of projects that they have come to us about, or that we have gone to them about, that one or the other of the parties has said no, and that hasn't broken the relationship. In some cases, it has, but in the ones we've been able to sustain, both people are allowed to say no, and yet there's still the feeling that you can come back with the next idea.

If theatres don't often structure their companies around the principles of relationship and commitment, such principles may still guide their thinking. "I don't ever want to say yes to a writer if I don't think in my core I'm going to want to say yes again," an Off-Broadway artistic director asserts. Making "home" might be as simple as being available, offering hospitality without being asked. The dramaturg at a large institutional theatre expresses these virtues in cultivating regional writers. One "house writer"

> enjoys a literal drop-by status. I will drop everything, unless I'm in a meeting, to spend time with her if she drops by. She doesn't abuse that. She's very much part of the life of the theatre. When someone's under commission, it's important that they can send an e-mail and you will make time, and that you get in the habit of inviting them to everything. That if they're lonely and not writing, they can drop in to the theatre and have coffee with you and talk about the things that are in their heads.

Although the longing for home may reside in the writer more than in theatres, there is little disagreement about the altered environment. "The sense of a home for a playwright has changed," says one veteran of the new-play-development world. "It's not the way it used to be. There are fewer homes. It's a business on both sides. If a playwright has a play that can be produced anywhere, they want to get the best production they can, and, conversely, a theatre wants to do the best work they can." The associate producer of an Off-Broadway nonprofit attests to the effect this climate has on writers: "They're very suspicious. [Playwright] Theresa Rebeck in her book has a great quote—'when a theatre tells you that you have a home, what they really just mean is that they want the right of first refusal on all your plays and they don't want to have to pay you for it.'"*

Inevitably, theatres weigh their commitment to their favorite writers with the desire to open doors to new voices. It's

---

* Theresa Rebeck, *Free Fire Zone: A Playwright's Adventures on the Creative Battlefield of Film, TV, and Theater* (Manchester, NH: Smith & Kraus, 2007), p. 79.

part of the struggle of growth and change within the institution itself. "It's tricky. It's wonderful and beautiful to have an artistic home, and to have a commitment to playwrights, to artists, and to maintain that," reflects the literary director of a large regional theatre.

> The danger can be that then you end up producing the same artist all the time, and nobody else has an opportunity. There's always that balance that needs to be achieved—How can you both create an ongoing commitment to artists, and leave some avenue open, not just because it's good to support other people, but because we need to continue to have change in terms of the kinds of voices that we have on the stage?

The head of a "downtown," developmental theatre in New York City seconds this commitment to rotating opportunity. "I have limited resources and limited space for artists to work. I am trying to keep including more artists. I'll make a commitment to an artist for four or five years, but I only have a limited number of opportunities."

This tension, between commitment over time and the need to spread resources around, between continuing and fresh relationships, is indicative of the many tensions that appear as our snapshot of the nonprofit new-play world comes into focus. Though some of these tensions stem from intentions and practices gone wrong, many seem natural, inevitable, conflicts between people and principles meant to complement each other. Over time, some of these tensions, such as those between playwrights and theatres, have been exacerbated by systemic changes. Some result from confusions of purpose, a lack of clarity about who or what is served at any given moment—the work, the makers of the work, the audience, or the institution. Some, as we'll see, have economic origins, like the difficulty of sustaining writers through mid-career in a culture that stresses emergence. Finally, we find conflicts that grow out of changing values in a field where, possibly, creating homes for few has been trumped by the desire to create inclusion for many.

We began with examples of playwrights at the center of theatres and end this first chapter with the full awareness that they now find themselves on the outside looking in. Our next questions are practical ones with answers based less in perception than fact: How do the economics of playwriting contribute to this sense of exclusion? What can be done to make our writers feel at home again?

TWO

The Lives & Livelihoods
of Playwrights

I don't want to give up the idea that we can make a life as playwrights. I want health insurance. I want kids. But I can't do it as a playwright. You go from scarcity to "that'll work for four months." I'm trusting that there is some continuity, some way to say, "I am a professional playwright; I make my living as a playwright." I don't even know that that's in the language of most of the playwrights I know. That to me is sad. —PLAYWRIGHT

PLAYWRIGHT Robert Anderson, author of *Tea and Sympathy* and *I Never Sang for My Father*, coined the phrase, "You can make a killing in the theatre, but you can't make a living." Later, with the decline of Broadway as a home for straight plays and the proliferation of Off-Broadway and regional theatres, he rewrote his maxim: "You can't make a living in the theatre, but you can make a life." Does his revision still hold? Can a playwright today earn a living *as* a playwright? What does it mean for a writer to "make a life" in the American theatre? Is it possible to make one?

Although no two playwriting lives are exactly alike, commonalities abound. We've culled data on economics, education, productivity, and production, among other things, from surveys of 250 playwrights at all stages of career, and from conversations we held around the country. The picture that emerges is not, practically speaking, a pretty one. It is, largely, a picture of precarious personal economies, a lack of continuity in relationships with producing theatres, new-play development that does little to further the development of the playwright, a downward spiral of expectations about opportunity and artistic scale (e.g., "size" of plays, size of spaces, size of audiences), lags and gaps between output (the writing of plays) and fruition (seeing them staged), the attractions of television (which are artistic as well as economic), and the loss of the "mid-career" playwright in the United States.

This chapter probes the space between what playwrights need and what they commonly get. Even as we make grim report of the facts, however, we wish to convey a sense of the diversity and vibrancy of the American playwriting profession—both of which may be greater than at any time in our national history. We'll investigate race and gender here, and how these factors impact writers' careers and potential for production. Funding figures powerfully in playwrights' lives as well, affecting the ways in which writers define themselves in addition to how they sustain themselves.

Please note: The playwrights who we surveyed/interviewed for this study are all working professional playwrights. They are among those who have risen to the top of the crowded field at each career stage. They have gone to leading schools, gained entrance to competitive playwright centers, had productions on major stages, and won prestigious awards. We gathered their names from sources recognizable within the theatre as indicators of success. What follows, then, is a group portrait of the playwrights who are "making it."

Playwriting Lives: The Facts

YOU CAN'T MAKE A LIVING

Looking at the statistics, it's tempting to rephrase Robert Anderson's proposition even more bleakly: You can't get rich writing plays; you can't even get by. Financially speaking, there is no way to view playwriting as anything but a profession without an economic base. It's not a romantic notion that playwrights must be prepared to be poor. It's a sad fact.

FINDING: The average playwright earns between $25,000 and $39,000 annually, with approximately 62 percent of playwrights earning under $40,000 and nearly a third making less than $25,000.

This statistic may seem striking on its own, but it is made even more sobering by a couple of other discoveries. For example, **half of the playwrights surveyed live in New York City and another quarter in Los Angeles,** cities where low incomes crash up against unusually high costs of living. Additionally, when you consider that **the average playwright in our study is thirty-five to forty-four years of age** and that almost a third of the playwrights in our study were older than that (in other words, a full two-thirds are thirty-five or older), it becomes clear these financial straits aren't places on the map of some youthful Bohemia. Nor are they a phase playwrights pass through. Economic hardship is, for these artists, a chronic condition.

Of course, the dire economy of playwriting is not new. What is new, though, is the professional not-for-profit theatre that has grown up over the past several decades, in part to sustain those who work in that theatre. Unlike forty years ago, thousands of theatre professionals across the country are employed and paid some kind of living wage by this network of nonprofits. And, though each new season offers a few examples of successful plays that earn their creators a decent, if temporary income, most take home neither a salary nor a living wage.

The following writer's assessment may sound self-dramatizing, but it's true. "Most playwrights live on theatre at a poverty level. A production every other year if you're lucky, or a commission we can't afford to live on."

It is uncommon for a working professional playwright in America to earn even $20,000 a year from writing for the theatre. Playwrights, for the most part, need to work outside of their field to make ends meet. More often than not, they piece this work together. Of the great number of playwrights whose so-called living is derived from work unrelated to playwriting, 56 percent do temporary or freelance jobs, as opposed to 44 percent who hold full-time and/or permanent ones.

Start with our playwrights' average profile: older than age thirty-five, almost certainly college educated, very likely possessing an advanced degree, and living in a major urban center. On average, over five years, this writer will bring home $25,000

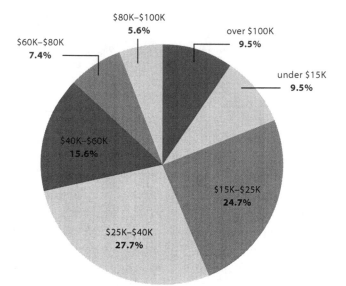

2.1 WHAT HAS BEEN YOUR AVERAGE ANNUAL INCOME OVER THE PAST FIVE YEARS (INCOME FROM ALL SOURCES)? *

> **FINDING:** Slightly more than half of the total income earned over the past five years by the 250 playwrights surveyed came from sources *unrelated to playwriting*.

* It's interesting to note that the same percentage of writers—9.5 percent— earned over $100,000 and under $15,000.

to $39,999 a year. Take away half of that, the half earned by unrelated, often temporary or freelance work, and you begin to see the real earnings playwrights derive from their art.

If you probe the phrase "playwriting-related," you can identify other disturbing details.*

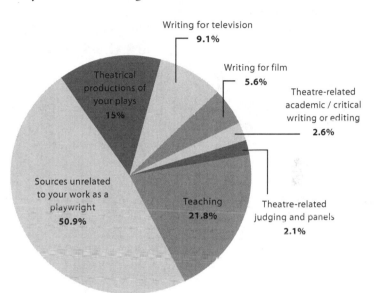

2.2 PLAYWRIGHTS' EARNINGS, BY SOURCE

> **FINDING:** Although approximately half of playwrights' total income came from playwriting-related activities—teaching, TV and film writing, and such—only 15 percent of that income came from their plays.

* In Fig 2.2, and elsewhere in this study, the total reported exceeds 100 percent. Our survey allowed playwrights to answer within a range of income percentages rather than with an exact percentage. As a result, our tallies, while providing an unmistakable snapshot of trends and financial realities, are less than exact.

The bulk of income playwrights describe as "coming from playwriting" is only indirectly related to the writing and production of plays. Eighty-five percent of their playwright-related income actually comes from teaching and writing for television and film (this accounts for more than 36 percent of total income). As writers report higher earnings, the likelihood substantially increases that they're either teaching or writing for television. (It's unusual for playwrights to do both.) Often success in one area goes hand in hand with opportunity in another. For instance, playwrights with higher incomes, earning a greater percentage from teaching or television, tend to be older, have more plays written and fewer plays un-produced. Once a playwright earns more than $60,000 a year, the likelihood is that approximately 70 percent of that income is coming from television. Again, even the high earners rarely take home more than $20,000 annually from playwriting itself over an extended period of time.

PRODUCTION DOESN'T PAY

The head of one play-development center expresses the outrage many feel about economic inequality within the field itself:

> Playwrights have historically been expected to do their work for nothing. Why would they put their time into a play that they're not going to get commissioned for, that they're not going to get paid for, from which the royalties are not going to be of any substance? It's hard to gauge who are the most exploited artists in the field, but most of us who are working in organizations are getting paid. We have health insurance. We have a salary. I am working with writers who are forty- or forty-five-years old. They have never had health insurance; they haven't been to a dentist in twenty-five years. Even the actors get a salary and hours toward insurance.

In probing these financial findings, perhaps the most shocking discovery is that **a mere 15 percent of playwrights' earnings come from their plays.** That money includes grant and award money, commissions, publication advances and royalties, and licensing fees, as well as production royalties. It gets more shocking. We asked writers to break down play-related income and found that only a small part of that figure derives from production royalties. Seventy writers provided us with such a breakdown, and this is what they said (figure 2.3):

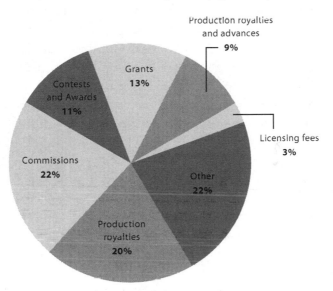

2.3 APPROXIMATELY WHAT PERCENTAGE OF YOUR PLAYWRITING INCOME COMES FROM...

FINDING: If these 70 writers are representative, 20 percent of 15 percent of their income is likely to come from production royalties. In other words, playwrights would ordinarily reap only 3 percent of their incomes from production.

Thus, an average playwright, making $39,000 a year (the top end of average), might make $14,700 (49 percent) from playwriting-related work, $5,850 (15 percent) from their plays generally, and $1,170 from production royalties. At the bottom end of average, the reward would be $12,250 from work related to playwriting, $3,750 from the plays themselves, and a paltry $750 from royalties.

Again, it isn't only early-career playwrights who face extreme or devastating financial constriction. Most established writers have it no better. The leader of a laboratory for writers and other theatre artists recalls seeing her community's most prominent playwright at a Theatre Communications Group conference. She quotes the writer as saying, "'I need health weeks; I need health insurance.' He had like five or six productions going on, and he still cannot support himself as an artist. And we in the community look at him as a success."

This isn't merely the playwrights' problem; it's the theatres' as well. "We lose a lot of talented people," one artistic director laments, as many others have done for years. "They burn out and leave the field because of that financial struggle. They start having kids, lifestyle things come up, and they don't have the level of support they need to stay in the field." As we'll see, often the people who leave—by their own volition or of necessity—are the very ones who have established their voices and honed their craft, who have had moments of artistic success without the concomitant financial sustenance. The economics of playwriting are akin to those of a hobby; you might make a bit of cash by buying and selling old comic books, but you don't plan to live off it.

The lives of plays should, by all rights, be long (witness the Greeks). There are always more theatres out there to produce them, to add to the playwright's income stream. In reality, this isn't so. Certainly, there are, every year, successful plays with numerous productions, as well as plays by major writers that enter the repertoire and continue to be produced for years. On average, though, playwrights have only one or two plays professionally produced three times or more, a significantly low number—proof that the American theatre suffers from what has been deemed "premiere-itis," that is, the overvaluing of first productions and the devaluing of subsequent ones. (We discuss this more in Chapter IV.) "Premiere-itis" undercuts the ability of theatre writers to maintain an income stream over time from royalties.

Production, the grail of playwriting, can be a losing proposition, as playwrights receive no pay for the time spent in rehearsal whether in their hometown or elsewhere.

> How do you pay your rent when a production pays you $3,000 or $4,000? They expect you to be there for a month without any per diem, and you can't work on anything else for a month. At the end of it, you spent money to eat and take care of yourself, and then you go home and you don't have any other income because you haven't been selling anything for a month.

As this scenario demonstrates, **there are many instances in which production actually costs playwrights.** There are many more instances when almost everyone involved in a production—actors and technicians on a weekly salary, directors and designers paid a fee—earn more than the playwright, despite the years of solitary labor that precede production. In theory, this investment of time is an investment in the future earning potential of the play. If it is only produced once, though, as so many plays are, the writer can never make good on the investment.

Some of the economics of production are hidden. For instance, although most theatres fundraise to supplement ticket income—50 percent raised/50 percent box office is, roughly, a common split—the income playwrights derive from production is not similarly supplemented. There is no similar adjustment available to them. Commissions and grants are meant to supplement royalty income, but, as we'll see, their impact, though cumulatively greater than royalties, adds too little to change the picture. In essence, theatres produce on a not-for-profit model, but playwrights, dependent on royalty percentages from ticket sales, mostly earn as they would in a commercial, for-profit world.

Playwrights complain that new-play development programs "fundraise on the backs of writers," because, although
artist support justifies the programs, the artists themselves rarely
benefit from such funding. They get paid nothing or very little
(expenses and travel at best) for their participation. In most
theatres, writers must rely wholly on box office for their royalties.
Moreover, since theatres often slot new plays into smaller spaces
with fewer seats and lower ticket prices, sometimes discounting
previews as well, it is the playwrights, with no way of making up
the difference, who pay the price. On top of that, many theatres
work to cultivate and expand audiences through discounted
tickets, free nights of theatre, and "pay what you can" nights
or, even, lower ticket prices across the boards. Playwrights
encourage and applaud these efforts. They share the theatres'
concern about ticket prices and the need to attract and grow
audiences. There are, though, no current efforts to mitigate, for
writers, the financial fallout of these practices. As one playwright
quipped after a meeting, 'Pay what you can' nights at theatres
are 'earn what you can nights' for playwrights."

In theory, new-play commissions and playwriting grants,
the other two largest categories of playwriting income, are
designed to supplement production royalties. Their impact
is, though, in the context of total earnings, weak. Playwrights
bring in slightly more money from commissions than they do
from production, even though a full quarter of playwrights have
never been commissioned. **The large majority who have been
commissioned received amounts averaging $3,000–$4,999. A
third of all commissions are for less than $3,000,** while payments
of over $9,000 are rare and over $12,000 practically unheard of
(see Figure 2.4).

In the realm of money for time, however, these figures
seem insignificant. A commission almost never pays for anything
near the amount of time it takes to write a play. According to our
findings, the average play takes one–two years from inception
to complete and six–twelve months from the moment writing
begins. So even a quick writer with a high average commission

in pocket—who collects $5,000 and conceives and pens a play in a single year—grosses only a little more than $400 a month for the effort.

Of course, for a playwright who writes a play on commission and then sees it produced, the initial fee is, presumably, prelude to greater income from royalties. For many writers, this connection is theoretical. It is unclear how many commissioned plays go on to production at theatres other than the commissioning theatre. Relatively few writers, however, have plays commissioned and produced by the same company. Forty-three percent of writers have either never received commissions or have never had a produced play begin as a commission at the theatre that produces it. Twenty-four percent of writers have had only a single play commissioned and subsequently produced by the commissioning theatre. In the context of total output, plays that bring in both commission and royalty money from the same theatre are rarer than rare.

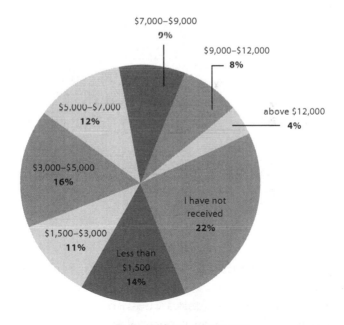

2.4 COMMISSION AVERAGES

Grants are often larger and almost always less complicated than commissions. The equation is simpler: direct grants—distinguished from commissions by not requiring the writer to complete a play—usually exist to buy playwrights time. Grants account for 13 percent of writers' income on average over the past five years. A large majority of writers (70 percent) have received them at one time or another. The size of these grants tends to be considerably larger than commissions. We asked playwrights to list their five largest grants and the granting agencies they received them from. One hundred and sixty-nine writers listed 442 different grants. The average playwright's largest grant is $10,000–$15,000, with other grants averaging $5,000–$9,999.

The granting agencies most frequently listed are:

FUNDER	RANK	FREQ	% OF TOTAL
NEA/TCG	1	29	6.6%
NEA	2	25	5.7%
Jerome Foundation	3	24	5.4%
New York Foundation for the Arts/NYFA	4	19	4.3%
Guggenheim Foundation	5	17	3.9%
McKnight Foundation	6	14	3.2%
New York State Council on the Arts	7	13	2.9%
Rockefeller Foundation	8	12	2.7%
Pennsylvania Council on the Arts	9	11	2.5%
Helen Merrill Foundation	10	9	2.0%

2.5 GRANTING SOURCES FOR PLAYWRIGHTS

One statistic offers a ray of hope: 18 percent of the 442 grants listed were in the amount of $25,000 or more. Sadly, we suspect that the hope is somewhat false. By far the biggest number of these large grants (twenty-two, or more than one-quarter) were given as part of one of two programs from the National

Endowment for the Arts and Theatre Communications Group, both of whose programs—the NEA Playwright Fellowships and the NEA/TCG Residency Program for Playwrights—have been discontinued (the Fellowships since 1995 and the residencies in 2007). The next largest number of equivalent grants come from the Guggenheim Foundation (12) and the McKnight Foundation in Minneapolis (5). Two main sources of $25,000 grants, however, have dried up.

LIFE AMONG THE MIDDLE CLASS

> *The days when somebody on their 1040 form puts "playwright" where it says "profession" are gone.* —PLAYWRIGHT

There are those who agree that the economics of playwriting are impossible, but express dismay that writers are surprised. Why, they ask, should any playwright expect to be able to achieve and maintain a middle-class lifestyle, unless they come from money or marry it? "Thus was it ever," says one artistic director, who takes home a salary well above the average for writers, and has the benefit of health insurance. He proffers the long, philosophical view of the problem:

> Is it different from at any point in time, either in our history or in Western history? As much as we all believe great civilizations revere their elderly, their teachers, and their artists, in point of fact, we don't revere them with money. I don't mean to be un-politically correct, and I certainly don't mean to suggest that artists don't deserve to live, because, God, they do; but there is a little something counterintuitive about the presumption of there being a kind of an economic level playing field.

Artistic directors are not alone in the view that, for playwrights, a middle-class life is unrealistic. We heard a similar argument from some older playwrights, specifically from those who teach fulltime. On one hand, there are those who have made careers in alternative theatre and seem to see the assumption that a playwright can earn a living from the theatre as part of the problem—the problem of professionalizing an art, the problem of fighting a losing battle to get produced by the handful of prominent and well-heeled theatres (mostly major LORT theatres or Off-Broadway theatres with a commercial presence), and the problem of a system of professional, MFA training that creates both debt and the false expectation that there's a living to be earned, if you just find a way in. "These people think they want to be middle-class and be writers, and I don't understand how that can happen," one veteran playwright/teacher declares. "That comes from institutionalized theatres like the Taper and Manhattan Theatre Club. The people [on staff at those theatres] have middle-class jobs, so playwrights think they will also have a middle-class job. Playwrights have to be out in the world for a while before they figure that one out."

On the other hand, there are well-established playwrights who make the case out of what they project as an earned realism. "It has not been true for a long time that there's a pot of gold at the end of a play. The lack of the pot of gold has caused the elves to go in a different direction." For the writer who wants to maintain a life in the theatre, according to this multiple award-winning playwright and educator, the two best, perhaps only, directions for the elves to go are musical book writing or a life given half over to television.*

Many writers are willing to sacrifice a great deal (usually money) in order to keep control of their work by keeping their copyright and authorial rights over that work, control that is in one way or another relinquished in television and film. Even so, some writers refuse to buy the argument that a middle-class

---

* It's important to note that the educators voicing these sentiments were, to a person, well-known, highly acclaimed writers who continue to have significant careers. In other words, these were not the sour grapes of writers whose only option was to teach.

living is too much to ask for. "I think that that old artist/garret thing is ridiculous," one scoffs. Another seconds that emotion: "The notion that that's the only style of life that supports true art is nonsense. And it's demonstrated over the centuries and decades by writers who lived and enjoyed living middle-class lives. I wanted to take my kids to Spain, you know."

Many writers, though, are quick to point out that they aren't looking for a pot of gold, or even for a particularly high standard of living. Often they are simply looking for places they can work and live, for health care, and for ways to raise a family. It sounds remarkably humble. "I grew up on the Central Coast of California," narrates one playwright who has written extensively for children. "My parents were migrant farm workers. I still look at being a farm worker in terms of I couldn't make a living doing this. I've had to find another way to support my craft. I wanted to raise a family. I had to figure out how to do that so I can still write." Not every theatre boasts a large salaried staff, and no one working in the not-for-profit field gets rich. Nevertheless, this expanded not-for-profit theatre community comprises hundreds of theatres that employ, sustain, and insure thousands of workers in all areas of the theatre. Why has the nonprofit theatre movement made middle-class living possible for some in the profession, but almost never the writer?*

---

* The sustainable finances of most independent artists in the theatre are equally desperate, and actors, directors, and designers experience many of the same struggles we describe here. When looked at next to these other artists, playwrights have some unique disadvantages that are worth pointing out. They have no opportunity for the kind of season-long employment that a small (and dwindling) number of actors enjoy in resident ensembles. They are rarely seen as potential leaders of theatres, whereas the ranks of American artistic directors are drawn almost exclusively from directors, so that, in effect, dozens, if not a couple hundred, of directors have salaries and benefits. And playwrights are unable to work on multiple projects on a fee-basis, as designers (by necessity) do. Also, it takes longer to write a play than to direct, design, or rehearse one. Finally, these other artists are able to collectively bargain in a way that writers, who own their work, cannot. All this said, we must reiterate: The finances of almost *all* independent artists in the nonprofit theatre are desperate.

GENDER & THE PLAYWRIGHT'S LIFE

When it comes to the effects of gender on a playwright's ability to get produced, statistics and experience do battle with one another. What begins as a clear, if grim, picture, grows murky, complicated, and contradictory. First, the background: Our respondents were fairly evenly split between men (52 percent) and women (48 percent).

> **FINDING:** When separated by gender, male and female playwrights report no significant difference in the number of plays produced.

This is one of the study's stickier findings, because it flies in the face of what playwrights say they see all around them: stages, especially main stages and those of the largest and most visible theatres, are dominated by the plays of men, specifically white men. Few of the playwrights we met or interviewed believe that men and women are produced in equal numbers. Or if they believe it generally, they question its particulars—women may have the same number of productions, but not the same scale of productions.*

"Women are having productions in smaller spaces, at smaller theatres, and on the second stage at larger theatres," a Minneapolis-based playwright points out. "And men are getting the coveted spot on the main stage." The same point is echoed by

---

* It is important here to remember what we did and did not study. Our findings are based solely on information given to us by the playwrights themselves—numbers of productions, income earned, and so forth. Although we surveyed theatres on numbers of new plays produced, we never studied their seasons or compared playwrights' perceptions about their own representation on stages with the offerings of actual theatres in specific years. As a result, though disparities between men and women, or white writers and writers of color, may appear obvious to anyone who looks at theatre brochures or theatrical listings across the country, such disparities do not appear as starkly from the information given to us by the playwrights themselves.

a New Yorker, looking for distinctions in "levels of production." "Women get done at a lot of small, spunky theatres, and men are done at Playwrights Horizons, New York Theatre Workshop, and the Roundabout. Any of us can have maybe six productions at these small theatres, but Mamet and LaBute are going to be the ones that are visible." A third playwright boils it down to money. "Usually those [small] productions pay $500. And then you would make $3,000 a year. The level of production and the financial fallout of doing smaller productions as compared to main stage is huge."

This contradiction between data supplied by the writers (number of plays, number of productions, etc.) and the data of experience was brought home when, during the writing of this study, an ad hoc group of women playwrights in New York, studying the 2008–09 Off- and Off-Off-Broadway season at more than a dozen leading theatres of different sizes, discovered that of fifty plays by living writers scheduled for production, only nine were by women (one African-American male writer had a play on the docket and there were none by Asian, Latino, or Middle Eastern playwrights).* Similarly, a 2002 report from the New York State Council on the Arts Theatre Program, "Report on the Status of Women: A Limited Engagement?" by Susan Jonas and Suzanne Bennett, found that in 2001–02, according to listings of the TCG membership theatres in *American Theatre* magazine, plays by women made up only 17 percent of the season's offerings. (This number does not tally discrete women, so, for example, numerous productions of Margaret Edson's *Wit* or Yasmina Reza's *Art* would have helped elevate the figure.) The authors cited a 1998 NYSCA study that found, in smaller Off-Off-Broadway theatres (those with budgets under $500,000), representation of

---

* The theatres include the Roundabout Theatre Company, Lincoln Center Theater, Manhattan Theatre Club, the Public Theater, the Second Stage Theatre, Playwrights Horizons, the Vineyard Theatre, New York Theatre Workshop, Primary Stages, Soho Rep, Rattlestick Playwrights Theater, the New Group, and the Atlantic Theater Company.

women playwrights rose to 30 percent. Although this decade-old finding tests something we did not—the representation of women playwrights in current seasons—it nevertheless is consistent with the conclusions of the playwrights in our study's national meetings.

> **FINDING:** Though male and female playwrights at the same career stage report the same average income, the average career stage for men is significantly more advanced than that of women. As a result, the average income for women playwrights is significantly lower than men's—$25,000–$39,999, as compared to $40,000–$59,999 for men.

Although male and female playwrights report similar numbers of productions, the argument that women's work is relegated to smaller stages and less visible theatres gains force in light of overall income. There are no notable differences between men and women in the percentages of income derived from theatrical productions of their plays, writing for television, writing for film, theatre-related academic/critical writing or editing, theatre-related judging and panels, teaching, or sources unrelated to their work as a playwright. The portion of their income that comes from production royalties, commissions, awards, grants, publication royalties and advances, or licensing fees is, likewise, roughly the same. Only the total earnings, on average, differ.*

Several writers suggest that women's opportunities are disproportionately developmental. "That's the only time where I see the amount of women being the same as or more than men,"

---

* Since career stage was determined by the playwright-respondents themselves, it isn't possible to know what went into every self-designation. Presumably, though, level of productions received, prestige of theatres involved, and size of income earned all play a part. As one young writer puts it, the scale of theatres is a big factor in "how you define yourself: 'emerging,' 'early career,' and 'mid-career.'"

one writer claims. "It's only in the reading series or the developmental thing. Women get developed and men get produced."

Another suggests that women playwrights have to vie with each other for limited opportunities, and that they have to justify the structure and subjects of their plays in ways that would be unthinkable with men. "My female peers and I get pitted against each other in ways that are ridiculous. They do new plays by men a lot. And they think that the subject matter is more important if a man says it. Or more universal. It's smaller if a woman says it, or more personal."

Women may be rewarded on par with men at each stage, for each kind of work, but, apparently, men advance through their careers more easily and, so, earn more.

RACE & THE PLAYWRIGHT'S LIFE

On the subject of race and ethnicity, our findings are still knottier. Our responses from playwrights of color suggest both positive trends and chronic under-representation. The size of this response is too small, however, to draw solid conclusions. More so than in other areas, our quantitative results raise many questions and provide few answers. Although they were almost always viewed with skepticism and even disbelief, if not rejected out of hand, by our roundtable participants and interviewees, the data on race provided a starting place for discussion. More work will certainly be needed in this area, with access to a larger sample group.

Most problematically, the writers of color in our survey group reported receiving roughly the same number of productions as their white counterparts, at all career levels. Their survey responses indicate that they earn the same average income from a similar distribution of sources—teaching, film, TV, royalties, grants, for example*—as their white colleagues. The overall income of the respondents appears to be on par with

---

* One positive thing that can be said about playwrights across the board is that, while, as we've seen, the financial rewards of writing plays hover near the poverty line, there is pay equity at each level.

that of white playwrights. Unlike women writers in our survey, the writers of color did not self-identify at a lower career stage than white playwrights. If this equity held across the board, the field would have cause for celebration. Indeed, some cite these indications as proof that funding initiatives stressing diversity (as well as increased social consciousness about representation and diversity) have greatly expanded opportunities for writers from traditionally under-represented communities. They point to the considerable careers of a handful of high-profile African-American, Hispanic, and Asian-American playwrights as added evidence of increased inclusion.

And yet, writers of color consistently paint a discouraging picture. In meeting after meeting, playwrights and some artistic administrators of all ethnic backgrounds challenged the notion that writers of color are produced as frequently or as widely as white writers. One well-established writer, a white man, puts it simply: "Whatever the proportion of people of color in the United States now, that is not represented on the main stages of theatres." Another senior artist reflects the reality as she finds it:

> It's around "emerging," "new," "edgy," "under-produced,"
> "festivals," "reading series" where I meet the female
> playwrights, the non-white playwrights. It's assumed that
> if we're doing real theatre, viable theatre, theatre that has
> legitimacy, that is financially viable, theatre that means you
> have a career, we're talking about white men. Everything else
> is "new voices," "new," "emerging," "edgy," "festival," "small
> theatres," "bring it in and let's discuss it so we can comment
> on how to fix it."

A third writer, also well known in the field, insists that legitimacy—and the clout that goes with it—is bestowed by proximity to white collaborators.

> Race is one of the huge obstacles for many playwrights.
> Unless you are somehow validated by the company you're

keeping, you have no power. That is the elephant in the room many times—that we can't navigate without that champion next to us. Most of the time if I'm working on a project with [a well-known director], the theatre will pay attention. If I dragged in some unknown Filipino director I wouldn't get attention. They've got to feel comfortable.

Is this difference between the data collected and empirical observation simply a question of perception? Does it represent a weakness of methodology? The number of surveys we collected from African-American and Latino/Hispanic/Cuban writers is small: just 18 and 23 responded, respectively, out of a total of 250, accounting for 16.4 percent of that total. (Additionally, we received ten responses from Asian-American playwrights and four from Native American playwrights, another 4 percent and 1.6 percent of the total.) By any measure, it is dangerous to draw too many conclusions from this minimal sampling, in which the relative success of two or three writers might wildly skew the results.

One gauge of the strength, or weakness, of our data is to compare them to statistics for the U.S. population in general. First, a look at how writers identified themselves. The responding playwrights' ethnic heritage was 76.7 percent Caucasian, 9.2 percent Latino/Hispanic/Chicano, 7.2 percent African-American, 4 percent Asian-American, 1.6 percent Native American, and 2.4 percent Other, including those who self-report being Arab-American, Hawaiian, Armenian-American, and Jewish. Some playwrights didn't select racial designations and all were free to mark more than one that applied.

This spread falls fairly close to U.S. demographics for Caucasians (74 percent, including White Hispanics), Asian Americans (4.4 percent), Native Americans (.68 percent), and Other. The greatest disparity appears in the percentage of African-American playwrights (7.2 percent), whereas African Americans account for 13.4 percent of the country's total population, and Hispanics of any race (9.2 percent), who make up 14.8 percent of the nation.

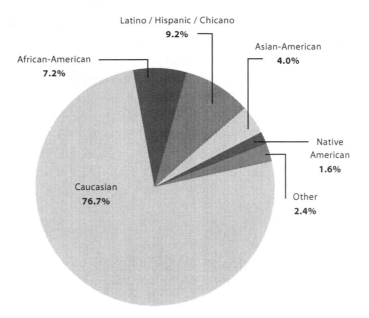

2.5 SURVEY PLAYWRIGHTS BY ETHNICITY

At such low levels these differences are considerable: just over half the national representation of African Americans in the U.S. population and more than one-third below that of Hispanics. Is this an accurate representation of the profession? Do black and Hispanic writers enter the profession in smaller numbers? If so, why? Do they lack access to the kind of schools and theatres and professional organizations from which we culled our lists? Do the harsh economics of the playwright's life make the profession less attractive (or viable) to people from traditional American minorities, already grappling with the economic affects of discrimination? Or do they choose to operate in a different theatrical universe? If so, how can these groups gain access to the part of the field covered here? Do the successes of a handful of prominent African-American and Latino/a playwrights mask the lack of opportunity for others? If opportunities for writers of color are so limited, do they leave the field in greater percentages than white writers, and, if so, does this shift the statistical balance to those with more robust careers and higher, more competitive incomes?

Amidst the data, two details stand out. First, African-American respondents were younger, on average, than other writers, raising the possibility that more young writers from this group are entering the field, unless, of course, more older writers have left it. Second, African-American playwrights tend to earn more from commissions than other groups. Might theatres be using such commissions to support and sustain these writers, to encourage writing, and keep them in the theatre? Or is this, as one African-American playwright calls it, "guilt money," given to support writers of color in lieu of producing them?

For writers of color, theatre lives and production can be complicated in ways that go beyond finances. All but the most conscientiously experimental white writers tend to be seen as "mainstream." So-called mainstream theatres, many say, produce predominantly "white" plays, by white writers, about white people, for white audiences. For writers of color, fitting into the mainstream, as defined by a largely white theatrical establishment, becomes an aesthetic issue. Can their work fit into this "mainstream"? Do they want it to? How does the mainstream theatre accommodate, or fail to accommodate, a variety of racial and ethnic backgrounds and modes of expression, across bodies of work? Do these theatres, once they have accepted a writer, allow that writer to change and grow, even if that growth leads them to tackle race in different ways, including dropping the subject altogether? When theatres consider their work, what judgments do they make about universality that differ from how they view the work of white writers? How does race itself become an issue in their work in ways that do not apply to white writers? One writer illustrates some of these arguments:

> When I first starting writing, I was just a writer. Someone
> said, "You're a Latino writer." I said, "Okay," and that
> became a brand that I was always uncomfortable with, but
> I somehow felt I had to speak to. The companies who say

they want to [produce me] are always telling me, "You aren't
Latino enough." I don't know what to tell you. If you can't
read it in the work, if you can't open up your point of view,
then it's a problem.

This expectation—that writers from non-white backgrounds will write about race in an explicit, explanatory way—
limits the writer's ability if she wants to get produced. One artistic
leader—who works at both an established theatre and a small,
young company—both racially specific—describes the schism:

> Some writers' natural sensibilities will lend themselves to a
> more mainstream, palatable aesthetic anyway. I don't think
> they're necessarily compromising. It's just that the things that
> they're interested in, the way that they situate Asian-American
> characters in the larger mainstream world, happens to match
> something that these theatres can produce more readily. For
> instance, sometimes they want to explore language. They have a
> certain poetic or violent sensibility; they don't want to deal with
> race head-on at all, but they want the characters to be Asian-
> American. The market for that kind of play is very rare, because
> you're not explaining race, which is what a lot of the crossover
> hits have been, but you want ethnic representation on the stage.
> It's very difficult to then funnel these playwrights toward the
> right places where they feel they can advance their career.

Writing about race—or about non-white characters—can
have practical implications for playwrights as well, especially
outside of major cities. "If I am going to write about Asian-
American characters," an L.A.-based writer remarks, "that limits
me. Some theatres in the Midwest, like Ohio where I've been
done, they say, 'We want to do it, but there are no actors.' Or
they'll say, 'Can we get a Hispanic?' This happened one time.
'Can we get a Hispanic person to play the Asian character?'" This
kind of practical limitation—and the attendant incomprehension
and insensitivity—constrains others as well, as one white writer

notes. "It affects anyone who's writing work for actors of color."

The lack of diversity on the staffs of the theatres themselves can provoke disturbing questions about the profession generally. Has theatre become like professional sports, where in the "big leagues" the front office is all white and diversity applies only to "talent"? What is the impact of this ubiquitous whiteness on play selection, marketing, and audience cultivation? Theatres may often be unaware of their own racism, as one African-American playwright observes:

> When I go to these theatres and do readings or work on a play, everybody on the staff is white. At [one large regional theatre], they were all lined up to meet the writer, and the whole cast is black. It was just funny. The actors were happy. They tell me, "This is the first time we've been in this [main stage] space." Then the theatre realized, these guys are great; "We'll do *Crowns* the next year." They didn't know they had all this talent just sitting there. It's unbelievable how racist this business can be.[4]

ON THE TRACK

Considering the financial difficulty, if not near-impossibility, of maintaining a professional existence as a playwright, it's unsettling to note that a professional or career track for playwrights seems to have emerged over the past few decades. This track leads through college training programs, specifically those offering Masters of Fine Arts (MFA) degrees in playwriting. As one artistic director argues,

> Those incredibly successful training programs have by their very nature limited the demographic range of who becomes a playwright—not by race or ethnicity or region. The people

---

* These issues change enormously when playwrights work in so-called culturally specific theatres. We'll address some of these differences in Chapter IV.

who become the voices of American playwriting are people who are culturally capable of feeling like it's appropriate to spend three years in an MFA program at Yale. That's dangerous, the idea that there is now a path for becoming a serious playwright at the nonprofit theatre that path leads through an MFA training program. We need to make sure that we are creating opportunities for the theatre, ways into this profession that are not through those formal training programs, that there are ways to hear the voices that can't find their way to Brown or Yale or UCSD.

It's tempting to infer from the rise of this track, via higher education, that playwriting has concurrently become a more solidly middle-class endeavor. An MFA track will, necessarily, filter out whole classes of people, including the working poor, immigrants, and anyone for whom elite graduate training is off the radar.

The training track for playwrights begins in college. Fifty-one percent of respondents received formal undergraduate training in playwriting, either as part of a Bachelor of Arts degree (43 percent) or a Bachelor of Fine Arts degree in playwriting (9 percent). A full 56 percent of the playwrights completed Masters (8 percent) or MFA (48 percent) level training, a figure that doesn't include the other 7 percent who attended the non-degree program at Juilliard. In other words, nearly two out of three practicing playwrights come through one training program or another. Older playwrights are less likely to have advanced playwriting degrees, further evidence that this "track" is a fairly recent development. Of the respondents with MFAs, almost three-quarters come through one of six programs—Columbia University, Yale University, New York University, University of Texas/Austin, University of Iowa, and Brown University (in order by number of graduates). Add the non-degreed Juilliard students and **seven schools account for almost nine out of ten of the study playwrights with advanced professional training** or 42 percent of all 250 playwrights. The picture that appears is not merely of a track for training, but a system, with a handful of prestigious graduate programs feeding the field,* offering entrée to their students where access might be otherwise more difficult.

Those who majored in playwriting generally feel that their academic training was helpful to their professional career. Fifty-seven percent found it helpful or extremely helpful, as opposed to 24 percent who found it not very helpful to their professional career. One young writer feels his graduate training instilled in him a necessary writer's discipline. "I can write when I don't feel like writing, which is a pretty important thing to learn in an academic environment." And for many, it's the collegial community that remains a lasting benefit of grad school. "It's the nexus of a network that you begin, depending on when you go and where you plug in. That's been the most beneficial thing: the people that I met, the relationships that I developed."

In the profession, despite the sense of looking to these programs for the "next hot young playwright," reviews are mixed about how effective and viable the training is. There's widespread concern that graduate playwrights don't get enough production experience—"one in their final year is not enough," one literary director remarks—or, if they do, they are working with directors and dramaturgs who know no more than they do, a potentially damaging circumstance. One artistic director tells of an MFA playwright he works with who's been in a leading program for three years: "He's never had a one-on-one with the director of the playwriting program about any of his plays. That's not what they do. He gets feedback from his peers, but they don't know any more than him. I was astounded."

Several complain that graduate programs, divorced from the

---

* Because these schools were also among the many organizations from which we compiled our lists of playwrights to survey (some gave us contact information, some didn't), any specific findings will necessarily be skewed. These particular percentages, therefore must be seen as descriptive of general trends, though in no way definitive.

practical side of theatre, actually train writers to pen unproducible plays. On the other hand, as one playwright/educator says admiringly of Paula Vogel's students at Brown University (Vogel has recently taken over the playwriting program at Yale), "They are encouraged to go to the wild side and be inventive and break rules. A lot of those students have done very well, not by following rules, but by creating their own rules." There are a few advanced training programs for playwrights that pay their students way, and others that provide assistance in the form of fellowships. The vast majority charge hefty tuition. For professions with significant earning potential, student debt can be a short-term burden; for playwrights, it can be a perpetual one. Playwrights, needing the time and access that MFA programs afford, rack up debt to enter a field in which they will never generate enough income to pay down that debt.

THE ADVANTAGES OF EMERGING

> "Emerging" is a catch phrase. I'm considered emerging because the theatres didn't fish me out of the pond. I've been slowly trying to emerge and I'm drowning. I have a voice, I have plays. They've been developed. Emerge me already! It's better to be labeled "emerging" because you could be the winning horse. Every theatre wants to say, I "emerged" her. —PLAYWRIGHT

The professional track continues after graduation, as funding for writers and play development programs often tends to encourage the newest of new—the emerging or early-career playwrights. Top training programs—and the connections students make in them—are one way, possibly the most common and influential way, for theatres and agents to identify young writers of interest. In fact, despite writers almost universally resisting the term, "emerging playwright" is a category that more than two-thirds of all playwrights see themselves belonging to, and even clinging to. Emerging is where the money goes. It's where the buzz about new voices can be heard.*

Our respondents cover an expanse of career experience, with just under a third identifying themselves at either the earliest or the most advanced stages of professional life ("new" or "early career" and "mid-career" to "established") and a little more than two thirds (69 percent) clustered around the complicated label "emerging" (36 percent "early career" to "emerging"; 33 percent "emerging" to "mid-career").

Left to themselves, playwrights tend to think outside of these categories, or to fudge them. "I don't know any writer who comes to me and says, 'I'm emerging', or 'I'm mid-career,'" one artistic director says. "Writers are writers, and they would like to get their work done."

In practice, though, playwrights must work with just such distinctions. Writers describe efforts to recalibrate their resumes to qualify for emerging-writer grants. "For those of us that aren't going to be Sam Shepard and Neil Simon, what are the signposts that you're not emerging, that you're emerged? How do you quantify that? I've played both cards. I have underplayed some things and overplayed others because the grant may not want you to be emerging."

As a result, most playwrights judge their own career advancement by the size of theatres producing them and by the income they generate from their writing, rather than by their artistic growth. In other words, as one young writer explains, they are defined in large part from the outside, by where their opportunities and access allows them to work.

* Our study left it to the writers themselves to identify their own stage of career, though we presented categories for this identification. We hoped to keep the categories fluid, slightly ambiguous, to allow for the writer's own sense of movement, growth, or progress and to avoid the implication that career categories had fixed definitions (as if they should know, for example, what an "emerging" or "mid-career" résumé must contain). Our career categories, therefore, were multiple: "new or early career," "early career to emerging," "emerging to mid-career," and "mid-career to established."

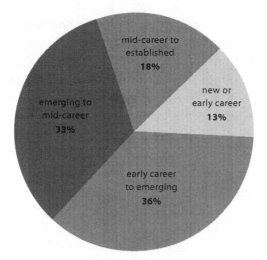

2.6 CAREER STAGE

The scale of theatres is a big factor. Where you see the potential for your career to go is going to determine where on that trajectory you think you are. Never imagining yourself on such-and-such stage is going to make it different for where you think you make that leap into mid-career or established or master, versus someone who does think they have a shot at that Tony Award.

The artistic director of a small experimental company seconds this analysis:

In the last few years it has become harder and harder to be produced at mid-sized or the larger theatres. There's more stratification in the kind of work as well. The less financially secure theatres that are doing the more experimental work end up with a certain kind of playwright. It may be that playwrights are incredibly active, incredibly well known among us, but they still consider themselves emerging because there is more of a ceiling to go through to get to a place where you might have a different kind of recognition.

The head of a playwright development organization casts the designation in economic terms.

> How many writers make a living writing plays? There are
> so few, so it's hard to think of yourself as beyond emerging,
> because "beyond emerging" probably suggests that you
> are making some kind of living at it. A lot of writers keep
> themselves at "emerging" because to have "emerged" means
> that you are supporting yourself on your writing, and so
> few writers do.

Or, as one writer puts it in this semi-satirical *cri de coeur*, "I have three resumes, according to my sense of, am I emerging or not? Drowning or floating, or what? What do they want? I would very much like to stop being emerging, but I don't know what it means. I would like the theatres to define 'emerging.'"

The head of an Off-Broadway playwrights' theatre tries to define it: "An emerging writer is someone who's not making a living as a playwright." Another artistic director counters, "That's just about everybody!"

Playwrights feel the pull to identify as emerging artists for as long as possible, since field support—new-play programs and, especially, funding initiatives—are heavily weighted toward supporting the young, new, emerging playwright at a moment of entering the field or gaining traction. You can hear the magnetism of the emerging label, even for the artist who has long since grown past it. "I call myself at this point an emerging master...I know my craft...I'm a brilliant performance artist, brilliant writer, brilliant choreographer, brilliant director...I haven't made $10 million, so I'm obviously an emerging master."

Most everyone we spoke to—individual artists and artistic administrators—finds the term slippery at best. "It's like pornography: we know it when we see it." For some it epitomizes an infantilizing that happens to writers in the theatre. "Emerging," according to one director of new-play development, implies that writers:

are not fully formed; their view of the world or their way of writing plays, or their aesthetic is still open for interpretation and to crafting by others. That becomes difficult for people who feel that they are accomplished, not in terms of number of productions or income, but in terms of their own aesthetic or their own world view. To be put into "emerging" tends to mean that they are still there to be taught.

In such situations, where the playwright is seen as someone to be shaped or taught, there's no guarantee that the artistic director or literary staff are, as artists, any more mature.

Here is a point of deep agreement between writers and theatres: **The "emerging writer" category is murky, overused, funder-driven, and should probably be retired.** The veteran artistic director of a small, experimental company expresses the same sentiment as the head of a large, LORT theatre. "That's such a wavy category. I wish we would drop it. For us it has very direct implications in funding. There are writers who would like to work at a small theatre like ours but who are not necessarily emerging, so I can't tap into emerging monies for them," says the first. "We don't use that term. But don't you find that the grant people do? It's grant-driven. It's certainly not internal to the theatre," the other agrees.

Playwriting Lives: The Fallout

THE DISAPPEARING MIDDLE CAREER

> You emerge for a while, and then you give up. It's rare
> that someone gets to stick with it, because it's a race
> against despair.

That is the way the next career stage for playwrights was described by an artistic director. Though this may sound melodramatic, it's not entirely wrong. To some the rubric of "emerging playwright" is a life raft that keeps them from drowning in the treacherous waters of middle career. Mid-career tends to be a time when grants dry up, teaching beckons, television becomes more alluring, and the ambitions of career and the demands of daily life grow less compatible, even as the small money of playwriting becomes less sufficient.

Moreover, in an ecosystem that defines itself by its newness, and that funds accordingly, there is no obvious way to celebrate the passage to maturity. At New York's New Dramatists, a developmental laboratory that grants playwrights seven-year residencies, alumni status brings with it mordant jokes about artistic identity: If you're no longer a New Dramatist, what are you—an old dramatist, a used dramatist, a used-up one?

Mid-career approaches differently for a playwright who has already had significant success and for one who hasn't. It's generally acknowledged that, even for a writer who's managed to "hang in there and develop a career," as one literary manager put it, sustaining that career is particularly difficult without a hit play, that is, one that received major awards or numerous productions or New York acclaim. "It only takes one play. It can be one play that makes that difference. But if you didn't have that one play, it's hard."

Even with one or more plays that bring in some money or renown in the small world of theatre or the wider world, breakthroughs are neither clean nor sustained. On one hand, very few playwrights get to production with a successful play without a great deal of time spent and debt accumulated. A Pulitzer Prize winner depicts the journey:

> You write early plays, and finally you get one that everybody perceives to be the one. That's going to be your flag, that's going to make your name. And that play, strangely and bizarrely enough, goes off on this long detour. It says "road to fame goes here," and that turns out to be this long, detouring route that ultimately ends up somewhere three or four years down the line in some sort of major production.

(Let's just say this is a happy story.) And what happens in the meantime is that this person still has no cash. So, now they figure out…you have to sell half of your time. You have to figure out who will pay the most for that half.

Versions of this story recur. Often, they're narrated with surprise that celebrated writers or those who have appeared to "make it" are, in fact, having trouble sustaining careers. An artistic director from San Francisco tells of having spent an evening with one such writer in Santa Fe.

He said, "The last two plays I wrote were totally unsuccessful." He had one production. He said, "There were too many characters in it, and I don't know how to write for my generation anymore." He was successful in his twenties and thirties as a playwright, and he's also now writing screenplays.

Another portrait: "a major American playwright" teaching "to keep his health insurance in force."

He's got a cult behind him. It's huge. But the people who do his work—they're colleges, so he gets eight dollars. If he has a new production every five years, that's a lot. And, at some point, he's done writing plays. Struggle, struggle, struggle, struggle, struggle. This somebody who is a prominent, dominant American playwright who has had a profound effect on the imagination of people and would be presumed, I think, to be doing very, very well, and he is just hanging on.

There are always new writers entering the field, though the number of opportunities remain relatively stable. In a system that stresses the new, experienced writers are forced to consider alternatives. The problem could be "classic ageism," one influential writer/teacher hypothesizes. "On the other hand, I'm rather lucky because I'm past sixty and I still can get produced. I'm a little scared about the future. It's another kind of diversity question."

Whatever the causes, it's evident that playwrights can rarely sustain consistent careers. The American theatre may celebrate a playwright for a time or reward a given work; it also has a short attention span and lacks the mechanisms to support bodies of work and lifelong careers. Another well-known playwright weighs in:

> We are only as good as our last piece. That tends to be a problem and even the most successful of us—maybe we had a gold card for five minutes. Theatre, by its very nature, is a very random business. You're visible and sparkling for two years, and then you become invisible.

In retrospect, many senior writers see this randomness as both natural and inevitable, if eternally galling.

> So many of the problems of playwrights are predicated on their assumption that they are entitled to a career. Why isn't it great to be a playwright and do one or two great things, and never do another? That's honorable. Careers are unsustainable for most people. It has nothing to do with talent. I've gone through periods where my work is hot and then other periods when it's not, and I realize it has nothing to do with whether I'm doing good work, or anything that I can control…I think, "Why have I wasted my life on this?" But, I have had sixty plays produced. Often in very tiny places, but they were still produced. A big part of it is my own ego. It's important that new writers be produced, and that means that I can't be produced as much. It's as simple as that.

Some go so far as to suggest that playwriting energy and playwriting careers have an inevitable life span. One writer notes the ways age and the clutter of life can impact not just energy but imagination.

> The energy that can get poured into making art, even when you don't have enough time, diminishes as you get older.

When there's a large chunk of time that has to be devoted
to something other than thinking about what you'd like to
write for the theatre, that time gets squeezed by other things
you have to take care of, and your ability to be imaginative
begins to shrink.

The head of a leading training program furthers this train
of thought, arguing that the way to keep writers in the field is to
support them when they're young.

We have a limited window of time in which to help writers,
and it is up until they're in their early thirties. After that they
will make other decisions. But if there are great plays to be
written by young writers, you've got to help them fast. And
you've got to help them by giving them cash so that they
don't have to go earn it, because that's the road to perdition.

THE TEACHER'S PATH

Looking back, older writers see the moments of possibility and
the almost universal moment of divergence, when playwrights,
for reasons of fiscal or mental health, lifestyle or ambition, choose
another path, either in addition to playwriting or instead of it.
Some writers stick with the theatre but enlarge their scope, adding
directing to their resumes, returning to acting, if they began there,
or running a theatre. Successful playwrights also argue that musical
book writing can bring financial reward, creative joy, and/or clout
when it comes to having their straight plays produced. Some
turn to other forms of writing, and occasionally score remarkable
publishing successes. One minimally produced playwright sold a
serial novel worldwide for huge sums and a more senior writer,
who claims not to know—or seemingly to care—how many
plays he has left in him, sold a food memoir "in four hours to
Penguin for a lot of money. It's a whole different world." He's still
writing, but he has achieved lucrative success in another—more
welcoming—genre. "You have to reinvent yourself."

Perhaps this perspective—in addition to the financial wall that nearly all playwrights hit—is one reason why so many accomplished writers turn to teaching in mid-career. Playwrights are more likely, though, to speak of the mission of teaching and its connection to their craft than of its pitfalls or economic expedience. "Your creativity as a teacher is huge," exults one. "You can inspire." Another refuses to separate the roles: "I consider teaching earning money as a writer." Indeed, the ranks of university playwriting programs—which have exploded in recent decades—are peopled by working playwrights of significant accomplishment.

Clearly this has been a boon to the field, in terms of creative mentorship. Despite a range of teaching philosophies, there is, possibly for the first time in our nation's history, a profession of educators who have come of age in the theatre, rather than in the academy. Their lessons reflect that experience. Earlier generations famously schooled their students in principles of craft, often captured in textbooks on dramatic structure and taxonomy. Current master teachers seem determined to train the whole artist. One influential teacher puts it this way:

> What I have to teach, if I teach anything, is to create an
> ego that can create. The ones who just want a set of rules
> are never going to get anywhere. The ones who realize that
> they're building an ego that is indestructible [will make
> things happen]. It's absolutely what you need to write a play.

Additionally, these artist-educators understand that their programs are as much about community building as they are about craft. "The other positive thing about these programs," the director of one explains, "why they're necessary, is that they're a substitute for bohemia. Students actually can meet each other. That's very good and it has nothing to do with our influence."

Certainly the infiltration of the academy by practicing playwrights has contributed to the creation of the burgeoning career track for writers as defined by a handful of advanced training programs. It has provided a way for playwrights to move more gracefully into mid-career without sacrificing their connection to the theatre. In this way, playwrights resemble other creative writers who sustain themselves in academia. "Most serious poets in America seem to make their living from university work, and that's quite acceptable," an artistic director notes. "It's not an issue about economics; it's an issue about the art and the work. I don't know if it's because we intersect with entertainment so much, there is an expectation that a serious writer has to make X amount of dollars as a living, and not really about the craft of writing and moving forward."

But for all the good of teaching, there are, as one longtime artistic and literary director elaborates, artistic pitfalls.

> The mid-career people are the ones that are taking teaching positions now, because you have to have some kind of track record to get the job. But there are a tremendous amount of writers, you can name twenty-five to thirty people, who are essentially functioning playwrights that have taken university jobs. I'm not advocating it. Academics is the perfect world—you're overpaid and underworked, you have a ton of time to write. It's a great job for a writer. The problem is, it doesn't seem to produce [the best] kind of writing, once they get in there.

Educators even rail at the students who think that there's a way to write a successful play, that their tuition money can buy them a career or the secret to one. "I don't care what style anybody writes a play in," the outgoing head of one program says. "But the more Ivy League the students are, the more that they want to dictate a certain type of style that they think will fit into the Manhattan Theatre Club or the Roundabout, and they are pursuing that style with a vengeance."

THE JOYS OF TELEVISION

Not long ago, the lure of television was financial. Things have changed. Money may still be the prime draw of TV, but it is clearly—and loudly—no longer the only one. Playwrights in large numbers are turning to television for its artistic satisfactions as well. We are, it is widely acknowledged, in a "golden age of television." Playwrights populate and lead the creative teams of such highly regarded recent series as HBO's *Six Feet Under*, *The Wire*, and *Big Love*, Showtime's *Weeds*, FX's *The Riches*, and network hallmarks such as *The West Wing*, *Friday Night Lights* and the many-tentacled *Law & Order*, to cite some of the most commonly noted examples. Writers on these shows work with other writers in often-satisfying collaborations. Along with the money comes increased responsibility and power, as directors, producers, executive producers. They can achieve a degree of creative control not previously found in Hollywood, because TV, unlike film, is a writer's medium. And more, they make something that reaches huge audiences, beside which even the greatest theatrical successes pale.

Theatres would do well to take note of this shift. Television is no longer something that playwrights are sheepish about pursuing, and the mythology of "selling out" rarely surfaces in conversation these days. Moreover, the craft imperatives of the form—its discipline and rigor—can strengthen their dramatic skills. The money also can buy them a sense of creative freedom in their theatre writing.

Testimonials abound. One television writer experiences a new authority in her theatre career:

> I feel freer. I can approach people at theatres that I want
> to approach and go, "This is the thing that I would like to
> do. Do you guys want to do this?" because I don't have the
> burden of saying, "This play is going to make you guys a lot
> of money." I write faster because of TV, because I have less
> time to write. The craft of television is to turn it around fast.
> That actually has been useful. I realized how fast I can write,
> because you have to.

For another, TV has freed her stylistically.

My plays are riskier now. I am getting the narrative part of me out in television, and I get to do the non-linear stuff in my plays. My plays are becoming more interesting to me, because there are no rules about what you write about in a play, because I assume that it is never going to be produced. I assume that I am writing it for me, so I might as well enjoy it. I'm taking more risks as a playwright and enjoying it more. The pressure is off of the play. When I was a playwright first and foremost, this play has to be produced or else I'm not going to eat this year. Now I'm eating, so this can really be about the art and it can be fun again. The writing work that's commercial is the safety job and the writing work that is my own is my own.

A third sees the opening of options for the stories she has to tell:

I made a very modest living from playwriting for a couple of years. You can't always count on grants. You can't always count on productions. I live in high cost-of-living cities, so I felt forced to look into TV as an option, because I don't have an MFA. Now I have options. If this theatre doesn't want it, maybe it could be a novel or a pilot. I have a lot more options instead of going, "Should it be at Actors Theatre of Louisville or Roundabout or Second Stage?" Now I think, "There's a story in me. What's the best way to tell it?"

Again and again writers describe their work in television (and, somewhat less prevalently, in film and other media) as releasing them from paying court to that handful of larger, more prominent theatres that offer the only, if still small, hope of notice and/or remuneration in the world of new-play production.

Far from selling out, television has become for many a key to job satisfaction and creative freedom that few experience in the world of new-play production. It does so on commercial (as opposed to nonprofit) terms. This needs to be underscored.

Embedded in these playwrights' descriptions of the joys and freedoms their television work has led to is a description of the American professional theatre: It is a field that does not support or reward their risks, that in many ways stifles their creative exuberance and squelches their sense of agency in their own work. Though other theatre people may still view TV as a deal with the devil, like the artistic director who described a playwright he premiered as "having the L.A. stink on him," playwrights are typically more sanguine. Says one, "People who go to write for *Friday Night Lights* are not really deciding, I can't really write good, so I'll have to write bad and get paid for it. They're just not."

Does television tarnish these writers somehow, spoiling their theatrical instincts or training these instincts out of them? Some artistic directors think so. Many contend that the medium of TV pushes writers toward naturalism at the expense of imagination, encouraging convention over invention, and stressing accessibility above complexity.* They complain that TV draws our most talented playwrights out of the field. "I'm making phone calls to agents and asking what about this writer or that writer," says the head of new-play development for one of the nation's largest theatres. "'They're not writing for theatre. They are doing television.'"

Even the writers who don't give over to television entirely, artistic directors argue, significantly reduce their theatrical output. For every example of a writer who "is writing plays seemingly at no changed clip than he was when he wasn't writing for TV," there are numerous counter-examples, the playwrights who, following some success in the theatre—or its opposite, a critical drubbing—turned to television and now go

---

* Interestingly, these are often the very charges that playwrights level against the new-play-development process at theatres. Playwrights, like this one in Minneapolis, fault theatres for unadventurous programming and for relying on the storytelling conventions—and conventionalism—of TV. "It's gotten away from what theatre is and toward what film and television are doing far better."

years between plays. New-play producers seem to understand the financial necessity of this work, and a few admit the creative draw of being present at a time of explosion, when innovation is welcomed and rewarded in the competitive world of post-network-only TV. One even saluted the possibilities: "God bless *Law & Order* that certain playwrights can make a living and pay for their families. It's a healthier scenario than it used to be, where you had two choices in life: to write for the theatre or not. You do have opportunities if you're lucky enough to do both."

Whatever new positivism exists about television, most playwrights say they would rather be writing plays—if they could afford to and if they found the theatrical climate more hospitable and vital. There's little romance about Hollywood as a cozy place to work among kind and noble beings eager to draw out the writer's best. But, as we've seen, there's little such romance about the not-for-profit theatre either. What does persist is a desire and determination among writers to keep writing plays, even when they doubt that anyone will produce them.

What Playwrights Want

> *I didn't become a writer to sit at home at the computer. I under-stand what the animal is when it's three-dimensional, and sensual, and it's on actors. What's gorgeous about theatre is that we get to sit in the room and take the thing on its feet all over the place and explore it in the collaborative process with the other voices. The thing, at the end of the day, has to be sensual, and three-dimensional, and dynamic. It has to move, it has to have a rhythmic quality. I don't know how to find that out when it's me and the computer.* —PLAYWRIGHT

The playwright's material life is, much more often than not, one of precarious fortune, economic scarcity, and rocky, desultory progress. It is—practically speaking—an un-life: uncertain, unmarked, undependable, and unsustainable. If material struggle is what playwrights get, then what do they want? Naturally, these struggles are, to some extent, offset by the other, obvious rewards—the joys and freedoms of a creative, self-expressive life. But this is a study of working, professional playwrights, not hobbyists. A professional artistic life requires fruition. For playwrights, that means seeing their work on stage, completed, realized, enacted. If this study establishes anything, it's that the centrality of playwrights in the American theatre, their ability to mature as writers, and their faith in that theatre are all being eroded by a lack of continuity of production. Few have the kind of ongoing relationships with theatres that encourage the cultivation of bodies of work. They are always starting over.

Let's look at the average playwright in this study: She or he has had five to six plays produced, and another five to six plays that get readings or developmental workshops but no production. This (roughly) fifty-fifty split between plays that go on the stage and those that stay in the drawer lines up with the statistic showing that our average playwright has written ten to twelve plays thus far in his or her career. With plays typically taking between six months and two years to write—from the time active writing begins—and a good deal longer from conception, it's apparent that playwrights who commonly see half of their work get to the stage can easily go two to four years between productions, a period of time that is stretched by the slow turnaround time at theatres, and the even slower periods of decision making and season planning.

DEVELOPMENT & PRODUCTION

> **FINDING:** Plays are only rarely produced by the theatres that "develop" them.

Statistics confirm what many playwrights have long been saying: New-play development, as currently practiced, does not truly lead to production. The average playwright has had only one to two plays produced by the same theatre that developed

HOW MANY OF YOUR PLAYS...	0	1-2	3-4	5-6	7-9	10-12	13-15	16-19	20+
received professional productions?	8%	22%	17%	15%	15%	7%	5%	2%	9%
had the professional world premiere in NYC?	45%	27%	11%	6%	5%	1%	1%	1%	1%
received more than 3 professional productions?	44%	23%	13%	7%	4%	2%	1%	2%	2%
were produced by theatres that had previously produced your work?	30%	35%	12%	10%	4%	3%	3%	0%	2%
received a developmental workshop/reading and production by the same theatre?	41%	31%	9%	11%	5%	1%	1%	0%	0%
received a developmental workshop or reading but not a professional production?	14%	24%	20%	17%	7%	4%	3%	4%	7%
What is the largest number of productions you have had of a single play?	12%	25%	14%	10%	8%	7%	4%	2%	19%

2.7 PRODUCTION ACTIVITY: PLAYWRIGHTS

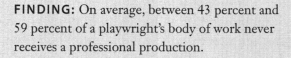

FINDING: On average, between 43 percent and 59 percent of a playwright's body of work never receives a professional production.

them. By contrast, the average playwright has had three to four plays produced by one of the theatres that previously produced his or her work. In other words **it is, typically, two to three times more likely for playwrights to have a play produced by a theatre that previously produced their work than to have a play produced by a theatre that gave the play a reading or workshop.** Or to put it in numbers: if a writer typically writes ten to twelve plays and has one to two of them developed and produced at the same theatre, the odds are quite long (one to two in ten to twelve) that development (readings or workshops) will lead to production. "What would help a lot," one mature playwright quips, "is if the theatres were actually producing, doing a production of at least one of the plays that they read every ten years in a play reading series. That would change the way that audiences came to those readings, and the nature of what the play reading series ideas are."

If developmental programs at producing theatres don't lead to production, then what are they for? On the upside, new writers meet people around the country and begin building a network of colleagues and supporters, especially within the literary offices of theatres. "From like the point of view of someone just starting out in their career," a young playwright affirms, "the reading experiences I've had, even though I had zero expectations that they would ever lead to production, have allowed me to meet artists in cities I would have never met otherwise, and gotten my work in the hands of people who give it to other people. It's a great career-development tool at a certain level of career."

Much more often, though, the lack of productions, in addition to its economic impact and the professional frustration it engenders, stifles creativity in unexpected ways. Whereas frequent production teaches playwrights about what one writer calls "the animal" that is the play and helps them mature as writers—furthering their stagecraft, increasing their awareness of audience, actors, and the limits of design, encouraging artistic risk and growth—infrequent production can lead to second-guessing, shutting down risk. As one playwright puts it: "When I get fewer productions I get a little conservative. This is your chance, and you feel that there is this scarcity in that. If I had four productions a year, in one I would like to experiment. Well, I don't."

The only place, other than consistent production, that playwrights say they experience the freedom to experiment and grow, is the new-play lab or playwright development center. These range in type from those that engage a dozen or so playwrights in an intensive summer retreat—the Eugene O'Neill Memorial Theatre Center's National Playwrights Conference in Connecticut or the New Harmony Project in Indiana, for example—to non-producing companies that sponsor a combination of retreat intensives and year-round programs to support writers—most notably the Sundance Theatre Lab in L.A. and Utah and the Playwrights Foundation in San Francisco with its Bay Area Playwrights Festival (BAPF). The Lark Theatre and the Cherry Lane Theatre's Mentor Project in New York City hold a combination of new-play development workshops and ongoing playwright developmental projects for select playwrights, to which the Lark adds international projects and ongoing writers groups. The Playwrights' Center in Minneapolis, Z Space Studio in San Francisco, and New Dramatists in New York support companies of playwrights (or, at the Z Space, other theatre artists as well) over periods of years, also combining programmatic offerings for both plays and playwrights, not the least of which is long-term collegial support from other talented writers. The flexibility, focus, and true writer-centeredness of these organizations allows playwrights valuable time in the laboratory, to attempt new things, explore, and grow without the pressure of "auditioning" for potential producers.

Playwrights are vocal in their praise of these organizations, distinguishing development there from readings, reading series, and the broad range of what are called "workshops" at producing theatres. One well-known writer, whose plays and musicals have been performed across the country, on and off Broadway, extols the virtue of this kind of freedom. "I liked working at the Playwrights' Center because they give you a lot of time to rewrite. Not having a production and having lots of rehearsal time, and then just sitting around a table or at music stands, is very, very helpful." Unlike the "cookie-cutter" development writers find at producing theatres, these labs allow them to suit the process to the artistic needs of the moment, safe from having to prove the worth of the play. "We need different things at different times in our artistic lives," he continues, "and part of it is flexibility. Every time you go into a theatre you're auditioning."

The value of these flexible, safe-haven laboratories is unquestionable. The necessity of production is absolute. We don't need playwrights to explain why productions are necessary. The artistic leaders of theatres can do it for them: "A play requires a production in order to have completion," says one. Others echo this sentiment: "Nothing competes with a production for a learning experience, for developing the playwright, for developing the play." "Playwrights grow and get better and write the next better play because the other one was produced with all its flaws." "Plays are written to be produced, they're not written like novels to be read, but written to be on their feet, and that is the way that playwrights learn and get better." Or, as an associate artistic director sums it up:

> If the complaint is valid that some playwrights don't know
> how to write for the theatre, or how to handle breaking
> form, they're not going to learn that just with actors around
> the table, they're not going to learn that in a three-week
> workshop, they are not going to learn from a reading.
> They're going to learn it because they had to go through the
> whole process and fight with the director.

In other words, **production is development.** It is the playwright's crucible, the play's forge. In the past fifty years of American playwriting, production has moved from the single means of new-play development to its last call. In the 1960s and

'70s, especially Off and Off Off Broadway, plays were thrown onto the stage in great numbers, hot out of the typewriter. Famously, theatres like La MaMa, Theatre Genesis, and Café Cino would give writers brief intense rehearsal periods and short runs. Theatres that now dominate Off Broadway with seasons of six or eight productions, at that time produced twice as many plays each year, sometimes more, exploding theatrical convention, filling the New York theatre with new energy, and creating a generation of playwrights who learned their craft in practice. Writers, as one playwright advocate points out, often find solutions to a play's questions in their *next* play. Theatrically, this kind of growth calls for continuity and the full realization that only production can offer.

For the past twenty years or so, development has been synonymous with "readings" and the ill-defined "workshops." Theatre seasons have, in many cases, shrunk. Productions grow more precious, and the stakes of each grow higher. Rarely is there heard this kind of fierce commitment to production as development that we heard from one "downtown" New York artistic director:

> The best development process is just putting on the play....
> Eschew everything and just put it on. Cauterize your
> audience. "This is it, get used to the rough edges; these
> are the plays you are going to see."

THREE

The Way of the Play

If you could imagine there's lots of planes in the air, but there's only so many places in the landing strip. That's the problem playwrights face. How do I get to the control tower so I can land? Otherwise, I'm just circling in this hell of development... — PLAYWRIGHT

FROM IDEA to draft, reading to workshop to production, premiere to ongoing life, the journey of the new play is tortuous, random, and unpredictable. The process of selection, hidden from the writer and often protracted over several years, can be a puzzle—even to the artistic staff engaged in the process. Across the divide, playwrights call for theatres to see the damage done by the current system—damage to inspiration, immediacy, plays, bodies of work, the vitality of the theatre itself. Theatres seek to demystify this "system," to cast it as a series of complicated human decisions based on institutional realism, yes, but also on passion. Playwrights seek access to theatres, specifically to the decision-makers, often finding entrée blocked. Theatres, especially the many small and mid-sized ones that dot our nation, seek access to writers and writing of the highest quality. They, too, often find doors closed by the very artists they wish to work with.

How do plays move through a theatre? Through the field? How do they get selected for production? Where do they get stuck? Some theatres effectively shepherd, develop, and produce new work. How do they do it? And what is to be learned from the most successful journeys? This chapter tracks the movement of the plays themselves: the access points, obstacles, support, selection, rejection, and development—the road to production. It addresses the question at the heart of this study: How can we clear the path for plays of merit to get to the stage? How can we open channels for the new?

The Chosen

GETTING IN THE DOOR

FINDING: Lack of access to artistic directors— the people who make the final choice about what plays to produce—is seen by playwrights as the single greatest obstacle to getting their plays produced.

Two-thirds of the working playwrights in this study believe themselves to be hampered by a lack of access to top decision-makers.* Compare this with the next-highest rated obstacle—the feeling that their plays are too unconventional—at 55 percent, and you see how powerfully access, or the lack of it, figures in writers' lives. Overwhelmingly, playwrights do not believe that plays make it to the stage by themselves. Rather, they perceive that plays are furthered by relationships. And as theatres have become bigger, relationships between playwrights and artistic directors have grown more distant, with literary staffs and others serving as intermediaries. These other connections have become more crucial to playwrights, especially those with literary

---

* The number is greater for playwrights in new, emerging, and early-middle-career stages. Between 67 percent and 72 percent of these writers agree or strongly agree that lack of access is a top personal obstacle. About half of the writers who identify themselves as mid-career-established also believe this to be true.

managers, directors, and even actors—all of whom are perceived as having easier access and greater influence than the writer.

Access, then, becomes the cornerstone of professional strategies. Playwrights look for and rely on "champions," from theatres or elsewhere, people who have the access or influence they lack. "In my experience and the vast experience of a lot of people I talk to," one writer explains, "it's about whether or not somebody on the theatre staff gets behind your play and champions that play and says, 'we should do this, and I want to direct it.'"

Playwrights know that the numbers are not in their favor; they also believe that artistic directors are weighing the concerns of staff, boards, audience, artists with whom they want to work, as well as their own likes and dislikes. A New York playwright does the math:

> I remember someone at a very large theatre, in the literary office, talking about how proud they were that they read 800 plays a year. Breaking it down a little bit: You do six plays. Of those 800 you read, 750 are [thrown] right out, and fifty maybe you do readings of. There's ten that maybe you do a second or third reading, or maybe a workshop. Of those ten, maybe three go on the table, along with the fifteen that the artistic director has already gotten from other directors and board members and other people, that he or she is already thinking about. Even if the artistic director really likes it, it's already one out of ten.

He poses the questions that all playwrights try to answer for themselves when they submit their plays for production: "Who actually makes the decisions? What's invisible in the process?"

LITERARY GATEKEEPERS

The larger the theatre the more layers of personnel playwrights find between themselves and the person who will finally decide whether or not to produce their plays. For most theatres, it is the literary manager who mans the gate through which most plays pass. It is, therefore, the literary manager who maintains the greatest number of relationships with playwrights and who, by reading hundreds of plays a year and by overseeing play readers who tackle hundreds more, tracks the plays being written. Literary managers are, as one agent calls them, "the book club," keeping eyes out for talent and possibility, and circulating among their colleagues at other theatres plays they admire, but which aren't right for their own.

Playwrights speak of literary managers with sympathy and sometimes affection. Many feel they have supporters in literary offices, people who read a lot and care about writers. Writers know that these literary managers speak to each other and recommend plays. Ultimately, however, most playwrights believe that literary managers have, at most, the power and responsibility to say no to a play, but that they lack the power to say yes. "A lot of the literary managers feel like their hands are tied," a Minneapolis-based playwright says. "I've heard of miserable stories of all these plays that they love that come across their desk, and they feel like they're never going to be able to get them past the business side. Or the artistic director is ultimately making the choices and it's really things that come across his or her desk that get to production." Literary offices serve theatres, not playwrights, observes another playwright with a longtime day job as a literary manager. "With very few exceptions, I haven't seen [literary managers] standing up for the playwright as much as standing up for the theatre's need to serve an audience or to serve the bottom line." One influential playwright, who at one time served as literary manager for a large regional theatre, is blunt about it. People on literary staffs are, he says, "neutered dogs biting their stitches. They are completely snipped by their artistic directors."

Within theatres, literary offices are seen more in terms of process than power. "My job is being a bridge," explains the head of play development for a New York City theatre. "It's about project acquisition, finding the writers and the projects that I know would be right for a production, which is defined as something that the artistic director would support and believe in." "Dramaturgs and literary managers are looking at plays differently than artistic directors," comments one artistic director.

> That's a good thing in a way—they cast their net a little wider, and they're more engaged in championing great voices, promising writers. Artistic directors feel the pressures of making decisions about slots, and whether we can invest, whether there's an audience for it, how it fits into the other things we're making choices about.

The head of a New York theatre, also a former literary manager, agrees. "It's the role of a literary department to fan more flames than the artistic director."

For at least one literary manager, who has worked at theatres across the country, the problem isn't the power structure within theatres, it's how that structure is communicated to writers. She believes there's "a field problem of how literary offices run. There often is not transparency in terms of how much power do you have or do not have."

The sad irony, many acknowledge, is that literary offices were established, in part, for the care and tending of relationships with writers. They were designed to scout out new playwrights, create developmental programs to help them, oversee commissions, and, in a sense, open up more access. The unintended consequences, as with so much in the institutional theatre, often run counter to these original aims, creating distance instead of connection. What were meant to be points of access have become buffer zones, used to protect the theatre (and artistic director) from the barrage of playwrights in search of production.

Many artistic directors agree that personal relationships unlock the gates for writers in the theatre. The head of a mid-sized theatre known for new work admits that, when it comes to reading a play quickly and considering it seriously, relationships—with the playwright or with colleagues in the field—are catalytic: "Most plays come to you through personal connections. Things that link to me personally always get higher and faster in the process." "Playwrights get productions through relationships that they cultivate themselves," says an Off-Broadway artistic director. The head of a different New York City company points to the access technology offers:

> Something that we didn't have twenty years ago: e-mail.
> I think about how often writers e-mail me and say, "Did
> you read my play?" It's kind of cool in a good way. It's
> created more lines of access. You can e-mail anybody. It has
> empowered playwrights to roll up their sleeves and make the
> contacts, rather than not being able to and being frustrated.

Indeed, playwrights' belief that relationships and personal access are key to the selection process is borne out by their collective experience. The most effective way for playwrights to get produced, according to those surveyed, is to submit their plays directly to the theatres. In order to submit directly, when fewer and fewer theatres accept unsolicited scripts (or plays that don't come from agents or colleagues), playwrights *must have relationships with those theatres*. Those relationships stimulate interest in their work. Those relationships lead to invitations.

> **FINDING:** 62 percent of playwrights have had two or more plays produced as a result of their own direct submissions.

Cultivating access works.

Some, on the theatre side, dispute the notion. One veteran artistic director strongly objects: "I've been saying to writers for forty years that the play speaks for itself; all you have to do is be able to read it. There is some perception that, 'Gee, if Sam just had me to dinner, he would do my play.' It's just not the case." Under questioning from the head of a new-play lab, he elaborates:

> NEW-PLAY LAB DIRECTOR: Does [a writer's desire for personal access] have to do with not knowing if the artistic leader is reading the work, as opposed to a *reader* reading the work?

> ARTISTIC DIRECTOR: [If so] they're calling you incompetent. They're saying whoever you hired is not suited to read my work. If I'm doing my job, somebody good is reading this play. If any of us who are running theatres had somebody reading our plays whose taste was completely different from ours, what are we doing? That just doesn't make sense.

> NEW-PLAY LAB DIRECTOR: Aren't there literary managers who are themselves frustrated because they champion writers and they can't get the work to the main stage? "I love your work, but I can't get [the artistic director] to commit to it, I'm sorry."

> ARTISTIC DIRECTOR: That's a dishonest response, a really chicken-shit response. There's a reason why this theatre's not doing your play, if you really want to get into it, and it isn't because, "I love it, if I were running this place, we'd do a whole season of you."
>
> There is something stinky on the table: What the literary person says to the playwright. We all have passions and things we delight in, but that's not our job. Seventy-five percent of the playwrights think that if only they could talk to the right people and get past this barrier that they would get produced. And if the reason they think that is because literary manager is saying, "God, I love your stuff," then "Here is why we can't produce it" has to be articulated.

Otherwise, the artistic director is painted into some kind of barrier or villain by the literary person.

I can understand the response of the literary person. You don't want to burn bridges. We want to keep writers enthused and favorably disposed to your theatre. But you're giving this completely mixed message: "Hey, I love you but it's something else." Telling the truth is [essential]. We've been talking over the last week on a piece that I'm really excited about. Maybe I'll do it, maybe I won't. I have two theatres. One's too small and one's too big. To produce it in the big theatre would almost kill it because it's not that big a piece. That's a specific response to a specific work. That's more honest, as opposed to some kind of general "we love your play." It's more work to do that, but it's more honest. Anything you could do to resolve that disconnect would be useful.

Writers' sense of being shut out of the system can frustrate artistic directors, especially those working for transparency and openness. Playwrights may be correct in their belief that personal access helps a play along, *and* they may be overstating the case. Either way, it's clear that some kind of mutual education is needed—for artistic directors to understand how playwrights are thinking about access and for playwrights to understand how play selection actually works. It's not an easy bridge to construct, as one playwright-turned-artistic director confides:

I've been in an artistic director position for a fairly limited amount of time, and I've been fascinated how people feel like they're excluded. Our staff isn't that big. My door is open. People can ask me questions all the time. I'm happy to tell them what we're talking about. It's not like we have a secret handshake. But people feel excluded from that conversation.

I've been on both sides of the divide—between independent artists and institutions. I don't know how you bridge that. If you could figure out a way for playwrights to sit in a room and watch a season planning thing happen, it would be like an actor actually sitting in on auditions, watch you suffer through them, how you wrestle with wanting the auditions to be great.

This notion of gatekeepers: It's one thing if you're having the playwright talk to a receptionist or an intern. Your literary manager is not just a gatekeeper. They're an integral part of the decision-making process. They're hearing those conversations. And yes, you trust that person to talk to the playwrights, just as you trust the associate artistic director. I don't even know that one-on-one conversations [would make a difference]. As soon as you tell somebody, "We're not doing your play," there is immediately, "I don't understand why because my play's brilliant. I don't know why every theatre in America is not doing my plays." That's just the truth.

WHO ELSE HAS A WAY IN?

Playwrights also believe that other artists, especially freelance directors, have easier access to decision-makers within theatres than they do. A New York playwright has "only had things happen outside of New York because a director got interested. It's also true in New York," he explains, pointing to the first New York theatre he got involved with. "They have their own tortured process of programming, but any number of things actually got on the table because of the director." Many share this sense that directors are closer to the selection process than playwrights. "Writers are generally a little more out of the loop. That is because so many artistic directors are directors. There's that sensibility [that] the director's the one putting the project together. So often the playwright is not around: Maybe they're in town, maybe they're not," this playwright hypothesizes.

Another writer presents her own experience as evidence:

None of my plays, with the partial exception of one, have been produced because a theatre picked it. Almost all of my

plays have been a director getting enthusiastic about it, and
charging around until they ran into an opportunity where it
could be produced, or even fundraising themselves.

The clout of a director with institutional connections
(and trust) may be more necessary for writers of difficult
material, or at least material that appears difficult on the page,
she adds, using her own work as an example. "It's weird to read
these plays. Because [unconventional writing is] so clearly not
going to make it through any kind of institutional way, people
may then engage with it more personally." In other words, the
theatre may trust a director's vision, even when that of the
playwright is harder to trust.

For the theatres with resident ensembles, actors can
provide a point of entry for a play. Sometimes, as described by
one co-artistic director, "the ensemble selects the season. The
other two artistic directors [and I] try to get the choices in front
of them. It is primarily from within the ensemble." A Chicago-
area literary manager describes a similar process. "The ensemble
is a very big component in our season planning process. We tend
to program, particularly in our subscription season, based on
ensemble attachment to projects….It may involve the willingness
of two or three of our ensemble to act in a piece or one director
and a couple of actors."

And sometimes—with less formal acting companies—
casting is where an artistic director begins. "I fall in love with a play
in the context of a cast. The two are so linked. There are plays that
I love that I wouldn't do because I feel like I haven't got the cast.
And there are people I work with, I'm thinking about what kind
of piece would I develop for them as performers, or what piece
would they shine in." Occasionally, a playwright discovers this in
action, as a young New York playwright recounts: "[A]n actress
who really wanted to play the part made a play go up. She was part
of a theatre company. She pushed the company that she was a part
of to do the play. I didn't even know her." Though playwrights
everywhere wish they had the kind of access that directors and

some actors have, they're delighted when productions come about through these—or almost any—channels.

IN WITH AGENTS?

As playwrights confront the problems they associate with access, the question looms: how much do agents help in getting plays produced? The answer, for most playwrights, is "not much."

> **FINDING:** 67 percent of the playwrights surveyed have had no plays produced as a result of an agent submission. Another 16 percent have had only one play produced after their agent submitted it. In other words, 83 percent of the playwrights surveyed have had one or zero agent-submitted plays produced.

The days of scripts appearing on a producer's desk and being snatched up and read because of an agent's name or an agency cover are behind us. This is one thing that playwrights and theatre administrators agree on. "I've never had anything come from an agent," one playwright says. "It's all about relationships, and they can come from casual circumstances or formal ones." "My agent negotiates the contracts, but most of the work that I've gotten has been through individual connections," says another. "Most [productions come] through serendipitous acts of fate and community," a third writer adds. A playwright, who has had significant success with experimental and site-specific work, puts it like this:

> The age of the really close relationships between writer and agent has gone by. I have an agent who is a really interesting person. As soon as I make myself famous, she's going to be able to find me a lot of work. My favorite thing about my agent is that she doesn't drop me. She's busy with the clients that are making her money.

The artistic and literary directors of theatres see a similar picture: "It's about relationships," the head of a Philadelphia company says.

> If you know the playwright, the agent is irrelevant until you
> get into a negotiation. If you know the playwright, you can call
> them up, and say, "What are you working on?" They send you
> a play. You say, "I like this, but I'd love to see where it's going;
> what are you thinking about?" All that leads much more likely
> to production than anything an agent's going to say.

Agents are rarely the people to whom theatres listen most closely. "We don't live in a world where we just open our mail and read plays," explains the dramaturg at one of the nation's largest theatres.

> We know actors; we go to the theatre. If somebody comes
> to visit you, a young actor you really admire, and says, "I've
> found this good writer I really admire," I would read that in
> a second. That's so much more important than coming in a
> William Morris binder.

Artistic decision-makers everywhere agree: "It's people that you trust in the field that you want to hear from. It's generally somebody you know well." The new-play development director of another large company explains the exact role agents play in the process of selection.

> I've never, in any theatre that I've worked at, decided to
> do a play based on an agent's submission. The closest I've
> come was starting with writers to look at, in terms of who's
> in somebody's stable. If playwrights think that agents are
> serving that role for them, it's not happening.

Few writers dispute the vital role agents play with negotiations, relationship building, creating reputations at theatres, and providing career advice and support. "I'm one of the few playwrights I know who actually thinks I have a fantastic agent and that he helps me enormously, and that I couldn't possibly have gone certain places without him," one writer enthuses, emphasizing the fluidity of their collaboration.

> I don't distinguish too much about whether it came from me or if it came from him, because if a production does arise I find him so instrumental in making sure the theatre is taking care of me. It's a partnership, a good relationship, and I feel lucky.

In the lengthy process of growing a career, a playwright never knows exactly what might take root. Agents "can help get the word out about you," a Los Angeles writer explains. "I have an agent who submitted me for a workshop. Seven years later in the same city, I submitted a play to a theatre and they read it because they had heard about the workshop seven years earlier." For those at a later stage of their professional lives, it's the agent who builds on the playwright's longtime relationships.

> Agents submit my plays, but then people know me by now. The ones that have gotten done have been because I've sent a play in. [Somebody asked,] or I had a relationship, or there was something going on where I thought it might [be right], like Louisville. I said, "Have you seen this one?" And it happened to catch their eye.

Theatre administrators value agents' contribution in many of the same ways. "Agents have been great, particularly for younger writers in terms of contracts," the artistic director of a mid-sized theatre says. An Off-Broadway artistic director says, "Playwrights get productions through relationships that they cultivate themselves, and the agents continually encourage them to cultivate relationships." Another New Yorker explains this cultivation process. "An agent may introduce a writer to a producer, and then once a personal relationship develops the writer picks up the phone and says, 'Would you want to read my play?'"

In the end, a theatre's relationship to the agent is just that—a relationship. And the closer, the more trusting that connection is, the more it will help in the first stage of a completed play's journey from the playwright's desk to the stage: getting to the top of the reading pile. "Something has to get a play onto the give-it-a-ten-page-read pile," explains one artistic director.

> Our official policy is…we only read solicited scripts. Anything from an agent is automatically solicited. We'll do anything we can to put something in the solicited pile. Any connection whatever, however tangential, we'll call it solicited.

Overall, though, these same company leaders believe that too many agents fail to tailor submissions to individual theatres. They tend to submit plays to theatres based on their sizes and prestige, not their aesthetics. This often limits playwrights' opportunities and draws out the time it takes for them to get their plays done. In fact, there are few agents working whose knowledge of the field artistic directors trust (the number floated by artistic directors at roundtable meetings was five or six, at most). Agents' lack of knowledge of the field, especially beyond New York and a handful of the most prominent theatres, certainly affects their success rate. "They don't know what's good," says the literary director of a prominent regional theatre, which has begun to ignore agent submissions. "They don't follow what other theatres are thinking about. It's a strange tiering system of, 'This will be good in the regions, and this won't.'" Most agents, she believes, "are not keeping up with the field."

For some agents, focusing on the top tier of theatres and ignoring the rest may be misguided strategy, a New York associate artistic director explains. "There are very few agents left in the business who target specific theatres because they think that theatre is going to be the right theatre for a given play. They start with the biggest theatres and let it trickle down. Once Lincoln Center, Manhattan Theatre Club, and Roundabout have passed on a play, we get it." Similarly, even sizable regional theatres with a history of new-play production aren't getting scripts the way they used to. Agents "have a real strategy now about how to place their plays," the head of one such theatre says. "I might get plays from other sources, but the plays don't come to me officially until everybody in New York has passed."

Another aspect of this top-down thinking among agents, especially at larger agencies, is a trend toward packaging scripts with actors and directors—rather than circulating them—a practice whose roots are in Hollywood. "There is a trend now of packaging," says an Off-Broadway artistic director. "Agents are getting very sophisticated on packaging stuff and controlling where plays are going." This approach sometimes pushes writers and plays more quickly than may serve them, according to the leader of another Off-Broadway company.

> Something has happened in the last few years: There are a couple of aggressive and—this is good—younger agents who are representing very young playwrights. People who are representing a generation that normally would wait another ten years before having a high-level agent. The flip side is that sometimes they're trying to broker productions at major theatres for plays that are in a very early stage of development. It's competitive, bringing a film or television agent-ing style to young and promising writers. It's a double-edged sword. It's by and large good, but sometimes it scares me.

One ramification of these strategies, this single-minded focus on large theatres, New York theatres, and commercial packaging—is that agents are losing their clients production opportunities that may further their work and careers. A common complaint heard among small and mid-sized theatres is that they are off agents' maps, a geography that does a disservice to playwrights. "We don't get any [agent submissions]," says the head of an East Coast theatre that has focused on new work for more than twenty years.

They must have clients who would be happy to have us read the play, but I don't think they think there's enough money in it. So they don't care. They know who we are. They just don't think we're big enough. There's not enough money in this deal that it's worth their time....But there are a zillion of us out there....They're foolish, because if it gets done at a few small theatres, that's better than being rejected by one or two large theatres.

"Most [agents] just don't get it," exclaims the head of a small New York company that ranks in the top ten of theatre companies that have produced the greatest number of plays by surveyed writers. "They don't really understand that sending to us will help build careers." "You have to keep re-educating the agents," a colleague from Washington declares.

How can writers and their advocates learn more about the specific missions and aesthetics of theatres? Are there systemic ways to help in the growth of careers and the care and tending of new works, where theatres of different sizes and intentions work in concert to assist plays and playwrights at different stages of artistic and professional progress? And how can the whole field, playwrights and theatres, cultivate more, better relationships in a profession where, clearly, relationships drive advancement?

In the Way

How playwrights get rejected impacts the field in pervasive ways. For example, as seen above, literary managers who tell writers that they love their plays but can't convince their artistic directors to produce them—whether or not they are being honest—create a perception of divided artistic staffs: with literary champions on one side and, on the other, artistic directors who don't read, don't know the world of contemporary writing, or "don't get it."

Likewise, the widespread use of "This isn't right for our audience" as a justification for rejecting plays has led to a near-unanimous feeling among playwrights that audience is the chief reason plays are passed on. As one agent explains, when it comes to rejection,

> unless it's a flat-out pass, and they're just not interested in the play, the answer [from theatres] is always "It's not right for our audiences." One-hundred percent. I don't think all the time it's true. I think it's an easy thing to say without offending someone, especially if it's a writer that they like, but they don't like this particular play and they want to be in the running later on.

As we'll explore in depth in Chapter V, this language contributes to one of the deepest perceptual divisions between playwrights and theatres—how they think about audience.

The language of rejection needs to be rethought, and handled with probity and honesty, most agree. "It's partly our job as literary managers to make it clear, to articulate it, and to explain, 'There are a lot of factors and as a writer you're going to face a lot of rejection,'" the head of a literary office admits. Even though he tries to be "up front" with writers, he also feels the need to protect the artistic director from being pushed about the reasons for rejection. "He has to have the freedom to not have to explain himself," he adds. An artistic associate from the Twin Cities affirms the need for greater clarity. "We need to be a lot more honest about all of the reasons why we choose the work," she says.

It's not hard to understand why the language of rejection has become muddied. It's hard for one set of artists to rebuff another, and it's hard, in a world that requires the imagination to say "Yes," to accept "No." More muddying still is a deep confusion about the reasons plays don't get done. What are the most significant obstacles? It depends on whom you ask. Although playwrights believe that their own greatest obstacle to production is access to top decision-makers, when asked to speculate about the obstacles to production *within the theatres themselves*, they overwhelmingly agree: concern about the audience.

THEATRE PERCEPTIONS	MEAN PERCEIVED OBSTACLE SEVERITY †	PLAYWRIGHT PERCEPTIONS	MEAN PERCEIVED OBSTACLE SEVERITY †
Cast size or composition for an individual play	4.3	Expectations about audience reception and interest	3.1
Too expensive	4.5	Cast size or composition for an individual play	4.6
Technical demands for an individual play	5.1	Disagreement among artistic staff about the merits of a play	4.6
Hard to find work that makes an important artistic contribution*	5.5	A play or a playwright's production history	4.8
Expectations about audience reception and interest	5.6	Subject matter for an individual play too controversial	4.8
Availability of rights*	5.7	Expectations about response from critics	5.0
Theatre space	6.4	Too expensive	5.4
A play or a playwright's production history	6.5	Technical demands for an individual play	5.5
Subject matter for an individual play too controversial	6.7	Theatre space	5.8
Disagreement among artistic staff about the merits of a play	7.0	Past critical response	6.3
Expectations about response from critics	7.7	Availability of rights	n/a
Past critical response	n/a	Hard to find work that makes an important artistic contribution	n/a

FIGURE 3.1: HOW THEATRES AND PLAYWRIGHTS PERCEIVE OBSTACLES TO PRODUCTION

* Playwrights were not asked about availability of rights or the difficulty of finding work of artistic merit, so comparisons are unavailable.
† The mean answers appear on a scale from "strongly disagree" to "strongly agree." The number on the right is the severity mean, another way of saying something like "average intensity." The lower the number, the more intense the agreement.

Figure 3.1 shows the relative ranking, by artistic administrators and by playwrights, of obstacles—real or perceived—to plays getting produced. The differences in these two perspectives highlight differences in experience, as the artistic staffs of theatres plan seasons and playwrights make inferences from what they see and are told.

FINDINGS:

* Theatres see expense demands as a significantly greater problem than playwrights think.
* Playwrights think theatres weigh audience concerns and potential critical reaction far more seriously than theatre leaders report.
* Playwrights perceive disagreement among artistic staff as inhibiting production, whereas theatres do not. Artistic directors rank this next to last.
* Theatre leaders say they place less emphasis on a play or playwright's production history than playwrights think they do.
* Season planners express far less concern about controversial subject matter than playwrights suppose.*

Participants weren't asked to rank these obstacles, but their aggregate responses create the order in which they are seen to influence choices. The intensity with which they're believed to exert influence can be seen from the numbers on the right.

---

* In fact, some artistic directors say they wish there were more controversial plays out there. As one says, "I'd love to do plays that are controversial...I have a hard time finding plays that are good and genuinely controversial...[In] certain communities it's really hard to shock people."

The relative severity of these obstacles creates a statistical picture of stark differences.

> **FINDING:** 82 percent of the study playwrights believe that concern about audience reception is an obstacle to the production of their plays, making it by far the biggest stumbling block for a play.

This, then, is how playwrights in our study believe theatres operate—in anticipation of their audiences. They see concern about audience reception far outweighing any other reasons a theatre has to say no to a play.

When we asked the theatres to rank obstacles to production, however, we got a completely different view.

> **FINDING:** Theatres do not consider concerns about audience reception a serious obstacle to the production of a new play. Less than a third of artistic directors see it as such. They rate audience concerns fifth among potential obstacles.

This particular disparity is the subject of Chapter V. Whatever the reasons—the language uniformly used to reject plays ("It's not right for our audience"), denial on the part of playwrights ("They like my play, but feel it's too challenging for their subscribers"), or a lack of candor from theatres ("We only do plays our artistic director loves, and we trust that our audience will follow")—there is much confusion about the role of audience in play selection.

On the other hand, there is some agreement. Both playwrights and theatre leaders identify cast size or composition as
a powerful impediment to production. (We'll discuss dwindling
cast size in Chapter IV.) And though playwrights and theatres
have both gotten used to a diminished scale for casts, many fear
that the shrinking ensemble is leading to a shrinking of ambition
and imagination as well. All, naturally, equate cast size and cost.
"If I'm interested in a play but I can't do it, then the chances are
good it's because it's too big or because it's too expensive," explains
a Bay Area artistic director. At least one writer of color, however,
believes these terms—"cast size or composition"—are code, ways
of theatres begging off plays requiring actors of specific races or
ethnicities. "I don't think theatres want to identify themselves as,
'We shy away from anything controversial,' or 'We're worried
about subject matter.' It's easier to say, 'We might not be able to
find those actors.'"

A play's *technical demands*, too, are seen by both groups
as potentially somewhat prohibitive, a view that's only slightly
stronger for the artistic directors. "There are some incredible
plays out there that are daunting to do because of the technical
demands," the head of a long-standing small theatre maintains,
"because of the very creative mandate to write plays that are
impossible to do that you get from some of the great playwriting
programs." But what makes a play impossible? Are production
managers driving the conversation, telling artistic directors
what can't be done? Do producers at large theatres believe
their audiences expect to see every setting fully and realistically
realized and, so, find themselves avoiding work that moves
through place and time or that works imagistically? Again,
playwrights, conceding that a play's technical requirements
can make it harder to get produced, complain that nonprofit
producers lack theatrical imagination. They take the work too
literally. Indeed, the very plays that seem technically challenging
for larger theatres are often done at tiny theatres, with little
money and a lot of imagination.

THEATRES DENIED ACCESS

Everybody wants the same ten playwrights.
—ARTISTIC DIRECTOR

When it comes to access, playwrights are trying to find a way into theatres. Theatres, meanwhile—by their own admission—are trying to gain access to a small group of playwrights and a handful of plays—often the same playwrights, the same plays. For some artistic directors, especially in small and midsized theatres, two obstacles go hand in hand: 1) the belief that it's difficult to find work that makes an important contribution, and 2) the unavailability of rights to the work that does. This combination has many theatres scrambling in the same direction. The artistic director of a theatre identified by peers as one of the leaders in new-play production tallies the competition:

> As someone who commissions a lot and produces a lot, the competition for plays of merit is very high. When I go to commission a playwright—often a mid-career or early playwright—I find that they have four or five commissions lined up. Their writing schedules are full. It changes the equations. My guess is that a dozen or more, maybe twenty, are these writers who are being competed over. I'm about to go out to fairly prominent writers, and I know I'll have to go to four or five before I find one who can do it. Twelve to twenty [will be] backed up with three, four, five commissions.

"It's also very difficult to commission playwrights of a certain stature," offers the artistic director of a smaller theatre, who reports trying to commission a writer—name withheld—well known to everyone at his meeting. "I was told they've got six commissions out and there's no way that they could even talk about it."

The aggravation of being shut out can boil over: "Do you know how hard it is for me to get on some new playwrights' lists?" asks the head of one major city's third-largest theatre.

It's really hard. I've got to beg somebody to email me something. Who do you got to blow to get a copy of [Sarah Ruhl's] *Dead Man's Cell Phone*...? Twenty percent of my work is actually, "No fucking around, I'm doing your play." I pull the trigger faster than almost any artistic director in the country....I put my institution right on the line. And I don't get the latest Sam Shepard or Caryl Churchill.

Even if this rage is expressed somewhat ironically, it's fueled by real frustration over the clout that institutional size confers (on others) *and* by a sense, at least implicit, that there's a scarcity of plays of merit and playwrights who can write them.

The competitive angst over a small pool of talent and plays operates at all levels of the field, theatres large and small, in and out of New York. An artistic director in Chicago defines the stakes, using examples of two very different theatres from his community:

Victory Gardens wants to be on that list [of new-play producers], and Goodman wants to be on that list, for many reasons. It's not necessarily about ego. It's about, wow, the next time great playwright X writes a play or is thinking about writing a play, they're going to call you. It's to be able to retain access to those works.... The more new plays that we produce, the more world premieres that my company does, the more chance I have of getting a really interesting world premieres from more and more accomplished playwrights.

This rivalry over a handful of writers happens at both ends of the career spectrum, too, as an Off-Broadway producer explains:

Enormous institutional theatres...Roundabout, Lincoln Center, Manhattan Theatre Club—have made a conscious choice, both in programming and grantsmanship in the last few years, to offer mainstage productions to the writers who would be normally cutting their teeth at letter-of-agreement theatres or smaller [venues].... In some respect it's good for the writers…very new writers who haven't even had a production anywhere. I'll take an interest in the play and suddenly my offer to do the play is leveraged…by a major theatre. It's happened three times to me this year. All the experiences were very positive. They are writers I'm friendly with….I would never begrudge them. I'm excited when a writer I like gets that opportunity, but the scary part is when the plays are not done well.

This struggle for access to plays even extends across the Atlantic. "I'll see a play in London," says one artistic director, "and be interested in doing a second production and find the rights held up for years and years and years, until I'm no longer interested."

Why do so many theatres contend for so few writers and plays? As we discussed in Chapter I, opinions about the abundance or scarcity of good plays vary widely. Some believe that American playwriting, despite a high level of activity, is in a dry spell when it comes to quality, making it hard to find exciting, stage-worthy plays. If this is true, then it's easy to see why theatres seek access to the same group of playwrights. They represent rare quality. But at least as many, probably more, artistic leaders profess to believe that ours is a fertile moment, that there are more good plays than they can possibly produce. So why do they want the same plays? Why do they wish to claim the same writers?

Is this struggle over a small group of proven writers and plays about box office potential? Is it ego—the desire to be the theatre in your area to produce the most prestigious works? Is it a matter of artistic security, that there's less risk in turning to known quantities? Or are the people in charge of the nation's theatrical vision swayed by their peers and, more by their peers' successes? Competition is a great motivator, according to one playwright advocate. Play selection, he believes, always seems to become about something other than the play.

A perfect example is *Fuddy Mears*. Everyone loved that play at Manhattan Theatre Club. Why wouldn't they just commit

to it? They loved it. Wouldn't commit to it. It wasn't until
[the playwright] David [Lindsay-Abaire] won this award at
Primary Stages, and all of a sudden there's other interest,
and then, it happened....That was really the reason they
ultimately decided to do it, and, I think, for the most part,
that is the reason for most theatres. Other interest is really
the reason they ultimately commit.

Nearly everyone has a story about a play that was
rejected by numerous theatres over many years and then, after
a successful production—usually in New York—was suddenly
in demand, including at the theatres that originally rejected it
(think Margaret Edson's *Wit*). Do decision-makers change their
opinions of these plays, suddenly seeing value in works they
once dismissed? Have they been waiting all along for colleagues
or audiences to confirm their initial (but maybe timid) liking
of these plays? Are artistic leaders actually jockeying for field
position by fighting over "hot" playwrights and properties (i.e.,
to show that they are the tastemakers or the ones who can
attract the top talent)? Is taste a collective, almost viral thing,
as opposed to something that individuals exercise and, so,
distinguish their theatres?

Whatever the reasons, this competition by the many for
the few underscores the field-wide homogeneity of taste about
which playwrights and others complain. At least in mid-to-
large-size American theatres artistic directors are, overall, as
homogeneous as their audiences—from similar social, cultural,
and ethnic backgrounds. They are monochromatic (i.e., white)
and (in LORT theatres) two-thirds male. Playwrights claim that
their own ranks—and their works—are infinitely more diverse
and varied. If both propositions are true—that playwriting is
thriving and broad-based *and* that dozens or even hundreds
of theatres all want to associate with the same ten to twenty
playwrights—then there is a gap between the reality and action,
between the fertility of the field and the perceived drought that
motivates behavior within it.

THE PATH OF A PLAY, OR WHAT'S LOVE GOT TO DO WITH IT?

> *I try to take every opportunity to walk writers through the puzzle of season planning, because I find that they don't have much access to it, and it seems too mysterious, and all they see is whether their play gets done. And while that basic thing will always be at rock bottom most important to them, [it helps] to know the number of pieces that go into that puzzle so it's not just about rejection....Do they have any idea that their play might not be getting done not because it's not a good play, but because it's got to fit into this larger ecosystem?* —DIRECTOR OF NEW PLAY DEVELOPMENT

How does a play get selected for production? What is its journey within the theatre itself? First, there are the sheer numbers, the plays in the reading pile. "We get a thousand plays a year," calculates the head of new-play development at a New York theatre.

> Every week we have a department meeting where we go through the list of plays that have been submitted. Some plays are priority. If it's a playwright whose work we don't know at all, and a play that we know nothing about, that would be a first-read, and that would take longer to get to me. Unless the reader loves it, then it comes to me more quickly. It's a filtration system. If a play is submitted to [the artistic director], she gives it to me anyway. Unless she has a very strong relationship with that writer, she's not going to read it immediately or any more quickly than she would if it were submitted to me.

As we've seen, the plays that move through a theatre aren't merely scripts; they carry with them relationships and history. Behind each play stands a network of people—writers, directors, agents, actors, colleagues—and its pace and ease of moving from the reading pile to the desk of the person who decides what gets done depends both on its strength as a script and on those relationships.

"In most theatres, you have to win the heart and soul of the person who's going to [produce you]. It's a marriage," explains an artistic director. As we've seen, playwrights and their advocates argue that play selection is too often a corporate process, founded in everything but passion—except, perhaps the passion to please a theatre's stakeholders. By contrast, artistic directors and their literary and producing associates insist that love stories are the aim—between producer and play. "If an artistic director makes a strong connection with a play, a way will be found to make that play happen—which is an amazingly great thing," enthuses one director of new-play development.

> I don't know that playwrights know that this actually still happens, that that's still fundamentally what everybody is looking for. There is the economic side that we can't all do as many new plays as we want, but there aren't that many plays where that kind of love affair actually happens between an artistic director or whoever gets to make those choices, and a work. When it does happen, almost every other consideration becomes moot.

For some the costs of working any other way are high. "The times that I've done a play that I haven't loved, I regretted every second of it," confesses an East Coast artistic director. "You have to love it, or it's just not worth it. We are passionately interested in reading new work that will excite us." The founding director of a mid-sized company shares these feelings.

> Playwrights don't really appreciate that artistic directors…are hungry for plays they want to produce. There's a voracious appetite. We all have to find those plays that will excite us and will fit our mission that we can contribute to….We're all hungry for exciting voices.

The question, then, beyond how to gain access to the people whose passions dictate theatres' choices, is what will stir those passions? "How you capture that heart is personal," notes an artistic director. "The ugly truth is that writers feel their work is valuable, but if I don't find the play valuable to me, that is my prerogative. What I've been hired to do is exercise my taste. Their play may be worthy but I may not want to do it, or I may not find it important, and I may be wrong. You have to be able to live with that." In other words, "'Producing is personal,'" as a former literary manager recalls her boss saying. "'It's as personal as I am an artist. You can send me lots of plays of merit, but I might only like one.'" The head of the literary office at a prominent New York theatre puts it another way, responding to the playwright's natural question: "'Why won't you do this play?' The answer is, it's either kingly or queenly whim."

Artistic directors have different loves, different concerns and chemistries, and different notions of quality. The founder of a theatre that performs in nontraditional settings has one response. "When I fall in love with a play, it's always partly based on my sense that my audience will too. My sense of what my audience loves is part of what makes my love affair work." The leader of a theatre with affiliated playwrights has another.

> My selection has a lot to do with the ongoing support of the writer. There's a corps of writers that I am inclined to continuously support. The question comes as to who's ready to go into the game, who's got something that's ready to go and who [does] not, either because they have a longer gestation period or because the play is not yet ready.

A veteran artistic director looks for "stuff that's applicable to empty space, because you can do incredible things." He continues:

> It has to make an emotional connection. It's important to hear *this* story at *this* time in history. I don't think about

whether it's going to be important 100 years from now. If
it doesn't make that emotional connection to the audience,
no one is going to hear it. I try to keep myself really open to
what that connection can be.

Whatever the point of personal passionate contact may
be, according to this artistic director his peers share one basic
concern: "Everybody's looking for something they hope will
speak to the condition of the audience."

In the real world, though, every play selection is not a
love story. "That doesn't happen six to fifteen times in a year,"
admits a new-play-development director. "Then all of those
other considerations about other people you're responsible for
besides you and what you love come into play, which is everyone
from your audience to what your production staff can build, to
who's in your acting company, what the balance is in terms of
kinds of stories you're telling, and points of view and all of that."
Those "other considerations" are too complex for even those
making the decisions to parse. "There is a perception," says one
artistic director with decades of experience producing new work,
"that somehow, here's the play, the artistic director is totally nuts
for it, they'll find a way of doing it—and that's true. But that's
when the play hits the bull's eye and all the bells are going off
in terms of the artistic sensibilities of the artistic director." He
continues:

> There are plays which are still worthy of being produced,
> that you as an artistic director could say, "This play could
> work in this particular slot depending on this and that,
> because of budgets and all of that."…There might be three
> plays that we could be considering that could work, and
> we're going to choose one, or maybe two…. Finally, there's
> that aspect of putting a season together. Those are legitimate
> concerns, that there isn't enough money to do this; or the
> only place that is appropriate is in this larger theatre and the
> budgetary ramifications just don't make sense.

Also, the desire for a balanced season can grow as a theatre grows, as this artistic director observes: "Do you find yourself thinking more about balance than you used to? I do. I used to not think about it at all. Whatever four, five plays I fell in love within a year—I don't care [if] they're all about violence and killing your mother—I'll do them all."

Every situation brings a new set of ambitions and concerns to the process of programming a season. One literary director outlines the myriad considerations weighed by her theatre's artistic leader:

> Ultimately he makes all the decisions, but there is an artistic collective, and that is a part of how the season gets picked— who has projects that they are bringing to the table....In terms of new plays, there are a few things that make it seem like [something we] would do. His sense is what we can do is ambitious in terms of scope, size, theatricality, and ambition. That's what I try to bring to him: rangy and epic. It doesn't mean it has a huge cast. It may be ambitious in its scope, or it's really trying something new. That's a reason for us to do it: that we could do it really well, whereas other theatres would not be able to do it.
>
> The other reason is the artists themselves; either that the playwright is someone we should be supporting because artistically they have something to offer, or there's a collaboration, particularly because ours is a director's theatre. If I can make a case for not just the play itself, but for the production, and how we can envision the production, that's an important thing.
>
> The community and the audience is a big part, the diversity of the community. There has been a conscious effort to program work that reflects [the city], because of the size of the theatre. Not all theatres necessarily have that responsibility to serve the entire community, but we do. When we are looking at the breakdown of the season, which could be an obstacle. "We might really want to do

this play, but we need to do a play by an African-American writer." [Ethnicity] is more a part of it than [being] tonally or aesthetically diverse.*

Thinking about what can work in our spaces is something that we think about. That comes up a lot. The kind of work you are going to do in the 800-seat house and the kind of work you are going to do in the 350-seat house are different.

The reason I promote certain plays is because of the [relationship]….Does it feel like this writer deserves the support and exposure that a production at our theatre can offer?

In addition to the complex artistic factors that guide the process of play selection, numerous institutional concerns come to bear, including the very ones for which playwrights reproach the theatres. An artistic associate in New York is candid. "Plays don't ever get chosen in a vacuum," he says.

It's not a pure process where you're just looking at texts and deciding which ones are interesting. Some of the factors that can advance that process are, Who brought you the play? Is

---

* The speaker here is clearly describing her theatre's attempt to represent the broad range of the city's population by selecting plays by writers from different races and ethnic backgrounds. This kind of thinking is both applauded by playwrights and held in suspicion. On the positive side, writers hope for seasons that will speak to diverse audiences and enlarge the traditional (and traditionally white) nonprofit, subscriber base. On the other side, playwrights are weary of theatres using "slots" to program diversity. We heard many references to thinking that may be called "only one of each" programming, where Latino playwrights, for example, know that, if a theatre produces the work of a Cuban-American writer one season, a playwright from a Puerto Rican background will have to wait for another time. African-American writers often joke sarcastically that theatres only produce them in February (Black History Month). Why, they ask, are writers of color forced into competition with each other for isolated slots, when a theatre thinks nothing of offering a season predominated by white writers from similar backgrounds?

it a director, or is there an actor attached that you want to
fit into your season? When are they available? How much
are they pushing? Increasingly, is it attached to commercial
money? The producers who are offering that money might
have an agenda about when they want to do something,
or how.... Playwrights very often assume that it's a purer
process of aesthetic judgment than it is—why things get
produced. There are so many reasons.

At the end of the day we try to make sure that it's always
about admiration for the play. We try not to be persuaded to
do plays that we don't actually like or don't think have merit
for our audience, but for the fact that some star is attached
or that someone is giving us a lot of money. There are a lot
of incentives one can find: [for example,] it's a salable event
that's going to buoy the rest of your season, or give you the
opportunity to take another risk with somebody else.

We will discuss the relationship between the commercial
and nonprofit theatres—including enhancement money—in the
next chapter. It's important to flag these commercial questions,
though, because they echo concerns playwrights voice about
the direction of the not-for-profit theatre. Among this speaker's
blunt admissions, though, is another that confirms the critique
of playwrights across the country: that play selection is based on
many factors that have little to do with the play's artistic merits.

A New York playwright offers simple idealism as an
antidote to the complications that conspire against the producer-
play love match. In lieu of obligation, she asks for honesty.

If a theatre company doesn't feel like it has seven new plays
that it loves to fill a season with, I don't think it should touch
a single one. It should feel under no burden. It should do all
plays that it loves. If it feels for funding or community service
reasons that it really wants to do new plays, it needs to have a
second stage. Get the artistic associate involved to stock that.

It sounds so simple: A theatre should do only what it loves. Is this a reasonable aspiration or a naïve misreading of the realities of producing for the stage?

Commissions: Getting Plays Written

My sense of commissions is that a theatre that likes you gives you money so they won't produce you. —PLAYWRIGHT

I just got my first commission. I'm totally thrilled. They said to me, "The chances of our actually producing this are so small. We're giving out so many commissions." I'm so happy to get the money. I'm so happy to have a deadline. I have no expectation they'll do it. It seems all good to me. —PLAYWRIGHT

Separate from economics, playwrights consider commissions a mixed bag. They appreciate the money; they almost always need it. Commissions are a vote of confidence for many. They are also, as one writer puts it, "a hammer. It's hard sometimes when you don't have anybody pushing on you, sitting on your head, waiting for your play." But as our economic statistics make clear (see Chapter II), commission money, which averages between $3,000 and $4,999 and exceeds $12,000 only 4 percent of the time, rarely buys them anything like the actual time needed to move a play from conception to realization on the page. Playwrights appreciate being in the commissioning theatre's sights and good graces, but most prefer commitment to commission.

One artistic director, who is also a playwright, hypothesizes that, "If you ask most playwrights what they would rather have— three or four productions of their next play at professional theatres at whatever level versus a $50,000 commission—they'd take the productions. The productions are what they're writing for." Certainly, he's right. They are also searching for a mutual investment in a project's success, from start to finish. To most writers, the true worth of a commission is the production it's meant to lead to.

Some theatres strive for this commitment. "We only commission those things we hope to produce. We're not in the development market at all," the head of a large East Coast theatre asserts. The director of a music-theatre company articulates a committed, collaborative approach:

> The assumption every time we commissioned a piece was
> that both parties would always say yes, although we had the
> option of saying no. But the assumption was that if we were
> offering a commission that, of course, we would always take
> it to production, and that it was designed over the course
> of a two-year period to go to production, unless something
> happened—unless there was a major detour.

But for most theatres, firm commitments at the outset, though desirable, may carry too much risk. "It's tricky," the literary manager of one of the country's largest theatres says. "That can be a good idea, but it's hard. You are saying you're going to produce it, and you don't know what it is."

One of the benefits of commissions with commitment (or at least a solid determination to try to produce) is that writing for a particular theatre and audience or acting company can focus a writer's efforts. "I've had a wonderful experience working with children's theatre companies," an L.A.-based writer says. "They commission the work, and you are writing for a very specific group of actors." Some theatres desire this kind of quick turnaround, too, as an Off-Broadway producer explains.

> I don't like to spend three years dilly-dallying. If I like
> something, I try to do it within a year, or not [do it]. I've had
> successful experiences with commissions when the writer has
> not already written the play, but has an idea that I'm excited
> about, thematically and structurally, and we just know it's
> going to work....When you truly commission something
> and your green light is what brought the sperm and the

egg together, you become like a parent, and then you're
nurturing it.

Of course, contexts vary. Theatres interact with their
communities in specific ways. When Los Angeles's Cornerstone
Theater Company engages a writer on a project, for example,
the writer is expected to participate in community meetings,
story circles, and feedback sessions over the course of the play's
development. Similarly, children's theatre companies that
commission often play a guiding role in the selection of source
material. A traditional commission lies on the other end of the
spectrum—money for a play of the writer's imagining. One
writer sums up this ideal: "For me the best possible scenario
is no strings attached. 'We believe in you; here's some money,
and you write whatever you want. If we like it, we'll produce
it. We'll certainly want to look at it.'…No-strings cash sounds
good to me."

A handful of theatres provide just that. They seed many
more plays than they can produce, and they let playwrights know
upfront that this is the case. An artistic director explains that
writers he commissions can afford productions at other theatres,
since he helps pay for their work ahead of time:

> One of the reasons [we] commission four to six plays a year
> when we only have six productions is because we're targeting
> a lot of emerging writers....It's important that writers are
> getting money somehow, since they're not being compensated
> for many of the productions that they're enjoying.

From the writer's point of view this kind of un-possessive
support can be freeing:

> I got one of the little commissions from Playwrights
> Horizons. They were like, "Don't try and write a Playwrights
> Horizons play." They meant that in a good way. "We can't
> produce everything that comes through our door, and we

want playwrights to write more plays. So here's some money; go write a play."

One novel, "extreme" strategy was tried in the Twin Cities, according to a writer there:

> There was an artistic director here in Minnesota a number of years ago who called up three playwrights—I was one of them—and said, "I have some leftover money in my budget and I have to spend it, so I'm going to pay you this amount of money to write a new play that we'll listen to one time and we're never going to produce. And after you're done writing it, you own it."… I thought, "That's a brilliant notion."

Agents, too, can champion this kind of pact, even as they warn their clients against intrusive or directive commissions. "I love commissions," one agent enthuses,

> but we've been getting into a really dangerous territory with commissions over the last five years, which is, let's sit down and meet with the artistic director and tell us what you're going to write about. That is not the point of commission. What a commission does is buy you the option on a play, of a writer that you like, and it buys some exclusivity from that playwright. It buys their time. If they're saying we have to talk about what it will be, I run for the hills, unless they're saying, "We want you to write our Christmas show for the next 10 years."

However theatres approach commissioning, a playwright warns: "What they [shouldn't] have is an option that allows them to sit on it for a year, and then not do it." This opinion is shared by playwrights everywhere. When theatres commission work and then hold on to it for as long as they can before deciding not to produce it, playwrights are hamstrung. They are denied the chance of earning on the play. The play runs the risk of losing its immediacy or timeliness, if it deals with current events. Moreover, other theatres are denied access to this work. When the play is released, the normally prolonged period of circulating that play to other theatres with equally lengthy selection processes can add years to the writer's waiting.

Theatres with playwright support as part of their mission can help playwrights sustain periods of writing. South Coast Repertory in Costa Mesa, California, has proven visionary on this score, by creating an endowment more than two decades ago and dedicating it to supporting new plays through commissions, readings, festivals, and productions. SCR gives out numerous commissions. Moreover, it's not unusual at SCR for a playwright to receive a second commission before the theatre has decided whether or not to produce a first commissioned play. Some of the wealthier theatres have tried to imitate this procedure of "rolling commissions," as one director of new-play development acknowledges. "A writer will write a play, we'll either do it or not do it, and regardless of whether we do or don't do the play I commission the writer again, in many cases."

Other companies have begun to help plays they commissioned find production elsewhere. The boldest example: Yale Repertory Theatre recently received $600,000 (of a $2.85 million grant from the Robina Foundation) partly to generate premiere or second productions at not-for-profit theatres of plays commissioned (and premiered or let go) by Yale Rep. In other words, Yale will extend its support of commissioned writers by offering financial incentives to other theatres to produce them. "I'm totally happy to be a cog in that machine," one playwright confesses.

Again, with direct funding to writers scarce and the money earned from royalties low and unpredictable, commissions offer one of the few ways for playwrights to earn to actually write plays (as opposed to teaching or writing television, for example) during the long periods between productions. No one suggests curtailing them. Still, writers voice real complaints about the way commissions are handled. "Let me talk about commissions," one playwright insists.

> They're inhumane. When these theatres want to do a
> commission, chances are they don't want to do any of the
> plays you've already written. They like the way you write,
> but they want you to write a play with their idea. You have
> to say yes, because you need money—I actually like to eat.
> So I say yes, and then I write the play they want. They don't
> have to commit to doing it. You spend all this time with
> this little money you've got, you work on this play, you give
> them what you think they want. This is not really what I
> want to do with my time. You're trying to write your other
> plays, and work. You send the play in, and they don't do it.
> It shouldn't be commission. It should be commitment. They
> should have a ceremony where you sit and you commit to the
> writer: "We're going to do this play whether we like it or not,
> because we like this writer."

For writers of color the problems of commissions are
compounded. Commissions, many believe, offer a way for
theatres to look like they're diversifying without doing so in a
real or substantive way. "Sometimes these commissions are a way
to look like you're doing all these new plays and writers of color.
It makes your roster look good. And then you don't commit to
[producing] them," an African-American writer explains. She
adds, "No-strings money is great, but if your pieces never get
done, what's the point? A play that isn't being seen is really sad
to me." In this way, many believe, theatres can make their case in
marketing or to funders without changing what's on their stages.
Playwrights of color note the way they do readings or workshops
at theatres that never produce them and then see their own
photos in those theatres' annual reports, even on the covers.

Some artistic administrators see the problems with
commissions, too. "There's not enough money to actually live
on...and it's not a big enough investment to make the theatre
vested in producing the play," an associate producer admits.

"People embarrassedly call commissions 'the money they pay me to go away' or 'the money they pay me to put me on their brochure until they raise more.'" An artistic director recounts an idea he heard from a colleague to address this complaint.

> Let's say you commission a play and it doesn't fit your criteria for what you want to do in your main stage season. But you're committed to that playwright. Why don't you go back and do a production of that playwright's work that has been done before and needs to be taken to the second step? So that you're committed to the artist and not the play.

Clarity and honesty go a long way, playwrights offer. "It's only a drag if you think they're going to produce it," a New York writer says. "The idea of getting commissioned for a play that you were going to write anyway is better than not getting a commission for a play, especially if the theatre probably isn't going to do it anyway." Or, as another playwright puts it, "It's a matter of managing expectations for the playwright. I wouldn't want to do anything to discourage theatres from giving money."

Development: Getting Plays Ready

> *The development process in the theatre takes a long time and we want urgent plays that speak to us. We can't find them. Is it because we're killing them? Is it because it takes so long to get to production?* —ARTISTIC DIRECTOR

The idea the plays are "workshopped to death" or "dramaturged to death," in common usage for more than twenty years, has itself been reiterated to death. New-play development, however, is part of the ecology of getting plays to the stage, and, so, we need to touch on it here. If "the road to hell is paved with good intentions," the same might be said of standard-issue play development, which began in the late 1970s and '80s with the best of intentions. As one associate artistic director recalls,

> It's ironic that the new-play development machine has
> become this monster in American theatre, because part
> of the impetus behind the idea of institutional producing
> organizations doing readings and workshops and new-
> play development was to create this kind of access, and
> community between artists....[Ideally] writers and directors
> and actors have access to each other and writers have access
> to the artistic staff, and everybody sits around a table and digs
> into a play and talks to each other about how the story affects
> me, this is how I think it will affect my audience.

Even now, playwrights fondly describe their work at
retreats, developmental centers, and new-play labs, because of
the time and focus it allows them, as well as the freedom to direct
their own process toward their own artistic ends. Time is in
short supply in the rehearsal process, and anything that can add
time—for reflection, experiment, dreaming—may be beneficial.
"Because theatres have shortened production schedules, we've
bought into this notion that conceptualization, meditation, is
not part of the process anymore," a playwright in L.A. laments.

> When I first started I used to go to six- to eight-week
> rehearsals. Now the conceptualization time is gone too—the
> time to dream, the time to think. Recently, going to see a play
> in New York and hearing about a three-week rehearsal process
> was really interesting. It's two days of table work; you try to
> get it up on its feet. There's a week of tech and then you're
> done. There's no time to dream, no time to change your mind.

Previews, too, which allow writers to work out kinks in
production in front of actual audiences, are, in the words of one
playwright, "so condensed, especially in smaller theatres. It's
usually a final dress, it's not even in front of an audience. I don't
think I've ever had more than a week-long preview process, and

usually that's been about trying to deal with tech cues and not the actual script."

In the best of all worlds, developmental workshops can add time up front, allowing a playwright to make changes and revisions not possible in truncated rehearsal and preview periods. When that time is suited to the specific, immediate needs of the writer and play, its benefits ripple through the entire process, including final production. An Off-Off-Broadway artistic director explains one way that changing an early stage of process can affect outcome:

> Especially with things that we sign on for fairly early, we're
> trying to think more in terms of *production* development than
> *play* development. The 'a couple months before' model is just
> not working, especially for the kind of work we do, which
> is trying to push the aesthetic to be more experimental.
> Design is a really important part of the kinds of plays we do.
> If you say, "Here are your designers," right before [you got
> into production], it isn't going to work. We're making the
> actual design process, or at least design consultancy, part of
> even our smallest workshop. We're insisting people have the
> consulting designer in there to give that perspective. We're
> trying to get the conversation started early.

Flexibility—the avoidance of what's often dismissed as a "cookie-cutter approach" in developing plays—serves playwrights well. It can also serve theatres. Creativity requires flexibility. The rules that apply to one process rarely fit another, as another artistic director, known for his idiosyncratic producing style, elaborates:

> There's so much alchemy involved in the making of a play.
> I don't feel there's one rule of thumb. I've seen many plays
> suffer through a series of processes of being produced in
> various venues, different sets of input. One play in particular
> at my theatre went from almost the first draft immediately

into an initial production that was the best production a play could ever have. It's about the strange chemistry and magic and chaos and craziness of making theatre. There are no rules. Often you're asked [in grants, for example] to regulate this process and it's a very tricky thing to do, because often the best process is no process. It's just doing it and putting the right group of people together.

But rethinking process for each artist and play takes organizational flexibility and time, both of which many theatres lack. It's easier to resort to the established structures: cold or under-rehearsed readings, followed by staff critiques and/or audience talkback sessions.

By these methods theatres often act as though their job is to fix writers' broken plays, even when those plays have already been produced. An entire playwright chorus echoes Richard Nelson's assessment of this "culture of help" (see Chapter I):

ONE: It's so hard to go and sit someplace and hear your play be read when it's already been produced, and hear people talk about it as if it doesn't work. There's this odd notion in many places: we only read the new plays that are broken, or that need fixing; and we are bringing the playwright in here who needs our help.

TWO: The whole way of looking at a play in a workshop as being broken has even infiltrated into the artists that work there. I've done workshops where the whole audience is artists of some kind, or writers. These people are supposed to be speaking the same vocabulary, but you get the "I didn't understand when ..." and "I didn't like it when this happened."

THREE: I've had the experience a number of times where they'll have a reading of the play and then want to talk to me about further developing the play. I'm like, "The play is finished." I'm done with the play, but they really want to hear, "Oh, this has been a valuable process." Part of that auditioning process is, "Will this fit into the contingencies of this grant that we have to produce this play in our new-play slot that has to have some development in it?"

For playwrights stuck in the phase of career where readings and workshops are all they get, the protracted and random journey of development can be particularly destructive—to the play and to the spirit. "I've had a lot of workshop situations where I've completely ruined something and then had to go back," one recalls. "It can feel depressing, and it can make you not want to work on a specific play anymore."

The problems of development compound when the reasons for doing it get confused, when agendas get crossed. As a former literary manager, now associate director of a new-play lab, points out:

> At a theatre where I used to work, they were using development to answer questions that were unanswerable, [such as] "What's the guaranteed success of this work?" This development didn't yield anything except frustration. There were mixed messages about why a reading was there or development was there, and nothing that they read ended up produced.

Though at least one artistic director thinks that the "workshopped to death" problem is receding, and that more theatres are only developing work headed toward production, the majority of voices, inside and outside of theatres, still believe that theatres sponsor developmental activities as substitutes for production. "Companies do reading series and workshop series in lieu of producing new plays," claims an artistic director. "So they feel that they have done new work because they did five readings. Everybody now has a new-play festival, and that new-play festival is their new work, but they have no intention of producing anything that comes out of that, or if you're lucky, one thing." In many cases, as we'll discuss later, the agendas that get mixed up with artistic development are vital to the theatres in other ways: for example, donor cultivation, audience development, education, and community building.

Developmental activities that don't lead naturally and directly to production can stall the life of a play. They even erect barriers between the writer, who has moved on to other projects, and the work, which no longer feels immediate to its creator. "The amount of time it can take to get a production of a play can be exhausting. You feel like you've moved so beyond that particular play, and suddenly you're right back there," one playwright explains. Too much time between a play's genesis and its fruition (on stage) can also deprive it of urgency, which in turn becomes a barrier to production. "Certain subject matter you want to be relevant now," contends a writer whose recent work includes several plays based on current, global political situations. "It's important that theatre accommodate subject matter that's relevant. A lot of times if it doesn't fit in a season, it's not topical anymore." The lag between writing and production can demoralize a writer. "It's almost like screaming in a box for months on end, and then putting the box aside," this same playwright admits. "Sitting behind my computer day after day writing plays that may or may not be produced makes me crazy."

One large regional theatre addresses this issue of lag time in whatever way it can, according to its associate producer.

> We don't want plays to linger in development. We say it's two years max, and we want to do it; but what if the play isn't quite ready? Maybe we have three pieces that are not really quite ready but we want to produce them in some way, and we do a festival…so that we're actually getting them in front of an audience. They'll find a space, be launched, and have a second life after that. It's trying to find a way of producing the plays in the right space and give them an opportunity to find their audience. Maybe that audience at the beginning is a smaller audience. We no longer use the words "new-play

development." We use "new-play production." We're trying to find a way of developing less and producing more.

Perhaps, as one artistic director suggests, development, which began to cultivate relationships as well as plays, has been focused on the wrong thing all along.

There is a certain hubris on the part of theatres when we start talking about developing plays. In my own work I have been looking at, for the past couple of decades, the idea of developing playwrights or developing artists, and it's a pretty crucial distinction, not just a verbal tic. To develop somebody that you're committed to on some level, and to be able to say, "We're going to establish a relationship and do your work over a period of time and provide resources that may or may not result in a production depending on what happens." I don't think we develop plays. Theatre companies don't develop plays. We think we do, and sometimes we get out of hand in our thinking about that. What's this year's flavor? Everybody is looking for their two-character, one-set play that is going to go around to a bunch of different places. We're looking for properties, as opposed to developing relationships—which is much more difficult and much more time-consuming. It's much more effective, but it's much more inefficient, and exasperating.

How much more exasperating can this relationship building be than what one playwright elegantly calls, "the treacherous and torturous and marvelous road of development"?

FOUR

New Plays Onstage:
Producing in the Real World

*In programming, I'm partly thinking, "How many factors are
there that I can sell?" But also, what's the appropriate space? Is it
a play with size or, is it an intimate play? Whenever you take the
leap on a play of size that doesn't have a lot of known quantities,
you hold your breath.* —ARTISTIC DIRECTOR

WHILE THE playwright's life appears precarious, even
impossible, under most lights, running a nonprofit theatre in
twenty-first-century America can hardly be called a safe or sure
thing. Many theatres consider themselves to be, as more than
one artistic director has put it, "one flop away from folding."
If there were any doubt of theatres' shaky footing before the
economic crash of 2008, life in 2009 provides instant proof.
Budgets are being slashed by 20 and 30 percent, staff members
laid off or furloughed, salaries frozen and cut, and seasons
shortened. Literary departments are being closed down. As of
summer 2009, many theatres planned fewer productions and
opted for smaller-cast plays. A tenuous situation became, by
some reckonings, dire. New-play production, seen by many as
particularly risky, even in the best of times, had, in tough times,
proved endangered.

The production of new plays adds uncertainty to instability.
How can theatres predict the success of the untried? How can
they market the unknown? If time and history are the final

arbiters of a play's merit, how can theatres calculate its quality now? Most important, how can they cultivate an audience who will appreciate process and support the adventure of new-play production through inevitable ups and downs?

This chapter maps out the real world of producing new plays. What drives theatres' choices? What is their funding agenda, their commercial agenda, their human agenda (jobs, benefits, and so forth) for the institution and staff? In part, this map is geographical. No two theatre cities are the same. New York is a world apart—a magnetic, defining world. In part, it's a map of scale, because in the world of new plays, size matters—size of theatre, size of space, size of play. It's also a map of difference: what goes for so-called "mainstream" institutional theatres may not apply for theatres typically referred to as culturally-specific. And as the map unfolds, it becomes clear that most roads lead to the *premiere*. This part of the report focuses on the emphasis on and desire for premieres, which to the theatres represent a kind of necessary prize and for writers too often mark the end of the road for their plays.

WHAT'S "NEW"?

> *The play can be new to an audience or new to an artist. To some degree, if a play hasn't been done in a particular city, it should still be a new play.* —PLAYWRIGHT

What makes a new play "new"? For some it means a work no one has seen before. More often, though, the word describes a play that is new to the place it's playing, or that hasn't yet entered the contemporary canon. A play may be new for years, or it may stop being new when responses to it have reached some vague critical tipping point. Many playwrights think of a play as new until they stop working on it, which, commonly, doesn't happen with the first or even second production. In other words, "new" is a slippery term, so quantifying "new-play production" can be slippery, too.

A play is no longer new when "it's had 'X' amount of productions," one playwright ventures. "Probably three. It's such a weird algebra, because it would depend on which three theatres. It might stop being new when it's reached a certain sized audience." Another offers, "Maybe it has to do with time. Maybe if it's produced in one theatre in 2006–07, and then in 2007–08 it gets picked up by a couple of other theatres who do it. Maybe it's a time-sensitive definition, so in those two years the forty productions of [Lynn Nottage's] *Intimate Apparel* would technically all qualify for a new-play slot. But if somebody did it now, it would no longer be considered a new play."

For theatres, newness is less important than first-ness. As a category of work, new plays are often considered a hard sell. Premieres, on the other hand—especially world premieres—are seen as having cachet. (The reasons for this, as we will discuss, may have more to do with institutional concerns than audience demand.) In the contemporary theatre, a track record of premieres bestows, or at least suggests, status on a theatre and, so, to fill new-play slots theatres often vie for world premieres and eschew plays that have been produced elsewhere, except for a handful of plays that have been anointed "hits" (usually Off Broadway). As theatres contend for premieres, a hierarchy emerges, based chiefly on the budget size of the theatre (large trumps small) and location (New York trumps everywhere else). "New" may be hard to define, but "premiere" is purposefully fudged by theatres and playwrights alike.

A Minneapolis-based writer riffs on the situation:

> A new play—I read in the papers—is something that has been done in New York and never done. I've seen plays re-virginated. They have a premiere here, and then suddenly they had a premiere there.

The Numbers: Productions, Premieres, Development

Because "new" and "premiere" are inexact terms, statistics about such plays in production are hard to evaluate with precision. Similarly, as we've seen, new-play development means different things to different people, as do the components of new-play development: "reading," "workshop," "residency," "developmental program." Categorically, however, the amount of new-play activity—productions, premieres, development—at theatres is extensive.

We selected approximately two-thirds of the theatres randomly; we selected the rest *because* we knew them to have strong track records of new-play production and hoped to learn from what they were doing right. Ninety-seven percent of this total universe of theatres currently produces new work. Here's what we've learned about them:

> **FINDING:** While an average season at study theatres includes *seven* productions of all kinds, they report producing, on average, approximately *nine* new plays over the past three seasons—*45.6 percent of their total offerings*. Of these nine new plays, produced over three years, theatres identify slightly more than five (or 30.7 percent of theatres' total productions) as world premieres. Fewer than two of these new works (less than one per season) *are second productions* of new plays.

What do these statistics tell us? First, new-play activity is exceedingly high across the country. If these theatre statistics are indicative, new plays represent almost half of what lands on the nation's stages. Again, while it's impossible to know precisely what these theatres consider "new"—a play never seen before or, at the other end of the spectrum, a five-year-old work new to the city or region—it's clear that nearly all theatres give significant weight to the production of contemporary writing.

In meetings across the country, we found that playwrights were sometimes skeptical of these numbers, questioning either the theatres' definition of "new plays" or their reporting. Skepticism runs even higher about the numbers of world premieres reflected in the study, including among artistic directors. In fact, few of the study participants believe the accuracy of reporting on the number of world premieres.* Certainly the majority of Off- and Off-Off-Broadway companies focus almost exclusively on actual premieres or those new works that, having proven themselves in well-regarded regional theatres, are "re-virginated" for New York. But whether or not this reporting is accurate or inflated, it demonstrates a prevalent emphasis on world premieres.

Why are world premieres weighted like this? Why, by contrast, is the number of second productions of new plays so low? What do these numbers says about the values and priorities of the theatres, about our nation's system of new-play production?

---

* A recent study by the National Endowment for the Arts (December 2008) puts the number of U.S. professional theatres with annual budgets exceeding $75,000 at 1,982. Our sampling represents approximately 5 percent of the total. If our group, claiming around five world premieres every three seasons, reflects the field, then the American theatre produces approximately 10,000 world premieres every three years, which, of course, seems highly unlikely, if not impossible. (Certainly the rate of new play premieres contradicts everything the playwrights in this study report.) Against the backdrop of this theatre boom—with the number of theatres up 100 percent in the fifteen years between 1990–2005—the NEA study shows the audience for straight plays falling off precipitously, from 25 million (adults attending a play at least once in the year) in 1992 to 21 million in 2008.

PREMIERES: TO HAVE AND TO HOLD

> *What is the lure of working on a new play? It has something to do with the joy of collaboration. The actors and the designer and the writer and the director are all creating something that is incredibly unique. It's lonely to be a playwright, and it's sometimes lonely to be a director…If you have a relationship where there is a trust and a commitment on everyone's part to doing the best work that they can in representing this playwright and this play, it's really quite fulfilling.* —ARTISTIC DIRECTOR

For theatres the premiere—especially the world premiere—makes the most of newness, sells the event as well as the play, bestows on the institution the privilege of discovery, first-ness, and, therefore, a sense of ownership. Playwrights, by contrast, believe that the health of a new play often depends not just on being produced, but on being re-produced, being staged more than once. Multiple stages and multiple audiences help a writer see her work, refine and complete it. This is not a new idea: Out-of-town tryouts were once an important part of the Broadway system. But the "road," which long ago came to an end as a path for new plays headed to New York, has, in literal and figurative ways, been closed.

In a competitive marketplace, premieres are currency. If a title or author name is meaningless to the audience, the rubric "premiere" becomes a hook. If they can't sell the unknown play or the category of "new work," theatres hope they can sell the distinction of getting there first. They bring enormous creativity to marketing that distinction: "World premiere," "regional premiere," or "[City's name goes here] premiere."

Theatres prefer premieres for many reasons. Premiering new work might be part of a theatre's mission. It might be attractive in and of itself, because creation is an exciting process. "There is, from a very selfish artistic point of view for those of us who are directors, the thrill of working on a first production," says one artistic director. The head of an Off-Broadway theatre elaborates:

About 80 percent of the things that we do are world
premieres. I don't want to pat myself on the back but it's
not exactly common among the smaller to middle-size
theatres. It's not [out of] any kind of possessiveness, although
that exists; it springs out of my personal interest in forging
relationships with artists I like, being there at the birth of
the baby, and being a creative artistic director who likes to
contribute to the process. On some occasions we've done
shows which have been premiered elsewhere, but only when
I and my company can bring something of value to the play.

The rewards are both spiritual and tangible, as an artistic
director, whose theatre is frequently cited as a leader in the field,
explains: "New-play work is less ephemeral than the rest of what
we do. There's a bit of a legacy in having a hand in creating new
work. You will be listed in the scripts for years to come."

What some call "institutional ego" might play a role. "Even
if it doesn't sell that particular show, [a premiere is] important
in terms of the perception of what kind of work the theatre is
doing, its reputation," a literary manager explains.

I deal with board members who are on our new-play
committee. They want to know that our theatre came up
with it, like suddenly we invented this idea of this person or
this play. There seems to be a desire that somehow you found
this person under a bush and nobody else has heard of them.

Building a theatre's reputation by mounting premieres can
be important strategically. "World premieres are the first plank of
our new four-year plan, to do at least one a year," one Chicago-
area artistic director explains. "We felt it was important for us to
be able to raise the theatre's national profile" by premiering work.
Efforts to enhance a theatre's profile nationally have a practical
side. Premieres beget premieres, he continues, and producing
them helps the theatre fulfill its mission by eliminating a key
stumbling block to doing new work.

It's not necessarily about ego. It's about wow, the next time great playwright X writes a play or is thinking about writing a play, they're going to call you. It's to be able to retain access to those works. The more new plays that we produce, the more world premieres that my company does, the more chance I have of getting a really interesting world premiere from more and more accomplished playwrights.

Locally, too, doing world premieres lends a competitive edge, says another Chicago-area artistic director, by garnering press coverage.

The competition here is fierce, and so how many times can you do *Biloxi Blues?* You end up looking for stuff that's challenging for you as an artist individually, or the directors that you work with. Sometimes that's an old play that they want to do as a new play. Sometimes it's an absolutely brand-new play. If you end up doing replication here, you're not going to get any press out of the *Tribune.*

The press contributes to the prevalent premiere hunger. For arts journalists, first productions offer a built-in story, a justification for a preview piece or artist profile, much sought after as free publicity prior to a show's opening. Moreover, a theatre's involvement in those productions helps establish an identity, an institutional or curatorial voice to distinguish that theatre in a crowded field.

Despite these benefits, premieres don't automatically increase ticket sales, and artistic leaders disagree about how much audiences care about the distinction. "I don't believe our audiences are that keyed in to know or care about premieres," one artistic director says. A colleague agrees that a "world premiere" label "doesn't do a lot for the particular production. It's got to be a good show." But a literary manager from the Southeast argues (about musicals, in particular), "Our audiences love world premieres because they love the bragging rights."

LOVE OR MONEY: FUNDING NEW WORK

> *There's "premiere-itis" just as much with the funders and with*
> *the foundations, the corporations. They will not support you unless*
> *you "pop the cherry."* —ARTISTIC DIRECTOR

The realities of funding also add to "premiere-itis."

There are numerous granting opportunities for premieres and few for second productions. This fact has a deleterious (though unintentional) impact on the field. For funders, a theatre's claim to being part of the genesis of a play is a quantifiable outcome, as well as being feathers in their caps. The list of premieres underwritten by a particular foundation or corporation may be more impressive to its own board of directors (the funders' version of institutional ego). For any funders, including individual donors, who want to underwrite measurable change, thus leveraging their funds to have the greatest impact on the field, premieres offer "more bang for the buck." It's easier overall to raise money for first productions than for later ones, as this artistic director explains:

> With the world premiere, it hasn't been proven that it sucks
> yet, it hasn't had that proof that its mediocre, so if you can
> tweak the things that were exciting to you about it and speak
> about that, you can get people excited, and the hope of the
> unknown can sway it in a way that is not necessarily true of a
> show that's already been out in the world.

The funding climate for new writing has changed considerably in the past twenty years. One commercial producer, who has collaborated with numerous nonprofits, sums up the history:

> In the Reagan years we had [federal and state] subsidy
> cutbacks. That put the not-for-profits in the extremely
> unfortunate position. The idea behind subsidy, we all believe,
> is to allow risk taking and to allow failure. As subsidy was

cut back, that took that ability away from them, because
they had to compete for foundation, corporation and box
office dollars. The corporation will tell you, you got a great
review in the *New York Times*, your show transferred to
Broadway and you got a Tony nomination. That became a
mark of success. [As a result] the institutional theatres have
to compete on a different playing field. You can't afford to
say, "Our subsidy is to allow us to fail." You have to say "we
have to have five million more subscribers," so we have to do
A Christmas Carol every year. That led playwrights to write
less adventurously and artistic directors to program more
conservatively. The more conservative they became in their
programming, the fewer opportunities there were for people
to make a living in the theatre.

A San Francisco–based artistic director tells a similar story
in a personal vein.

I came of age in New York twenty years ago, when funding
went to the most adventurous stuff. Funders—the
professional philanthropic impulse—were to give you
support for something that you weren't doing to reach an
audience that you weren't reaching. Now, the fundamental
philanthropic impulse from professional foundations,
from family foundations, from everybody else, is very
corporate in its mindset. What are the outcomes? How
many eyeballs? How much money did this make? Theatres
are becoming, by nature, more timid, because they have to
be, because the outcomes are being measured on a whole
different playing field.

At the same time, and in part as a result of attacks on the
National Endowment for the Arts—especially over art deemed
controversial by its critics—funding for individual artists, e.g.
playwrights, dried up. Playwrights grew more dependent on
institutional theatres for funding their work at all stages of

development. These theatres, meanwhile, judged by a new metrics, were focusing on audience outreach and development, especially the development of racial and ethnic diversity in audiences. Funding for new-play development often dovetailed with these initiatives, as one senior African-American playwright explains. Major "foundations were trying to do that audience-development grant thing."

> The dramaturgy of the theatre became a big issue, [i.e.]
> how they connected with the community, whatever that
> meant. [These programs] began to include emerging voices,
> playwrights. There was more and more money available to
> do these readings series at institutions all over the country.
> We did these reading series but we knew…that [the theatres]
> were not going to produce them…

As the mandates of funders and donors become more specific and prescriptive, and as the universe of funding for new work narrows, the question of who is leading the programming comes up more often. As an artistic leader at a major institution tells it, programming is increasingly directed at

> the narrow universe of people who invest in institutions
> for their own reasons by serving on Boards or as program
> officers. [The theatres] know them very intimately. And those
> people tell us, "This is what I was expecting or this was not
> what I was expecting." And so what the theatre perceives
> as for its audience is being shaped by those people with an
> investment telling us what the connection is between their
> investment and the stage.

In other words, subsidy for process and production, experiment and attempt, has become investment. And investment seeks specific, quantifiable returns.

Whatever agendas guide funders to support new work, those seeking support have one pressing agenda: they need a lot of money to do this work, money and the freedom to spend it to further development in ways that don't always conform to funding initiatives. As we've seen, cookie-cutter approaches to new-play creation strangle the artistic process as much as they benefit it. Theatres wanting to avoid such one-size-fits-all approaches to new plays need *flexible* funding. "What we need at our theatres for development is not programs," asserts the head of a mid-size theatre, devoted to new plays. "We need money. We need a pot of funds, an opportunity fund to draw from, to use in whatever way it's needed on any particular project depending on the relationship—as compared to cookie-cutter programs— money for furthering particular relationships and processes."

Playwrights have no illusions about the cost of these efforts, as this writer succinctly acknowledges. "It always comes back to the funding. People aren't going to take risks unless there's a safety net." The producing artistic director of a national playwrights' lab concurs, describing a culture of new-play development that is "all wrong":

> Really investing in new work takes so much time. The only
> way new work can thrive is if it gets the kind of attention
> to take it to a place that it's ready for production. You can't
> usually rehearse a new play in three or four weeks' time. It
> really takes a familiarity with the play over a period of time to
> understand what's in it. Successful plays are [when] you have
> the same actors who have worked on it for two years, the
> writer has worked on it for two years, the artistic director has
> worked on it for two years.

Recognizing these demands and lacking funds, small theatres may avoid the long-term cultivation of new plays altogether, as the director of a Minneapolis company explains. "We don't develop work, because we can't afford to develop work. To have an ongoing relationship is almost impossible for us, as much as we would like to work with some of those writers on an ongoing basis. To provide real financial under-footing for this is

almost impossible for an organization our size." Small theatres in
the Bay Area have found support from large, local funders, but
even this isn't enough to cover all phases of new-play development
and production. One artistic director there spells it out: "We're
being supported by these big foundations, and it's really the only
way we can do this, I think. Without that support, the money's
just not there. And then of course if you do get the money to
commission a piece, getting the rest of the $90,000 to actually put
it up is the challenge." When the money isn't there, theatres have
to rely on each other, she adds. "That's where the partnerships
have to come in. We have to join forces with one another. That's
the future of producing. I don't know how else to do it."

The problems of funding new-play development and
production compound when theatres are compelled to justify
the costs of the work in light of minimal financial return. One
veteran artistic director tells of having to cut her theatre's new-
play festival altogether. A premise of the festival was the five-
dollar ticket—to make the work "free or almost free." When this
experiment made it impossible to generate income, the theatre's
board and the festival's funders, questioned the value of the
enterprise. "It just seemed like an obvious thing to chop away at.
You also have to say, what's bringing in the money?" When an
individual donor pulled out, the festival was cancelled.

SUBSIDIARY RIGHTS: INCENTIVE & OBSTACLE
Producing world premieres also can yield tangible economic
benefits for theatres, including money from subsidiary rights.
John Weidman, a musical librettist and, during the years of this
study, president of the Dramatists Guild of America, sums this
concept up this way:

> Subsidiary rights are secondary rights, which a producer
> attempts to acquire in a play when he or she options it for
> production. These secondary rights entitle the producer
> to a share of the playwright's earnings from the play from
> productions subsequent, to the production mounted by

the producer, and from any dispositions of the playwright's audio-visual rights in the play.

Currently, that producer's share runs from nothing to as high as 40 percent of the author's earnings, depending on the theatre. (Broadway producers traditionally exact the higher amounts, as do two New York nonprofits that also operate Broadway theatres. Size and prominence are not always indicators; Lincoln Center Theater, for instance, takes no subsidiary portion from writers, nor, as of early in 2008, does the Center Theatre Group in Los Angeles.) "The rationale for this participation," Weidman continues, "is that the producer's production has added such stature and value to the play that the producer is entitled to participate in that value-added. Arguably, this is true of a Broadway production that transforms the play into a 'Broadway play.' It is clearly a good deal less true of any other sort of production."

When subsidiary rights were introduced in the 1920s, according to one theatrical lawyer, the language of value was very clear. "The original language started off by saying, 'In recognition of the value the production has given to the play.' And that's what it's all about." Another producer clarifies. "If you look at the old APC [the Dramatists Guild's Approved Production Contract], it's very clear that the subrights say: 'In recognition of the value of a Broadway production.'" Additionally, on Broadway, subrights money helps a show recoup, that is, it allows investors to earn back their initial investment, the operating premise behind commercial productions.

When Broadway was the world for new plays, the notion that a Broadway production added significant value to a play— making it possible to tour, get published, attract amateur productions, etc.—was hard to dispute. When the center of new-play production moved, the issue of "value added" became harder to quantify. Is there a difference between the impact of productions in Los Angeles, Chicago, or Atlanta? Of one Off-Broadway theatre or another? How does the size of the originating theatre alter its impact on the life of the play? When a theatre takes the first chance, assumes the greatest risk, invests the most money in a work, shouldn't it benefit from its continued success? What is the appropriate proportion of investment and payback? If nonprofits are, for new plays, the new Broadway, should they adopt Broadway practices, or does their status, do their missions, as nonprofits (who, after all, spend money from donors, not investors) require a different ethic?

Whatever specific practices make sense, it's hard to dismiss the theatres' fundamental reasons for believing they deserve subsidiary rights participation. From the start of the regional theatre's commitment to new plays, theatre leaders have seen commercial producers benefit financially from the work they've done, developing and premiering plays. When *The Great White Hope* became the first regional theatre production to move to Broadway in 1968, Arena Stage, which had produced the play with the same cast the prior year, received no benefit from the two-year Broadway run or the movie sale, while others, including the playwright, profited nicely from the play's continued life. It was a "never again" moment for that theatre, and, in some ways for the field. Other theatres have watched producers reap profits from musicals to which they've committed extraordinary time and money. They've also watched other theatres—most notably New York's Public Theater under Joseph Papp with *A Chorus Line*—sustain years of programming on the income from hits. Why shouldn't theatres that struggle to bring high quality work to audiences year after year benefit from their efforts?

While there are purists on all sides—those who argue that theatres should never take sub rights and those who argue that any theatre that adds value should get some stake in a play—there is growing concern, especially among playwrights and those who represent them (agents, lawyers, new work advocates, and even producers in both the nonprofit and commercial arenas), that more and more people are grabbing for a piece of the play. Increasingly, smaller, less visible regional theatres are demanding the same kind of subsidiary rights participation exacted by large Off-Broadway theatres. (To make matters worse for the playwright, some directors are similarly demanding subsidiary rights participation for their contribution to the play's development and production.)

Some theatres are calling for greater percentages for second and third productions of plays they expect will have a commercial life. Some theatres are asking for rights for workshopping plays, even when they don't produce them. In London, too, developmental theatres are requesting that American writers cede to them control over their American premieres, as one New York producer marvels. "A writer we've been working with on a couple of projects…I was stunned. She called me for advice because they wanted to workshop her play for two weeks or something, a very short residency, and they wanted a piece of the play, and control over the New York premiere." One commercial producer expresses astonishment that some major regional theatres are asking for subrights for revivals. "Revivals? There'll come a point when, why bother? What do some of those theatres stand for?"

"It inches up and up and up and up," an agent explains.

> If it's a premiere co-production, which happens a lot before
> it comes to New York, we don't want to give 10 percent; we
> want to give 5. You're putting it together, you're sharing
> the costs, you know. I mean, a lot of people have different
> ideas of what subsidiaries are given for. A lot of these smaller
> theatres where these writers don't make any money—they
> don't make any money and the exposure's not big enough at
> a small theatre like the Magic in San Francisco. Yes, they're
> doing it; they deserve some subsidiaries. But do they deserve
> the same thing as a playwright who's going to make $45,000
> at the Goodman in Chicago and also get much bigger press?
> I just think [those larger, more visible theatres] deserve more.

One leading playwright celebrates the example of Lincoln Center Theater: "Lincoln Center has the best contract for writers in New York, because they don't take any sub rights—

nothing." By contrast, the battle playwrights have to fight with other large theatres

> is fantastic. I said, "It cannot be that a significant portion of your budget is supported by a piece of the royalty I'm going to get for productions." Their answer is that it's a precedent, and we have to maintain it, because there'll be a pot of gold. You say to them, "Yeah, but you know what? The insignificant amount of money in your budget is enormously significant to the budget of the writer who is not getting the money." And they say, "Yeah, but fuck you."

From here, he extrapolates, articulating the case that more and more playwrights are forced to make about the creeping encroachment on their rights of authorship:

> In exchange for doing your play, people want things that they didn't used to feel they were entitled to. The deal at Lincoln Center was that you give us the play, and we'll give you a production. That seems like a fair deal, right? But, a lower and lower threshold at smaller and tiny theatres are now demanding, in exchange for a production, an ongoing participation in the authors' revenues from that play. The revenues from the play might never be significant, so it may not amount to a great deal of money. But one of the things that happens is that the play becomes encumbered as it proceeds, like a lien on your property, until it becomes so encumbered that nobody's interested in producing it. It has been understood up to this point, that the second theatre in line or the third in line will share with the others. So, the size of the encumbrance doesn't necessarily get larger. That concept's days are numbered if they haven't already begun to disappear. Say it's 5 percent for five years. Then there's another production who wants 5 percent for five years, so everybody gets two and a half. But it is becoming not five divided by two, it's becoming five and five. Equally alarming

are the people you pick up along the way who also either demand financial participation or right of first refusal if there's going to be another production. Directors routinely ask for that, one or the other, or both. A [director] a number of years ago said, "A friend called me. He's got a new play and he asked me if I could get a bunch of actors together in my living room so he could just hear it. What should I ask for?" He didn't mean 50 dollars to pay for the chips. It was like what piece of the play do you think would be fair for me to get as a result of this? I said, "Zero would be fair." It's out there, and it's hard to tell how much of it has to do with anybody's actual financial interests, and how much of it has to do with some seismic shift away from the idea that the theatre is about the voice of the playwright.

Some theatre leaders discount the potential to benefit from subsidiary rights income as a factor. The artistic director of a theatre devoted to playwrights believes that subsidiary rights are gradually losing their grip over programming. "Theatres have slowly figured out, 'Doing the world premiere allows me to have those subsidiary rights and income from that. But it's a twenty-six-dollar check,'" he says. Others argue that when plays do well over time, the income generated for the originating theatre can amount to a considerable sum, and constitute a significant revenue stream. This may be particularly true for plays that are, or are perceived to be, on their way to New York, and, indeed, the examples held up—Donald Margulies's *Dinner with Friends*, Jason Robert Brown's chamber musical *The Last Five Years*— began life regionally before coming to Off Broadway. Clearly, it affects Off-Broadway nonprofits, especially those with a history of commercial moves.

All this begs the question: Why should theatres' additional gains come out of the pockets of the playwrights, for whom royalties account for a tiny percentage of a barely livable income? Isn't supporting playwrights essential to the theatres themselves? If so, why take back money at the very moment that a playwright stands to earn some? Doesn't a successful play add value to the theatre's brand? A literary agent pulls no punches: Theatres "want the money. They want the subsidiary rights. It's ego and it's subsidiary rights."

The desire to maximize subsidiary income may also inhibit collaboration among companies involved in new work, one regional theatre artistic director says. Whether it's for 5–10 percent subsidiary rights, 1–2 percent of the commercial gross, or 5–10 percent of net profits, this participation impedes the progress of many plays. This artistic director describes the prevailing attitude, especially in New York, as, "Why would you voluntarily share in the wealth?" He counters that argument with one of his own: "Because we're not in this business to make money off plays. Anyone who thinks they're going to make lots of money off plays out there in the regions is pretty crazy."

ENHANCEMENT

> *You look at the not-for-profits and their appetite in New York particularly, but not all in New York, for a [commercial] transfer is as voracious as ever. The article that was in the* New York Times *about [an Off-Off-Broadway producer who] said, "I spend most of my time trying to find enhancement money." And I read that and I said, "Okay, now this is really full circle. A not-for-profit now is spending most of its time looking for enhancement money from commercial producers?" I thought they raised money from people who are donors who want them to do their work, not from commercial producers who want to give them money so they could benefit by the transfer.* —BROADWAY PRODUCER

As the line between contribution and investment has blurred, the involvement of commercial producers in the work of nonprofits— especially through revenue known as "enhancement" money— has grown more pervasive, thus further complicating mission-driven new-play development and production. The producer quoted above is one of several people who, having worked on both sides of the commercial/nonprofit divide, spoke frankly and at length on the subject. A different producer—also involved with nonprofit theatres—recalls his introduction to the practice, and something of its evolution:

> The first time I became familiar with enhancement, it was, "We really want to do this play and we can't afford to do a ten-character play with four harpists in a box, so we'll pay for six actors and one director, and you'll pay [the additional] costs." Now, enhancement is really just a dollar amount. [One major theatre] says, "Okay, we'll do your show." We spend X; you're responsible for everything on top of that. And then there are others that say, the cost of enhancement for a show is at least Y or Z and, so, it bears no relationship to extra costs. It's just another subsidy.
>
> I've seen [other people] say, we've got this fantastic play and it has commercial possibilities, and we'd like a couple of hundred thousand dollars extra to do it. In return for getting that money, the person who puts up that money will get the commercial rights.

In other words, enhancement funds—to cover unusual costs, a portion of the budget, or a previously set figure—buy the enhancer rights to transfer/produce the play commercially, should it do well enough at the nonprofit to justify transfer, and to participate in its future audiovisual life.

There are definite advantages to such an approach, as one industry professional points out. "It's much easier to take $100,000 from X producer than raise that $100,000. They call and say, 'Hey, we got this great play. You like this play? Give me $100,000 and I'll give you the commercial rights.'" It may be easier, but it also stands to distort the purpose of the nonprofits. One producer summarizes this often-articulated point:

> Everybody is having trouble raising money, but that's what not-for-profits do. They raise money. Other not-for-profits

don't have enhancement money. Does the Red Cross have enhancement money? When the focus becomes, for not-for-profits, getting plays that can attract enhancement, your focus is on commercial theatre. Because nobody is going to enhance a play for its own sake.

Is enhancement the exception or the rule? A New York producer's answer: "I don't know of one not-for-profit that doesn't seek or want to attract enhancement money." Anecdotally, this statement would appear to be true, especially of New York City theatres of some size and ambition and of larger regional companies. Statistics, however, tell a different, if hazy, story. Only fourteen of our study's ninety-four producing theatres reported producing a new play in the past three years due to an approach from a commercial producer with enhancement funds. Eleven of the fourteen theatres did so only once (theatres of all budget sizes, four of which were in New York City), one theatre did so twice and another theatre three times (both large theatres located in California), and one theatre produced ten new plays with enhancement funds from a commercial partner (a small theatre located in New York City).*

The prevalence of enhancement funding—or the quest for it—is evidenced in the statement of an Off-Broadway artistic

---

* We suspect a lack of precision (and, therefore, certainty) in this finding, due to the way we asked the question. The question posed to theatres was, "Apart from your own theatre's new play development, of the new plays your theatre has produced in the last three years, how many came out of...?" with "an approach from a commercial producer with enhancement funds?" as one of a number of possible responses. Because we didn't ask about the theatres approaching producers for enhancement money, these percentages may only tell half of the story. The example of the small New York theatre with numerous enhancement experiences may or may not be responding to the exact question of producers approaching the theatre, as opposed to the opposite. Had we thought to ask, "How many new plays has your theatre produced with the help of enhancement funds from a commercial producer?" we presume, from anecdotal evidence, a much larger percentage would probably have resulted.

director's pride at having funded a Tony Award–nominated musical without it. "We dedicated ourselves to do [this musical] without enhancement money. Find another theatre that does a musical without enhancement money! We had three times what's usually at stake financially on the table for us. We begged for money from everyone who loved us. It was an enormous risk."

It is important to note the distinction between two types of enhancement, and the artistic/ethical/legal distinctions between them as well. In one instance, the theatre seeks enhancement funds for a project *as* subsidy, by attempting to interest producers in a play or musical it believes in. The second type of enhancement works the other way around. A project comes to a theatre from a commercial producer who sees a life for the piece and wants to try it out in an environment with a built-in audience, some developmental expertise, and, presumably, more safety than the commercial theatre offers.

In Chapter I, we made the case that the traditionally close relationship between the producer and the playwright has been severed by the growth of institutional theatres. When considering enhancement as a means of funding new-play production in the nonprofit theatre, an additional wrinkle appears. Enhancement adulterates the role of "producer" itself, making it harder and harder to discern whether the theatre or the commercial producer is leading the process. If 15 percent of theatres (fourteen out of ninety-four) have produced plays brought to them by commercial producers with money, what does this say about the selection process at the theatres themselves? Is money leading the process? How strong is the lure of a play's commercial prospects? How do the theatre's internal play-cultivation programs compare or compete with the clout of outside producers? Are artistic directors still picking plays out of love, or is there a new calculus for a play's potential success? Are artistic leaders under pressure from managers or boards of directors to ensure that the work of a theatre has a future commercial life? And what are the implications of these commercial practices for the traditional funders of nonprofits? Do they know about enhancements? Do they understand the nature of the business arrangements and their relationships to the theatres' missions?

Unlike co-production between nonprofits, the relationship between a commercial producer and a nonprofit cannot legally function as a producing collaboration. One legal expert explains:

> [W]hen the show is being produced at the not-for-profit, they [the theatre] should be completely in control. Because, presumably, it is mostly their money and they cannot give control over to the producer. Now we know informally the artistic director is talking, "Do you like this star? You don't like this star." But as a legal document [the commercial producers] have absolutely nothing to say. The contract is strict.

As enhancement has evolved from providing 10 or 15 percent of a budget to two-thirds or more of the budget, in the case of some recent musicals cited, the outside producer, with more at stake, is less able to give over control to the theatre.

> Now, they still go through the charade of saying that it's the not-for-profit's production. It isn't. They're whispering in everybody's ear, "It's all my money. You'd better hire this director and hire this composer," and this whatever.

A Broadway producer, who has been involved in many such deals, elaborates:

> The nonprofit resents the commercial producer being around. You almost can't not be around if you're the commercial producer, because what happens in enhanced productions is the director will say, "I want to have that on the set," halfway to rehearsals. So if they need it, the institution will say, no, that's not in our budget, we can't pay for that. They run to the commercial producer, and the commercial producer says yea or nay, and it's then the non-profit theatre company says well, you've agreed to that, you

have to give us an extra $50,000 if you're going to build that and add it to the scenery. The lines are blurry.

From the point of view of the commercial producer, who has no ethical obligation to operate under the guidelines of the theatre's mission or nonprofit status, it makes perfect sense to want to be involved in producing decisions when you've put up a great deal of money and have hopes of moving the production on, according to this same producer:

> The other thing about enhanced productions is that enhancement money is not easy to raise, because there is no possibility you'll get it back unless it moves and it's folded into the capitalization. People do raise enhancement money—certainly on the level of a musical it's hard—but what is commonly quoted to a major theatre in this town [NYC] is like minimum $200,000 to join hands. It's very hard to get that money unless you get it from somebody who is rich. If I'm writing a big check, I want some credit. I just don't want to be anonymous. Then you have somebody who takes a piece of that pie. I don't blame the people who are writing the checks for wanting it.

Even as enhancement has raised questions about the theatres' domain over their own work, it has increased the pressure on playwrights to come to the theatres bearing money of their own. "A lot of playwrights are actually coming forward with enhancement money these days," one Off-Broadway artistic director asserts. "They bring in producers or other folks." The head of small playwrights collective suggests, "[It's] a small number of playwrights though, right now." But a third artistic director, from a major East Coast regional theatre, counters, "It's large and getting bigger." An industry professional explains the impact of this new pressure on the writer:

> And now the playwright ends up at the not-for profit, where he or she should feel incredibly comfortable to experiment

and do what he or she really wants to do, and what are
they hearing in the background? "We need enhancement
money."…So the playwright immediately is a self-producer.
Now the playwright is sitting with not-for-profits and the
theatre puts the pressure on the playwright or his agent to
find enhancement money? What have we come to?

Increasingly, this pressure shifts part of the burden of producing and fundraising to the artists themselves. Some sense that
this "enhancement mania may be subsiding." They point out that
too few enhancement productions actually make the transfer
to commercial runs. "That which succeeds commercially is
invariably that which you don't think will," a commercial general
manager observes. "I bet if you did a top secret analysis of enhanced productions at any major theatre across the country that
weren't preprogrammed for Broadway, you'd find that the ones
that were enhanced never got out of there." Another Broadway
veteran speculates that producers are growing resistant to giving
huge sums of money at the same time they are giving up control.
It may be more prudent to wait and see how the nonprofit
production goes before investing in it.

Clearly, enhancement is a symptom of commercial
pressure within the not-for-profit community. Theatre leaders
feel pressure from all sides: their boards, the press, and even
audiences. They are expected to program work that meets
revenue targets, that increases the national profile of their
institutions, and that might move to New York. Mere plays
aren't enough, especially in light of rising ticket prices. Artistic
directors must deliver *events*. They must make *hits*.

To the extent that they fulfill these expectations, theatres
become victims of their own success. Artistic directors experience
this "hit/flop mentality" from all sides. It leaves little room for
experimentation, the small play of modest ambition, or for what
Arena Stage founder Zelda Fichandler once called "the fifth
freedom"—the freedom to fail.

A literary agent casts a cold eye on the situation:

I feel like every time you're trying to get a play, or a musical on, for that matter now, it's always being judged by "Could this become commercial?" It's not just about "Let's do good work." Everything is judged by the future life, which is based on money coming back to the theatre in the life of the play, and that's where you get into dangerous territory, especially with new writers, because not everyone's going to write plays that are going to be commercial.

A theatrical lawyer goes even further, depicting a theatrical climate completely defined by the commercial. "I used to hear about it more ten years ago, that…we need to worry about more commercial material. I don't hear that so much now, and I don't know why. Is it because they're not even booking anything else? There's no longer a debate, because they don't even think about the experimental plays."

The Afterlife of a Play

PREMIERE-ITIS, OR ONE AND DONE

> *Many worthy plays, even if they get good reviews somewhere else, don't get done again. It's a crying shame. If one whole thrust of this survey is, How can we get more worthy plays to be produced at all? Another side of it is, How can those worthy plays that do get produced, get produced again?* —ARTISTIC DIRECTOR

The first production may be a peak in the life of a play; it is never, though, meant to be the end of that life. Writers often need several productions to refine their work. "Second productions are a great gift in terms of craft," one writer asserts.

> You get a chance to see your play in front of an audience and go, "I wish I had another chance to do this." I was able to see [one of my plays in its premiere production], and the artistic

director kept badgering me to cut scenes. I was like, "I'm not cutting them!" Of course, after the production, I cut them.

Other writers concur. A play isn't finished, they agree, until the writer has seen it on its feet, taken a break, and seen it again. "You learn so much from the audience reaction the first time." In a world where premieres have taken the place of out-of-town tryouts and where writers and artistic directors alike complain of having too few previews to make changes and work the kinks out, the most effective way for writers to re-work plays is over time, from one production to the next. Without these opportunities, the work doesn't get done.

Furthermore, playwrights write plays to be seen, and the audience of a single nonprofit theatre—no matter how large that theatre is—is small, numbered in the hundreds or low thousands at most. Moreover, the economics of playwriting are so dire, and the space between plays so long, that royalties from successive mountings may be the only hope for anything like an "income stream" to support their efforts during the inevitable lulls.

For playwrights, the institutional emphasis on premieres raises the stakes on what is already a fraught process of creative collaboration and public exposure. These stakes can only go higher when the first production may also be the last. Writers and their agents, therefore, struggle to manage their "one shot" strategically, in order to maximize the economic and audience potential of their plays. Inevitably, and unfortunately, given so many playwrights' criticism of the "corporate" feel of larger institutional theatres, they must focus much of their energy and hope on the very theatres that they often criticize. They distance themselves from the companies most eager to support them, smaller theatres that do new work.

With so little chance for a play to have an afterlife and so little opportunity for any kind of significant remuneration, how can a writer say yes to a small theatre willing to mount the work, knowing that (a) it won't get seen by many people at all; (b) it won't earn the writer any money; and (c) it may never get produced again? "When I send a play to a certain place, this is the place where it's going to get the one production," a playwright explains, adding, "I don't want to do it at this little theatre because it might die there." Artistic directors see the problem. "The second and third productions are the hard ones," an artistic director explains. "Generally speaking, a show has to get a pretty strong rave before it's going to get a second production." This system also discourages writers from creating their own opportunities, as many educators and older artists advise, including producing themselves. A playwright who began her career as a company playwright for an experimental troupe spells it out:

> It's a pretty deadly equation for work, the question of what size theatre can you do something at. As playwrights, it's both a literary art and has a practical aspect. You want to be rehearsing and getting things on their feet. But because you're supposed to hold things to the side to be world premieres, you then are discouraged from getting yourself a grant, which is sometimes easier to do than going to a theatre and doing it through them. You do your small production that you put up the money for. It does well and you maybe get a review. Then other theatres won't ever consider that play, because you already had a review. Coming from a place where I used to do a lot of self-producing and moving to this other playwriting model I feel like a deer in the headlights, not knowing what I'm expected to do artistically while I'm waiting around to be anointed, or chosen, or picked out of a pile. As an artist I want to be making art, and I kind of don't care where I do that. But practically, you want to be moving forward, artistically as well.

This is the way theatres get stratified, sometimes against playwrights' and theatres' best interests, the way the fixation on premieres creates a pecking order within the new-play community. One writer talked about having a play done in New York at the Summer Play Festival, which, offering writers week-long runs of plays without claiming "world premiere" rights, is conscientiously designed to introduce theatres to new work for subsequent production. Though the production went well, it was not reviewed in the press (none of SPF's shows are) and was, in a sense, stillborn. "My agent talked to a theatre in New York that does have a very sizeable budget, and they said, 'We don't do remounts of plays that have already been done in New York.' I thought, 'My seven performances with my $10,000 budget counted as being done in New York?' I can't explain that. It's a disturbing trend, because now they're counting that as a premiere and a production."

This situation is problematic for theatres, as well as for writers. Midsize and small theatres are often frustrated by lack of access to plays they wish to produce. Artistic directors confirm the observations that playwrights hold out for productions at a handful of big theatres. The head of a play-development lab held a small convening of playwrights in Los Angeles and came away feeling that playwrights wait for larger theatres in order to reach larger audiences.

> When asked, "Where do you want your play produced?"—in L.A. there are hundreds of theatres—it was five theatres. That was it. They had no interest in having their play produced in any one of the small theatres all over the city, any of them. They feel (a) they're not going to get the support that they need at a theatre that doesn't have the resources. They're not going to get the production they want. And (b) they're not going to get a big enough audience. They perceive the Taper and South Coast Rep as the places that have the subscription base. People will see their work. [Economics] didn't seem like the biggest issue. It really was about exposure.

Another Los Angeles–based producer concurs with the observation that only the largest, most visible theatres can earn a play a continued life. "In the smaller theatres—a play doesn't have a life after. You premiere it at the Colony or whatever, and it's not going to have a life in the regional theatres. Even if it's at the La Jolla Playhouse in a 100-seat configuration, that has a profile. It will bounce and move on." If only large theatres can earn a play continued life, why shouldn't a playwright hold out?

Of course, if there were more cooperation between theatres of different sizes, many note, or if larger theatres were more willing to offer second and third productions, the bind created by this economic pecking order might resolve into a more self-sustaining ecosystem. Developmental work could happen in new-play labs and small theatres; production learning could occur in smaller theatres where the risks are mitigated by lesser economic expectations; and more finished work, tested before audiences, could have spaces to grow into—i.e., the larger theatres with their bigger audiences. Playwrights would have more opportunities to follow their artistic affinities by trying out plays with smaller companies, to continue development after the first production, and to increase their income through multiple productions culminating at theatres where it's possible to earn higher royalties.

Playwrights and theatres alike search for creative ways out of the premiere bind, often playing fast and loose with the concept itself. A veteran writer relishes the story of bending the notion of premiere. "I world-premiered something about twelve times in about two years. Every time I did it, I had to say, 'Well you know, we had a world premiere three months ago with this piece, but [every theatre] wanted another one.' So we got another. I never really had a second production of anything." Not everyone shares her gumption.

As we've seen, the cachet of the premiere is often linked to the prestige of New York. The artistic director of a small San Francisco theatre produced a play the company subsequently remounted in New York. "The [New York] producers said, 'It's going to be a world premiere here. We're not going to talk about the San Francisco production and its success.' That was hard. We just shut our mouth and said, 'Here's a new play in New York. San Francisco didn't happen.'" Most agree that the process doesn't work in reverse; once a play "premieres" in New York, no other theatre can claim "firsts," which is why they wreak so many changes on the term—e.g., "West

Coast Premiere," "Pacific Northwest Premiere," and so forth. Additionally, a theatre's status might be determined by its relative size, as a New York–based writer explains. "If it was done at a smaller-scale theatre, they [the next, larger theatre] can say it was a 'workshop' at that theatre." In this way—by size, location—theatres with clout can and do obliterate the path that leads a play to them.

CULTURALLY-SPECIFIC THEATRES

In the case of culturally-specific theatres, to use an imprecise and, for many, problematic term, this stratification of theatres is complicated by race. Where do these smaller, culturally-specific companies in particular, sit in what some refer to as the "food chain" of the not-for-profit theatre community?

As we've seen, writers, given the opportunity, often gravitate towards larger, so-called mainstream theatres that can provide the greatest opportunities for high-profile production and economic support. These theatres become what some call "gatekeeper organizations." This way, they not only overshadow smaller, culturally-specific theatres, but may also cut them off from the very artists they exist to serve. As an associate artist at one such theatre says,

> Writers all know if you get a production at [our theatre], that's great; you get better as a writer. But the likelihood that you're going to advance your career, which is what any writer wants to do, [is nil]. They know which organizations they need to get it to.

Once they are produced by the major regional theatres, then, what, he asks rhetorically, do these writers need the Asian-American or African-American theatres for?

That puts culturally-specific theatres in a tricky position. Beyond their work with specific communities of artists and audiences, they regularly struggle with their place in the overall ecosystem of new play production. They find themselves competing with larger organizations for grants, and especially funds earmarked for multicultural work.

An artistic staffer of a 30-plus-year-old company that produces work by African-American writers says that her company provides a home for artists early in their careers, and for artists whose work often challenges the aesthetics and the politics of "mainstream" theatres. The larger institutions can offer development resources, larger audiences, and greater economic support. The playwrights then are adopted by the larger theatres where they become "darlings." Major regional theatres will develop the work of African-American writers, but, she says, they rarely produce it, a sentiment that echoes complaints voiced by writers of color. So the writers return to her company at the end of the developmental process. "The artists come to us. We put the work up. The artists get a chance to grow."

On the flip side, her theatre does not have the resources to commission new work, or even a literary department to support a play development infrastructure, as is the case with many theatres dedicated to such work. As a result, the more "challenging, gritty stuff," as well as social-justice oriented work, eschewed by mainstream theatres, falls through the cracks. There's no place to develop it, though it, too, needs development. "What we get that's developed [by large theatres] comes through a lens that we don't control."

> It's frustrating because it has to do with tokenism, it has to do with there being room for only a few voices, and it has to do with the fact that companies like [ours] are interested in teasing out challenging, complex work. It's frustrating to be the test place but we're also proud of that.

Culturally-specific theatres bristle at being pigeonholed, marginalized, seen as farm teams for the majors, which, to some, smacks of colonialism. They support writers at early stages of their careers and work that many theatres overlook. And there are important benefits for writers, working at theatres steeped in a particular culture or part of American society. As one literary manager puts it, the theatre one writes a play for affects "the way you treat or don't treat race, the way in which race is or isn't explained, the way in which you do or don't deal with the history of discrimination in your work." Some writers don't want to explain race, he continues, as they might in plays for mainstream theatres. They want to write from inside a culture,

> they want to explore language, or they have a certain poetic or violent sensibility. They don't want to deal with race head on at all, but they want the characters to be [racially specific]. The market for that kind of play is very rare.

Beyond that catch-22, writers of color are subject to the ebb and flow of formal initiatives at major regional theatres that do cater to their specific needs. With the closing of the Mark Taper Forum's playwright labs and the shuttering of South Coast Rep's Latino Playwrights Festival, for example, a playwright who is also the artistic director of a West Coast producing organization says that Latino writers

> are looking towards the mid-size and smaller Latino theatres to cultivate that work, which [is] an opportunity for those theatres. Playwrights who typically weren't going to those institutions, are now. [This has] empowered those theatres to take the lead in the development of that work. I don't think playwrights are not going to the Taper or South Coast Rep and trying to get their stuff done there. Of course they are; they're simply not seeing it as a place where they're going to specifically a Latino program. They are saying, "These other theatres are a real opportunity for me to at least develop the work, if not get it done now."

Permanent, stable, culturally-specific theatres provide vital services to writers of color—at least one reason why those writers need them. Are these theatres positioned to capitalize on these opportunities? Will writers receive the support they need in terms of both artistic and economic opportunity? Are there models for closer collaboration between theatres of different sizes and different missions—different cultural sensibilities—that are more mutually beneficial?

SECOND PRODUCTIONS

> *One of the great things that we could do for a writer would be to give him a second shot, and a third shot for that matter, for all sorts of reasons. The second production sometimes is better because there's more of a period of gestation and the playwright has learned from it.* —ARTISTIC DIRECTOR

Many artistic directors acknowledge the problems associated with this premiere-only climate. Some believe that the path to second and third productions is getting clearer or, at least, that there's hope for improvement. One of the field's senior dramaturgs sees a growing awareness that successive productions and producing partnerships can be good for a play, helping it reach completion:

> When we are feeling that a play isn't quite ready, the idea
> that we are co-producing it with another theatre and that
> that theatre is going to produce it first—somehow that helps
> to release us into deciding, "Well, let's do it." We have a
> couple of opportunities to continue to work on the play. In
> the past, the premiere-itis would have had everybody fighting
> for individual premieres.

Even in New York, the head of a theatre who is generally cited as a leader in new-play production is rethinking the necessity of premiering plays, focusing instead on his ability to finish the work on them and help the takeoff:

> I let go of this idea of the premiere as somehow the cachet.
> Out of the six plays we're doing this year, four of them

have had prior productions. I have a rule of thumb that it
shouldn't have had too many outside productions. I don't
see our role as to do something that's had ten productions,
because it's probably set. Our expertise is in development.
That's our mission, to premiere plays. It's perfectly valid
for plays to premiere regionally and be launched that way.
I'm looking to launch plays. That doesn't mean a previous
production precludes them, but it shouldn't have too many
because it should be still in process.

If these speakers are representative, the willingness to
collaborate with other theatres and, thereby, open up more
production time for writers to refine and deepen their work,
may be spreading. Statistically, such co-productions (shared
premieres) are still rare (though anecdotal evidence suggests
that theatres are turning to them more since the crash of 2008).
According to playwrights, theatres need more incentives for
mounting second and third productions. One writer argues that
this is particularly true for small theatres, more reliant on funding
than large ones with bigger box-office potential. "There are a lot
of grants out there that say they only fund world premieres. That's
a reason why a smaller theatre wouldn't do a second production.
I remember [as a literary manager] writing grant after grant after
grant that said it had to be a first presentation of a play."

How can theatres be encouraged to offer more second productions, especially of work that hasn't received national notice?
One answer is travel. Artistic directors often lack the time and
money to get out of their own theatres to see the work of their
colleagues. (Indeed, even among their own artistic associates, there
are some who strongly believe that these artistic leaders don't get
out enough, even locally, don't see enough work beyond their own.)
Certainly, many artistic directors make somewhat regular trips
to New York to see theatre, but this can reinforce the prevailing
sense that everything important is generated by a few theatres
in Midtown Manhattan. The harder circuit is the one between
regional theatres of compatible aesthetics and, maybe, similar size.

To this end, a little funding might go a long way. "We were recipients of a grant for play development," a New York artistic director reports. "I can [thus] afford to hop on a plane and go see [other productions of] the play that we're working on. It's not incredible amounts of money." Writers and artistic administrators alike suggest that artistic directors who are having trouble finding work that makes an important artistic statement (or work of sufficient quality) might find more of it at their colleagues' theatres. By seeing plays up on their feet, they may get more out of them, especially with plays that, for one reason of another, don't read as well or as easily as others. Also, by seeing these works in production, artistic directors might understand what their own contribution might be. Or, as one talent agent sometimes says when he pitches second productions: "Part of my strategy is to say, 'They screwed it up. You should do it right.'"

Word of mouth drives tickets sales, according to people throughout the profession. It may drive play selection as well, especially when it comes to referring second productions. As a Chicago artistic director puts it: "I think about the shows that I have produced that have been produced elsewhere and it's almost always a case where there's somebody who I really know and trust who says, 'This is a play that I think would work well at your theatre.' If possible, I go to see the production. That makes a huge difference."* Some theatres aggressively promote to the field the plays they premiere. "I have, in fact, offered to fly people in to see pieces. I call people all the time. I work for our playwrights. I go out and sell those things. When we do world premieres, I work for those guys." Some producers send their colleagues bulletins about their recent work, encouraging others to consider plays they have done first. An East Coast artistic director explains this push:

* Technology, specifically videos or DVDs of productions, could help solve this problem by enabling artistic directors to view work they can't get to due to a lack of time and/or money. But union agreements with actors and other artists have effectively prevented productions from being filmed for this purpose.

For all the complaining that the playwriting community does—I totally get it, I'm a playwright—it's hard to find a good play, as a producer, that you're really invested enough in. Once you do make that commitment, because you really love it, it's hard to see it not go on. Whether it's successful at your theatre or not, I want that play to get better and have another chance, if it didn't go well. If it did go well, I definitely want it to be done again.

Many theatres, though, don't act on these collegial inclinations, either to build on work done or to share their own work, an insularity that may stem from lack of interest or initiative. Some simply lack the resources, especially money to travel. Literary managers loudly claim to know the field, to track what others are doing; they sharply disagree, however, on whether artistic directors can make the same claim. Nevertheless, when it comes to producing recently premiered work without the imprimatur of New York, the numbers are discouraging.

> **FINDING:** Half of the theatres surveyed seldom or never even request scripts that have premiered at other theatres. Only one in five theatres regularly seeks scripts that have been premiered elsewhere.

SHARING THE WEALTH: CO-PRODUCTION

Co-production has long been hailed as a way for theatres to share the risk and expense of producing new plays, while giving the writer the time in front of an audience necessary to refine the work. These partnerships, generally involving the same director and cast, as well as time between stagings for reflection and revision, are the nonprofit equivalent of the out-of-town tryout in the commercial theatre, a chance for playwrights (and all the artistic collaborators) to test plays where they are most fully tested: in production.

Of course, the salient—and most positive—example of cooperation among institutional theatres is the career of the late August Wilson, and the journey of his plays. After his breakthrough work—*Ma Rainey's Black Bottom*—developed at the Eugene O'Neill Memorial Theater Center's National Playwrights Conference, under artistic director Lloyd Richards, and Yale Repertory Theatre, where Richards was also artistic director, Wilson's plays received co-productions in partnership with a repeating group of regional theatres (as well as New York's Manhattan Theatre Club) in varying permutations, before landing on Broadway. These various partnerships afforded the plays a series of productions—same cast, director, and design team—around the country prior to their arrival in New York. Benjamin Mordecai—a commercial producer and longtime managing director of Yale Rep—led the producing path and coordinated these efforts. Simultaneously, Wilson the writer was sustained with years-long residencies and services through New Dramatists in New York and the Playwrights' Center in Minneapolis, where he wrote and held readings of many of these plays, as well as by regular summers at the O'Neill, where the plays were workshopped. Even before he, Richards, and Mordecai began to cut this path, the Penumbra Theatre Company in Minneapolis, an African-American production company, had supported him consistently and produced his plays.

By the time Wilson and Mordecai died in 2005, all ten of the playwright's *Century Cycle* plays, each chronicling one decade of the twentieth century, had been mounted in this national fashion. Rather than refusing to be a part of the circuit of productions or fighting for world-premiere status or a greater share of commercial profits, the lead theatres shared in a single portion of monies, as a producer, long associated with these efforts, explains:

With August, we only have one amount of participation
and the theatres have to carve it up among themselves. And
we've always done it that way. And with August's plays, they
always sort of accepted it, because they just loved the idea of
getting his play put up on Broadway. They didn't really care.
And they were willing to take the one and a half percent [of
commercial gross] and carve it up four ways.

While the example of Wilson's journey is idealized by
many, it is rarely followed. The producer goes on to say,

If you're not an August Wilson, however, I can understand
that [your agent] is not going to want to be faced with three
not-for-profits or four not-for-profits saying they all want
one percent of the gross. You can't do that. I understand that.
That's a different issue, that if you four guys want to pool
money and you each want one percent, then you're going to
make the play [commercially] unproducible.

Statistically, co-productions play a negligible part in the
production of new plays. On average, **sample group theatres
of all sizes produce no more than one co-production in a three-
year period.** Moreover, **almost none of the plays these theatres
produce come to them through offers of co-production from
other theatres.**

Co-productions often flow from a personal connection
between leaders of theatres, and such relationships can jump-start
such projects. They can also smooth the potentially rocky path
of collaboration. Institutional affinity helps, too. For that reason,
co-productions mostly happen between theatres of similar size or
equivalent status on the national scene. One innovative program
for sharing productions is the National New Play Network's
"Continued Life of New Plays Fund," which helps fund three
(or more) companies to mount separate productions of the same
work, as a "rolling world premiere" (see Chapter VI).

More and more, playwrights and leaders of new-play development labs argue for a broader sense of collaboration—partnerships across budget size and type of organization (labs with producing theatres, for example, or small ensembles with large institutional companies). One playwright articulated this vision, going even beyond the bounds of traditional theatres:

> I've had producing experience like the Cornerstone Theater Company, where it's not just Cornerstone. The thing I did was with seventeen other organizations. A lot of people came together to make that thing happen. My Latino experiences have been like that. Theatres get together—because they're all small organizations—in order to get enough money. That cooperative idea is a great idea. What happens a lot in L.A. is it's a theatre with a social service organization—Cornerstone with the Gay & Lesbian Center, for instance. That kind of partnership is essential to making the art.

Where personal or institutional affinity is absent, even the search for partners can be frustrating, as a West Coast artistic director makes clear:

> I've worked very hard this year...to no avail to get someone to co-partner the development of a new piece. I was talking to people I don't know very well, and maybe that's the point: Who is this person and what is your aesthetic? How do your aesthetic and my aesthetic match up? What do you see in this piece that I don't see?

Geography can be a help or a hindrance, especially when the co-production involves a New York theatre. There is general agreement that these associations work best when New York is the last stop, when the kinks of a play and production are worked out before facing the hazardous scrutiny of the New York press. There are other reasons for New York to come later. One regional theatre artistic director describes a pair of successful co-productions with the same New York theatre, both of which started at his company and moved into Manhattan. A third project moved the other way around. As a result, "we lost the whole cast." An agent explains: "The time span is usually horrible for actors. They don't want to spend five months doing the same play that's not in New York or Los Angeles where they can be auditioning, or [available for] pilot season."

Theatres hedge their bets on committing to unproven work. The head of new-play development at a large West Coast theatre explains:

> What happens is, I go to see a play. I go, "I really love this piece and it's kind of risky, but I really want to do it," and then another company is interested. It's after the fact. Then other theatre companies go, "[These two theatres] are doing it, so we'll do it."

This tendency to sign on after a play is proven underscores one of the riddles of our findings: While experience (including season brochures and published schedules) shows again and again that theatres across the country fill their stages with plays that have succeeded elsewhere,* especially in New York, their survey responses tell another story: seasons containing twice as many world premieres as other new plays and even fewer second productions.

---

* For the year 2008-09, for instance, *American Theatre* lists fourteen productions of John Patrick Shanley's *Doubt* (there were thirty-five the prior season) at TCG-member theatres (there are approximately 460 TCG theatres), thirteen of David Lindsay-Abaire's *Rabbit Hole* (twelve the previous season season)—both of which premiered at the Manhattan Theatre Club, as did Theresa Rebeck's *Mauritius* (eight productions that year). Conor McPherson's *The Seafarer* had twelve productions this season, and Sarah Ruhl's *Eurydice* had eleven. (Ruhl's *The Clean House* had twelve productions the previous season.) All of these plays had significant New York productions in the two years preceding these listings.

The Downsizing of Expectation

CAST SIZE

If there is any one thing that I could ask for, it's support for big-cast plays, to just get the humanity on the stage. Classics are very, very successful for us, and part of the reason is there are [so many] people on the stage. —ARTISTIC DIRECTOR

Size matters. Cast size, venue size, and the size of a play's aspiration—all these play a role in the ecosystem of new-play production. Even as artistic directors and others decry a lack of scale and ambition in contemporary playwriting, they agree that economics make it nearly impossible for playwrights to get large-cast plays produced and for theatres to stage large-scale works. As playwrights are assailed for "writing small," new plays are more and more consigned to the smallest of spaces, as if new work by its very nature can't rise to the expectations of a sweeping stage or a large audience. Ultimately, it seems, most everyone involved with new work has seen their expectations for that work downsized—the scale of the plays themselves, of the spaces they occupy, of the opportunities for consistent production, of a shared sense of artistic ambition. As a result, the linked ecologies of new-play production and consumption have slipped into a downward spiral of diminished expectation on the part of artist, administrator, and audience alike, one that will inevitably impoverish the art form.

Cast size may be the most obvious example of the scaling down of our theatre. **For artistic directors, "cast size and composition" is the most severe obstacle to producing a play. "Too expensive" is the closely related, second-greatest obstacle.** Playwrights have no illusions about the theatres' inability or general unwillingness to produce big-cast plays. "We're all being trained now not to write fourteen-character plays," one writer asserts, picking a number that, given national realities, seems ridiculously high. Says another,

My plays are of a size and a scope that seems preventative. I tend to write plays with nine characters, and the most frequent response I get back from theatres is, "If there were six, we would probably do it." My most produced play is a one-person show. Not all big plays are meritorious, and there are certainly ambitious four-character plays, but in terms of filling up a 600-seat theatre, a play with twelve characters seems totally reasonable to me.

"Very few new plays are written with many characters," agrees a regional theatre artistic director. Indeed, theatres seldom receive large-cast submissions, and only a handful of large plays receive productions. "I worked [as literary manager] at a theatre in Los Angeles for a couple of years," one playwright says, "and if a script came in that had fourteen characters, they wouldn't even look at it, because they knew they just couldn't do it." Even with a known-writer, an expansive cast list leaves little choice but cutting or doubling, as an East Coast artistic director illustrates: "We're doing a new play next year by Richard Nelson that I fell in love with. At this point it calls for fourteen actors. We're trying to get it down to eleven, but it's still going to be big. We figured out how to make it work because I read the play and I said, 'I have to do this play.'"

No one suggests that solo pieces and small-cast plays are in themselves less worthy of production, that small casts mean small ambition, or that bigger is always better. But the fact remains that theatres are, by analogy, producing string quartets and sonatas—intimate chamber compositions—while eschewing symphonies. Playwrights have mostly abandoned writing the equivalent of full-scale orchestral works. If, as playwrights tell us, writing big requires "a different skill set," how do writers get to practice it? One writer, who has enjoyed the rarity of regional productions of large-cast plays, finds the scale of her work rewarding, if anachronistic. "I happen to love it, but it's so old-fashioned. I feel like I'm making the last buggy-whip in America."

This shrinking is relatively new. Until fairly late in the

twentieth century, American playwrights took for granted casts of a size that seem exceptional now. Arthur Miller's *Death of a Salesman* (1949) has a cast of thirteen and Lorraine Hansberry's *A Raisin in the Sun* (1960), eleven. The Kaufman and Hart comedy *You Can't Take It with You* features a company of nineteen actors. The small town of Grover's Corners in Thornton Wilder's *Our Town* needed fifty-one actors to populate it. Playwrights like Tennessee Williams and Eugene O'Neill wrote large (*Camino Real*, thirty; *The Iceman Cometh*, nineteen) and small (*The Glass Menagerie*, four; *Long Day's Journey into Night*, five) as subject and inspiration required. Flip through early- and mid-century production photos: crowd scenes; populated courtrooms and town squares; contemporary work with a classical sweep. Even seminal new plays from the regional theatre boom came peopled: Howard Sackler's *The Great White Hope* premiered at Arena Stage in 1967, before opening on Broadway, with a cast— unthinkable today, even by musical standards—of approximately 63 actors playing 247 roles. Arthur Kopit's *Indians* also began at Arena before opening its 1968 Broadway debut with cast of forty-seven. An early transfer from the Mark Taper Forum, *The Trial of the Catonsville Nine*, debuted on Broadway in 1971, its ensemble a mere sixteen.

    Theatres continue to mount a certain number of large-cast productions, though not usually of new plays. Shakespeare, other classics, and well-known early- and mid-twentieth-century American works, as well as musicals, are routinely staged with respectable-sized ensembles. (Paradoxically, the few remaining acting companies of any size, mostly at a few Shakespeare festivals in rural America, have the capability and, with salaried actors to keep busy, the need for larger-cast plays, even new ones.) Theatres devote resources to classics instead of new plays because, as we discussed earlier in this chapter, they are seen as less risky. Ironically, their reliability may be partly due to their scale. Size can sell. Intimacy can be a selling point, as theatres have long understood, but so can "big." "There seems to be a correlative of economics in terms of larger plays that might appeal to a larger audience," one playwright observes, because "you have more people represented." This truth seems to have eluded artistic directors, another playwright comments. She calls attention to the finding that artistic directors view cast size as the chief obstacle to production, "but then they say it's hard to find work that makes an important artistic contribution, without realizing that maybe those two things are connected."

Size wasn't the only reason Alan Bennett's *The History Boys* and Tom Stoppard's *The Coast of Utopia* captured the New York public's imagination, but it was surely part of their appeal. Both originated in Britain, as products of a subsidized development system with the capacity to nurture projects of scale through the way stations on the road to production. Without such subsidy, big plays are the exception, rather than the rule, on this side of the Atlantic. Tracy Letts's Tony Award– and Pulitzer Prize– winning *August: Osage County*, a commercial Broadway hit with a cast of thirteen, first produced at the not-for-profit Steppenwolf Theatre Company in Chicago (a company rooted in its large acting ensemble) may be an exception that proves that rule.*

While today's writers have faced the limitations of size head-on, bringing theatricality and invention to bear, we can only wonder what the long-term implications are for the health of playwriting, of new-play production, and the field in general when the dramaturgy of contemporary playwriting is so radically circumscribed.

---

* In a June 1, 2008, *New York Times* "Arts & Leisure" essay, anticipating a best play Tony Award for Tracy Letts's Pulitzer Prize–winning *August: Osage County*, critic Charles Isherwood points out that, should *August* win, it will be, with Alan Bennett's *The History Boys* and Tom Stoppard's *The Coast of Utopia*, the third large-cast play in a row to receive this honor. Isherwood, for once, seems to agree with American playwrights (more on this later), as he argues that scale and ambition fill an audience hunger "...for drama on a grand scale, the kind of big, broad, juicy plays that were once a staple of any Broadway season but that have become increasingly rare as the American theater has gone on a slimming diet for the last few decades." That "slimming diet," of course, refers to the small, less expensive plays that have been the mainstay of the nonprofit theatre (and the bane of playwriting ambition) for years.

SHRINKING THE SPACE

Our theatres are smaller. We purposely built theatres that we felt were sustainable for new work. —ARTISTIC DIRECTOR

Artistic directors who produce new plays pride themselves on presenting that work in the best possible situation, fitting the theatre space to the work, finding the right audience to appreciate it. More and more, by all reports, the right space means a smaller space.

Slightly over half of the theatres studied program for more than one space. Typically these theatres target a variety of distinct audiences in these different spaces. While most of the theatres put new work on their main stages, the range of programming they do on those stages targets a wide audience—subscribers, single-ticket buyers, and diverse mainstream audiences—through a spectrum of work, including new plays, revivals, adult and children's theatre, large musicals, tours, and rentals. In their second spaces, theatres are more likely to program less established writers, writers of color, and "riskier" fare, and to market their plays to more sophisticated theatregoers with an affinity for new work. As might be expected, those second spaces tend to be much smaller than main stages. Primary theatres hold an average of 399 seats (median or midpoint in our sampling is 250), while second stages average a capacity of 270 (and a median of 200). Third or "other" spaces are considerably smaller, with a median of 140 seats. As spaces diminish in size, ticket prices, predictably, do as well.

There is wide agreement that the default choice for most new plays is the second (or third) space. Here's how one playwright, whose work has been seen on Broadway and in many regional theatres, describes a typical exchange: "I have a new play. A theatre wants to do it, and they said, 'We'll do it on a small stage, because it's a new play, and it has a small cast.'" Only the addition of a "name" director, he continues, precipitates a move to the main stage.

In essence, playwrights confront a kind of catch-22, in which they are expected to write smaller and then criticized for lacking ambition when they do. This attitude is typical rather than exceptional, as evidenced by the push in recent years to build and produce in ever-smaller spaces. Rather than challenging the assumptions of a shrinking scale for new plays, artistic directors believe that these new, smaller venues are better suited to today's new plays. They can accommodate the audiences that such works attract—i.e. smaller ones. The solution—tinier theatres—may be adding to the problem by discouraging artistic ambition in other ways, too. **When talking about obstacles to new-play production, artistic directors list "technical demands" third, after cast size and cost.** As the literal space for new plays shrinks, playwrights' attempts to imagine their ways towards bigger canvasses— multiple locations, unusual environments, theatrical effects to make up for diminished scale—may further prohibit production of their work. New plays, then, must avoid both pitfalls: they mustn't be *too big to do*, and they mustn't be *too hard to do*.

Theatre companies have built, are building, and plan to build smaller and smaller spaces, primarily to house new work, and the leaders of these companies hope to add even smaller ones next. "We have a [new] 300-seat space now," says the associate producer of a large institutional theatre, "to be able to produce plays that feel a little more fragile and smaller. We also want an even smaller space, a little, 100-seat, 120-seat house. Then we can do smaller plays that are more intimate." The artistic director of another large theatre, echoes this common aim, ramping down expectations about attendance over the course of a run: "We're trying to find a way to have a place where writers don't have to appeal to 18,000 people but rather 1,800, or even less—800." As venues shrink, the already troubling economics of playwriting become even more problematic. Smaller plays produced in smaller theatres yield smaller royalty checks without increasing commissioning fees or increasing the likelihood of multiple productions.

Is this downward size spiral an endgame of niche marketing? An admission of defeat in the broad cultural marketplace? An honest appraisal of what audiences these plays can be expected to draw? Or is it just hard-boiled economic realism? Intimacy is the most common artistic justification for the shrinking of performance space, but pressure from trustees to maximize income can work against the desire to achieve intimacy. The head of new work at a large West Coast theatre explains:

> We recently built a [flexible] new space that was supposed to accommodate anywhere from 50 people to 450. Since it opened, it's been in the 300 to 400 range. Someone, before the theatre opened, said to me, "You'll do the max rather than the smaller," and that's what it's turned out to be, because the board wants earned income. The board also wants all of our spaces to be filled with new work and exciting things, so it's between a rock and a hard place in terms of money available for new-play development and doing smaller plays. It's easier in the sense that we have space. It's harder because we don't have the economic resources to produce the smaller works, the riskier works.

Smaller and riskier—again and again, the words appear together.

For artistic directors who take seriously the notion of matching the play to the venue, a smaller space enables the theatre to produce challenging work without the pressure of having 1,000 seats (or even 300) to fill at each performance. One conversation between colleagues from neighboring theatres—about a disturbing, even confrontational play dealing with drug addiction—exposes the poles of thinking about size and challenge:

> PRODUCER X: [The play's] very hard in terms of tone. It's very poetic but it's assaulting, and it may not be the kind of thing that our complete subscribership will connect to. What kind of space do we produce the piece in? If it is a huge space, we aren't going to be able to get an audience. There is an audience out there, but we really have to find it, and maybe it's not going to be 300 people at each show, but 150 or 120.

PRODUCER Y: We keep talking about, "We have to do it smaller," which I totally understand. Who's going to see this play? I know what this play is about; it's tough. But the big question is, what's happening to the American theatre audience and why are they less likely to see a play that requires a certain challenge?

Another artistic administrator puts it this way: "New and risky is fine if it's in a bubble. We've put the riskiest thing that we do in a bubble, because it's easy to avoid that way." Are theatres condemning themselves to a world where "challenge," "risk," and, even, "new" always mean "small"? And will this downsizing implicitly train audiences to expect that new plays are difficult, precious, small things, an acquired taste, whereas classics are big and expansive? As new plays and the spaces they fill shrink, so may audience expectations and, consequently, the audience itself.

ARTISTIC ASPIRATION

Writers hold many opinions on this trend toward the small. Some playwrights see value in the opportunities for deeper connection that more intimate venues allow. Some even argue that major regional theatres should, instead of pouring resources into a few large-scale productions, produce a greater number of plays on lower budgets in littler venues.

What if a theatre, like the Guthrie, which spent millions of dollars on those beautiful new theatre complexes, instead had built ten small theatres and divided their resources to ten small productions a year, rather than two mega- and one medium-sized one? There are a million reasons why they wouldn't do that. Part of the issue with these bigger houses is that they're required, in many ways, to choose failsafe plays that have a very broad appeal. People aren't allowed to have specific tastes.

Many writers however express alarm.

We've been ghettoized to the smaller spaces. If you're doing
Endgame, a little space works, because it was about people in
confinement. But most plays want some space and dimension
and depth, and they do not belong in these little ninety-
nine-seat houses. It completely changes the perspective of
the audience on a play. Plays need height and air and depth,
and you need more than fifty people to see them to even
understand what's funny, much less what's part of the civic
conversation. That's our challenge, getting plays in those
places where they can do them properly and they believe in
them and they're willing to take a flying leap and fall flat on
their face.

For playwrights who write comedies, this downsizing may
be particularly damaging. Large audiences can be essential for
comedy. Laughter feeds laughter, while too close quarters and
too few people can inhibit it, making everyone self-conscious.
Even as they assail this current, diminished state of the art, many
playwrights seem to have accepted it as the only one they'll ever
know. One writer, at work on her first play for young audiences,
believes that this production is "the only time I'll ever see my
work done in a 750-seat theatre."

Whatever their personal response, there is little disagreement that the viable dramaturgy of the American theatre has
been downsized. Small leads to smaller. Plays shrink along with
expectations for them—how and where they should be produced,
who their audience might be, what reach they might have. If
things continue as they are going, a generation of playwrights
will never have the opportunity to write big. They will rarely,
or never, have the chance to see their work on a sizable stage
in front of a large audience. The question is: with little hope of
realization, how long can writers' large-scale ambitions—their
more monumental imaginings—live?

The rampant, pervasive downsizing of the new-play theatre,
with its multiple causes and diminished outcomes, has already and
will continue to seep into our national dramaturgy. One artistic

director spreads the blame between the theatres and the writers, even as he captures the shrinking canvas of the American stage:

> New plays tend to get produced at small theatres, for rarified audiences ...Part of that is giving them the opportunity, but part of it is also making the demand on them by saying, "You know what? It's not enough to write plays that will satisfy ninety-nine people in a three-week run, it's not enough to make plays that your thesis advisor is going to think is brilliant. You need to write plays that will reach a broad audience." The big danger as reflected in the American theatre for playwrights is the privatization of playwriting. Many, many plays are beautifully written that are just taking such a small, small scale of interest.

If writers are to accept this challenge to write bigger, for a broader populace, then theatres must, literally, make room for them.

The Place of a Theatre

Decentralization is one of the signal achievements of the regional theatre movement in the past half-century. Professional theatres have, in that time, cropped up across the country, until a city or large town without a company of its own is the exception. Despite a climate that many playwrights and others see as increasingly homogenized, the local nature of a theatre impacts its new-play practices, as well as its relationship with writers. The most significant geographical factor in the world of new-play production is still how close a theatre is (physically, aspiration-ally) to New York City. New York casts an enormous shadow over the rest of the industry, and communities within that shadow operate differently than those outside of it. For companies working with little or no reference to New York, the spirit of their local theatre community can have a huge bearing on how they work with playwrights and new plays. We held meetings of theatre leaders in four cities where new-play production runs high to get a sense of how they differ in spirit and practice.

Chicago artistic directors speak proudly about the local theatre's vibrancy, a vitality born of the city's ensemble focus. With reference to the numerous ensemble-based companies thriving there, the head of one theatre depicts the whole scene there as a kind of inter-institutional ensemble. Another veteran of the Chicago theatre includes theatregoers in the formulation:

> Even though the Goodman, the Court, and Northlight are regional theatres, I think they would probably categorize themselves as Chicago theatres first. It's an attitude that has to do with the creation of this scene, focusing on the artists—meaning the actor, the director, the designer, and the playwright—for the ensemble of the audience. That's essentially our attitude, which makes a difference.

Can playwrights sustain themselves in this citywide company of artists? Chicago may not have enough of an infrastructure to support playwrights, a local literary manager posits.

> There is a strong playwriting community here. But Chicago could be more of a destination, a home for playwrights, in the sense of people both staying here when they're from here and building a career here, but also coming here, from all over, with some level of expertise, and making a career here. It exists, but it could be stronger. The level of sophistication in terms of the writing could be higher.

The artistic director of an ensemble theatre elaborates, "With the relatively low cost of living, we do have an ability for [theatre artists] to have lives," but without the film and television work available in New York or Los Angeles, he explains, it's more difficult for playwrights to earn a living.

Minneapolis/St. Paul, on the other hand, is a "writerly community," most agree. The unique funding climate of the

Twin Cities has made it one of the few places where playwrights have, in recent decades, been able to support themselves financially. Generous corporate and foundation support for playwrights, individual artists, and an array of theatrical activity is available there (notably, from the Jerome, Bush, and McKnight Foundations and the Target Foundation, formerly Dayton-Hudson). Said one artistic director, "There is a rich belief in supporting all of the disciplines in an artists' community that's living here and contributing."

The **San Francisco Bay Area** may be distinguished by an unusual measure of collaboration among theatre institutions in support of writers and new work. Partnerships among theatres of different sizes, sometimes involving developmental labs and universities, with underwriting from several key California-based funders, give the Bay Area the feel of an ad hoc collective. Some theatres literally "swap playwrights." Writers there have moved from theatre to theatre, sometimes working with more than one company on a single project. "The thing about San Francisco," one such writer claims,

> is there's a large number of small companies that do new work, and they very consciously link themselves. They have evenings where they all come, and local playwrights come. There's a conscious desire to be a fervent, fertile theatrical community. I've been wondering whether that exists other places. I haven't quite found it yet.

Los Angeles has a large population of writers. It is, though, a city without a center and, so, the theatre community is scattered. "It's a funny community geographically," says one veteran of the scene. "Everyone is spread out. When I'm in New York for a week, I bump into three dozen playwrights on the street. I never bump into anybody here, not even at openings at the Taper." The film and television industry creates opportunities for playwrights to make a living in a different medium. The Equity Waiver contract prevalent in Los Angeles, which allows actors to work for free, is, for writers, a mixed blessing. It generates a great deal of new-play production and enables theatres to mount larger-cast plays, but, with the capacity of waiver theatres topped at ninety-nine seats, it severely limits royalty income.

LOCAL WRITERS

There is no such thing as a local writer. As a writer, you have to move all the time. Most of them go where the work is. Even very accomplished writers are never home.

—NEW-PLAY LAB DIRECTOR

It may be true that playwrights have to follow the work, but it is also true that all playwrights live somewhere. They are all local writers. And most of them care about being produced both widely and at home. But even locally, issues of size, visibility, and economics come into play. As Gary Garrison, Executive Director for Creative Affairs at the Dramatists Guild, writes in *The Dramatist*, "It's not about just getting produced in your own backyard, it's about getting produced by one of the named theatres that's in your own metropolitan neighborhood." For most writers, this rarely happens. Major regional theatres, according to most writers, rarely produce the work of playwrights in their own backyard.

Some theatres make a concerted effort to forge relationships with writers in their own backyards. Regional identity is especially important for theatres in certain parts of the country. "There is, throughout the South, a very strong support of southern writers," says an Atlanta-based literary manager. Her theatre shows this support by accepting unsolicited submissions only from playwrights who reside in the Southeast. "We check the zip code." Cultivating local writers takes time, she explains.

We want people who live in the Southeast, and especially playwrights from Atlanta, to start feeling like there's an open door. Why do so many playwrights have "drop-by status" with theatres in New York, even though it might take five years to do a play? Because they live in the neighborhood. We in Atlanta have to start having coffee dates with people who live here. Maybe we'll discover a whole class of people.

Local writers and local settings—as opposed to, say, plays set in Manhattan—can be a draw. "When you do a play that's either by a local writer—not in New York, but in Philadelphia, Chicago, a lot of other places—or something germane to that city," one artistic director points out, "you're going to do better than the same playwright from somewhere else, or about something else. That combination has sellable potential." He offers the example of a play inspired by events in his city; it sold better than any other play in his theatre's history. "It got funding, it got press and, it sold well." Interestingly, the show also played well, in some cases even better, in other cities. It goes without saying that all local writing can speak universally—think Chekhov's rural Russia—but not all local writers are seen that way. Even in Minneapolis, a community with what many agree is a critical mass of playwrights, few plays by writers from the area get produced in the area. As one artistic leader marvels: "I have seen tons of new work that comes out of here, and how little of it gets produced locally is always stunning to me."

If local writers have trouble getting a hearing in their own neighborhoods, it may be even harder for them elsewhere— which may account for the fact that three-quarters of America's playwrights live in only two cities, New York and Los Angeles. An artistic director from Northern California fumes, "We've got a play that we did last year that was one of the best-selling new works we've ever done, and nobody will touch it. It's by a local writer." A colleague from across the bay shares his vexation: "It drives me fucking crazy that people do work here, and it's not seen. Or it's not known, or we don't exist. Once you go north of L.A., we're not quite there. That's a major problem."

Some theatres bring writers who excite them into their city and encourage them to write plays specific to the community. A Southern California artistic director explains why.

Sometimes I say to my audience, "We live in a unique and interesting part of the world. Wouldn't you like to see a play about where we live, instead of Manhattan?" A truly regional theatre makes theatre for the community that it works in. Often the playwrights who we partner with in this process say it's the most difficult and the most rewarding experience they've ever had. They're not alone in the apartment going, "God, what am I going to do next?" They're involved with the community of people, both artists and what we call "community dramaturgs," making a work about what they can see and hear and taste and smell.

NEW YORK, NEW YORK—DESTINATION & SOURCE

The question of New York—it's not just because the theatres want to have a hit, it's because the writers want to make a living. New York as a destination is endemic to the contracts. Almost every contract anyone's working under has a provision to go there. —ARTISTIC DIRECTOR

Though many theatres operate completely outside its orbit, New York is the 500-pound gorilla in the new-play ecosystem. Fifty percent of the nation's playwrights are congregated in New York. In their words, they live there to be "closer to the action," because the city has "a greater density of artists," and a greater "variety of work" than anywhere else in America. Many writers of color find broad peer communities there. It's also easier to get teaching jobs and residencies, if you're based in New York, and, because of the proximity to many East Coast cities, it's cheaper to commute to them.

Moreover, the amount of new play production in New York provides incentive. When playwrights list the companies that have produced the largest number of their plays (in fact, the first, second, and third largest numbers of their plays), two-thirds of the companies are *in* New York. (By contrast, two-thirds of the theatre companies listed by artistic directors as leaders of new-play production are *outside* of New York. Again, playwrights and artistic directors look at the same picture and see two very different things.) New York outstrips any other city in the amount of new-play activity it generates. At the same time, New York's nonprofits—with the exception of a few of the largest ones, most of which operate partially within the Broadway system—provide a much-lower scale of compensation to artists, including playwrights, than do most sizable regional companies.

Sixty years after the birth of the regional theatre— intended as an alternate universe—many nonprofit companies, especially larger ones, still perceive New York City as the seat of risk and reward. (The same may be said of playwrights, who often pin their hopes on the benefits of the high-profile exposure possible there.) What happens there influences what plays get produced across the country and informs the expectations of audiences and artists, critics, funders, and theatre leaders alike. Many nonprofit companies calculate success by the number of plays and musicals they've transferred to New York, and they tout those successes in promotional materials. As we've seen, too, in their contracts with playwrights, not-for-profit theatres' practices hark back to the days when Broadway was the center of new-play production. The contracts, more often than not, provide for a New York move.

The magnetism works in both directions, pulling plays toward New York and pushing successful ones away from this city. In this way, the New York theatre serves as both destination and source for the rest of the nation. The literary manager of a large regional theatre spells it out. From New York: "We do a lot of new work. If we're going to do something from New York, it has to be a hit. It makes us look silly, actually, if something has done really badly [in New York], and then we do it." To New York: "Our audiences love the world-premiere musicals especially if they're headed to New York. They're more interested when we program things on the way in [to New York], rather than on the way out." They want, she says, "bragging rights."

Who is driving this New York–centrism? Credit (or blame) is due all around. In Chicago, for instance, a self-sufficient theatre community if ever there was one, the tension between the notion of local theatre for local audiences and the brass ring of New York comes from some unlikely quarters. Apparently, it is not coming from playwrights. "Don't you think playwrights from other communities have their eyes straight for New York, and playwrights in Chicago are not as focused in that way?" a local artistic director asks, and his colleagues generally agree. On the other hand, he complains that, in his city's critical climate, reviewers too often value work through the lens of "Will it go to New York?" Another artistic director elaborates, "We're making plays for here, and hopefully, if we do a good job, then they'll be interesting somewhere else. I don't think anybody's saying we're going to make it to go to New York or somewhere else, and yet that's how it's being critiqued." The head of a third theatre chimes in, joking that one prominent local critic dispenses advice about tweaks needed for the future life of the play. "He wants to be your dramaturg for the New York production."

In Chicago, New York's complicating presence may result, ironically, from the Windy City's own track record, which includes dozens of productions that did in fact move to Broadway and Off Broadway—from Steppenwolf, the Goodman Theatre, and other local companies. But whatever the originating city or town, our national system propagates the notion that the New York production is the definitive one, the one that really matters, and that a play is not truly finished until it appears there. A playwright with a hefty resume of both nonprofit and Broadway productions sums up this attitude:

> We in the New York–centric theatre world accept that
> implicitly, in the sense that when plays finally come to
> New York after having been done in England or all around
> the country, it's still, "Wow, this is the play's premiere."

The New York theatre establishment certainly seems to
believe that the measure is whether they've seen it before.
Not when it was written or how the author feels about it.

Another seasoned writer frames the question that resounds
in many corners of the national theatre: "How do we move our
attention away from New York?"

> I find doing a play in New York nerve-wracking and insulting
> and demeaning. It ghettoizes theatre, because only in New
> York do people read reviews to find a reason *not* to go to
> the theatre. I have a new play and I'm not eager to bring it
> to New York, [even though] it's done very well around the
> rest of the country. The health of the play depends upon
> *not* coming to New York. We have a morbid situation in
> New York. It's a *schadenfreude* festival—at the intermission,
> everybody with their cell phone going, "You can't *believe* what
> Steve Sondheim has done!" It's not fun. It's not interesting.
> It's not healthy.

Regional theatre leaders grapple with the same question:
how to move our own attention away from Manhattan. "Part of
the goal is really to speak to our audiences and do our art. It's
not about, 'Is it going to make it to New York or not?'" a West
Coast artistic director says, echoing a sentiment voiced across
the country. One theatre in Southern California has stopped
figuring New York into the equation at all, according to one of
its leaders:

> We're not concerned about taking a play to New York where it
> will run for three years and we'll be rolling in dough. The odds
> of that are slim. All our experiences in New York have been
> unpleasant. Why put yourself through that? We do our work
> for our audience, and let whatever life the play has beyond that,
> that's great. We'll do everything we can to spread the word.

The bottom line, a veteran East Coast artistic director believes, is that "there are a lot of reasons why you need to get that New York stamp of approval still." New York's imprimatur is necessary for national recognition and subsequent production, as well as to get a play published. One theatre agent is more blunt. "If it doesn't get on in New York, then it doesn't have a life, most of the time."

Clearly, the pull of New York has nothing to do with the articulated missions of most theatres. The unwritten ambitions of many of those theatres, though—increasingly shared by trustees, managers, and artistic leaders—lead them away from their missions. The leader of one regional company is not alone in taking her colleagues to task for allowing New York to derail them.

> I think the regional theatres have not kept up with their missions. If they loved a play before it opened in New York, and then it got a bad review, they're not going to put it into their season, even though they do a whole lot of things out of New York, second time out. That's wrong. It has to be addressed.

CRITICAL APPROVAL

The bar in New York is as high as it gets for the reception of a play. —ARTISTIC DIRECTOR

Knowledgeable and thoughtful criticism is crucial in the realm of new work, because, as one artistic director says, "The way we are led to what is new is through critics." This has become "one of the stopping blocks. We no longer have critics who are operating from the point of view that part of what they do is educate and bring people to material that might be unfamiliar or scary to them. It's moved into the thumbs up/thumbs down."

All too often, New York's stamp of approval equals critical approval. Whether or not theatres nationwide focus their efforts on making it *to* New York, they definitely focus their attention on taking *from* New York, as their peers testify and their season schedules prove. "People say, 'I don't read the reviews,'" one influential playwright explains:

> But they have an enormous impact on the future of the play. If you've got a good review Off Broadway in New York, it's huge for regional theatres, because that's what they pick up. They look for the successful Off-Broadway plays that have gotten good reviews.

The phrase "good reviews" is probably inaccurate. Since this study began, the ranks of newspaper critics throughout the United States have been decimated. Artistic directors and playwrights agree that, even as the power of the press has been severely curtailed by a dwindling readership for newspapers and the increased power of Internet reviews and, even, audience blogs, there is really only one source of criticism left with impact, and that impact is seen to be outsized. In the minds of most artistic directors and playwrights, the single meaningful opinion for a new play—in terms of its continued life on American stages—is the one printed in the *New York Times*.

While the theatre community's feelings about *Times* criticism have been historically negative, the current situation is as hostile, even vitriolic, as anyone in this study remembers it. The vitriol is directed, most especially, toward a single critic who covers Off- and Off-Off-Broadway plays, as well as significant new plays and festivals across the country, Charles Isherwood. Isherwood was assailed on many grounds, including an overbearing hostility toward those playwrights whose work he doesn't favor. While some argue that a good review from this critic—or from the *Times*'s senior critic, Ben Brantley, who, concentrating more on Broadway and London, as well as the musical theatre, has less direct impact on the not-for-profit sector—does not guarantee a successful New York run, all believe that a good review from him can grant a play life outside of New York. Moreover, a bad review from Isherwood, it is universally agreed, will cut short the life of a play and can seriously damage a playwright's career.

Whether or not audiences read or care about reviews— and there is much disagreement about the impact of criticism outside of New York—playwrights and nonprofit producers agree that, despite the often repeated claim that they do not take reviews into account, regional theatre artistic directors are heavily influenced by *Times* reviews. The head of a prominent Off-Broadway theatre warns against allowing Isherwood to become the de facto "artistic director of the American theatre." "Why on earth," he protests, should this or any critic "determine what is seen everywhere?" This artistic director was not alone in stressing that it's up to his fellow theatre leaders to "protect and foster [new work], to improve the climate, which is increasingly harsh, with fewer and fewer plays being anointed."

New York gives life, and it takes it away. Indeed, the toll of New York on a playwright can be devastating and lasting. The associate producer of a prominent Off-Broadway theatre cautions,

> If you do a play at a high-profile theatre and you're doing
> the world premiere, or even the East Coast premiere, and it
> isn't ready for that high-visibility production where the *New
> York Times*'s top critics are going to review it, the audience is
> paying a certain ticket price for it. They come in with certain
> expectations; it can end the life of the play, and it can be very
> damaging for the playwright.

The head of one Off-Broadway theatre considers this very fact in season planning. "There are things I like that I say no to, just because I don't think they're being served by having been done in New York. The last thing they need is to get beat up again [in the press]."

LIFE WITHOUT NEW YORK

Theatres think *toward* New York and draw material *from* there, but there is also considerable energy being spent thinking *around* New York. The question is of national concern: How can the theatre community support new-play production and the ongoing lives of plays without depending on the sanction of the *New York Times* or the pedigree of a Broadway or an Off-Broadway production?

Some current ideas are half steps, still involving New York City. One artistic director is giving more attention to co-productions with regional theatres, so that, by the time he produces the plays in Manhattan, they have already had some life, a track record, and maybe a handful of positive reviews, inoculation against the negativity of the New York press. Another artistic director, who is also a playwright, affirms this approach:

> A lot of us have hoped that you can give yourself the amount of time or productions your particular piece needs and keep yourself afloat financially. When you're ready, it can go to New York, and enough word is out there that even if one of the critics gets up on the wrong side of the bed and kills you, you can still keep it moving.

Sometimes this outside-in approach meets resistance from a playwright's own advocates, especially if a New York production isn't guaranteed from the start. At least one agent admits to this New York–centric worldview:

> I get scared of doing out-of-town shows, because if it doesn't get a great critical reception, it's really hard to get it on in New York. You're not always going to get a great director at some of these [regional] theatres, even the bigger theatres, or an ideal cast. I'm not going to lie. Unless the playwright says, "I really want to work on this out of town," my dream is always to find the right theatre in New York. If it gets mixed reviews here, it still has a chance of having a life. It may not

go into a commercial run—most things don't—but you've
got a better chance of getting it published and getting it
licensed, and the play will actually have a life.

Still others are exploring the more radical route—life
without New York. An artistic director within the National New
Play Network cites the long-term benefit of letting go of the
dream of a New York success. "If you can have a play that runs
around the regions and never makes it to New York, you're going
to have a better life than if you wait for that big New York hit."
Given the data, however, this "if" seems wishful. The economics
of playwriting must first change. New means of sustaining writers
over the longer haul have to be found, or a playwright's ongoing
success will continue to depend on success in New York.

The theatres that make up the world outside of New York
must regain their place as incubators for those playwrights who
write "the play that, for whatever reason, is not perceived to be
capable of going to New York and transferring to a commercial
run," as one veteran West Coast artistic director puts it.

> Those are the writers that we need to support the most, to
> write the play that may not be commercial, and who would
> be otherwise counseled, "Don't go there, don't write a big
> difficult play here, don't take on this subject, don't do that if
> your aspiration is to go and get validation back there." Rather,
> they should be counseled, "Please keep writing ambitious
> plays, paint on the broad canvas, and let's hope that there are
> enough theatres willing to commit to get behind you, so that
> you have some compensation for all the equity that you put*
> into it, and get something back." That's what in our small way,
> we're trying to do, to keep writers writing for the theatre.

Given our findings, this hope bears repeating: "that there
are enough theatres willing to commit to get behind" "ambitious,"
"broad canvas" plays, so that playwrights "have some compensation
for all the equity that you put into it, and get something back."

FIVE

Whose Audience Is It, Anyway?

The audience is not the enemy. —ARTISTIC DIRECTOR

ALL ROADS lead to the audience; what it needs, what it wants, what it will show up for. This audience, though, is no singular thing. Descriptions of the audience for new plays proceed, *Rashōmon*-style. There is the actual subscriber who returns year after year to a particular theatre. There is the audience in the writer's head when she sits at the keyboard. There is the perfect, potential audience and the imperfect, lost audience.

The perceptual divide that defines the landscape of new-play production holds firm when talk turns to the ticket buyer. The audience, as it appears to playwrights, bears little resemblance to the audience as it appears to the people running theatres. Writers and artistic directors do agree, however, that the audience is disappearing from the traditional theatre, graying, dying, and turning away from the form for more insistent, exciting, accessible, inexpensive media. An explosion of entertainment choices has marginalized a staid theatre.

Building audiences for the new-play requires building new audiences. Because we can't know that audience until it has arrived, we must begin with questions: What do audiences want? What do they fear? How much will they pay for experiences whose quality they can't foretell? How can they be educated to celebrate new work, even when it fails? How do we reach young audiences? How do we reach nontraditional audiences, specifically audiences of color? How do we enlarge the audience for work by artists of color? How do we keep them? Are audience and community the same thing? How new is "too" new?

Artistic directors worry about finding plays that will speak to their audiences, pleasing and/or challenging them. In their opinion, playwrights are too often unwilling or unable to make work that connects with a particular community, on one hand, or to a broad enough audience on the other. Writers complain that theatres are both constrained by their subscribers, and that they lack faith in their audiences' ability to grapple with challenging work. They see theatres as obsessed with marketing and ill-adept at it. Theatres, playwrights argue, don't know how to sell the things that make a play unique, nor have they found the way to market the experience of the new itself—new voices, new plays, new forms.

What accounts for these differing views? What are the demands of audience development, and what are the requirements of the creative process? How can they both be served without blocking each other? Do current marketing practices serve new plays? How does the race of the writer impact marketing, and how are writers of color impacted by it? What's being done to educate audiences about new plays? What more can be done? These are some of the questions explored below.

"My Audience" (The Artistic Director's Perspective)

> The truth is, the playwrights are the people who are talking to the audience. While they have to listen to their own muse, they also have to listen to the hunger, the intellectual hunger that the audience has. Otherwise audiences are just going to stop coming.
> —ARTISTIC DIRECTOR

Attendance at plays in the United States has been shrinking for several years, even as the population has grown. According to *Theatre Facts 2007*, published by Theatre Communications Group, overall admissions at a sampling of TCG member theatres has been in decline since 2003 (including at musicals, as well as plays; new plays are not reported separately). Total ticket sales at the 117 resident theatres tracked are down 6.1 percent over that period. The National Endowment for the Arts report "All America's a Stage" reveals that the percentage of U.S. adults who attended a nonmusical play over a twelve-month period fell from 13.5 percent (25 million people) to 9.4 percent (21 million people) between 1992 and 2008. The figures for Broadway are even more disheartening. Even as attendance at Broadway musicals continues to rise, the number of tickets sold to Broadway plays over the past five-year period has fallen 19.6 percent compared to the same period twenty years ago (1984–89). If we exclude revivals, the decline for attendance at new plays (or, more precisely at plays that were new to Broadway) over the same period is 41.6 percent.

In the grim view of one commercial producer, the whole field is at fault: "We're not developing new audiences," he said. "There are adventurous people out there, and they're probably the same percentage of the population that's always been adventurous. They just have more competition."

The audience is now *many* audiences, others worry, divided by generation, and interest. "There's a bigger and bigger divide between the baby-boomer audience and the next audience," one artistic administrator notes of this splintering, "but being a major regional theatre, where you really want to speak to a broad-based audience, I'm finding a more and more real, enormous division between maybe one, two, or even three or four audiences." Unlike cable television and the Internet, theatre hasn't known how to respond to this cultural shift to niche audiences. Moreover, there is an increasingly large group of people that most theatres struggle unsuccessfully to engage—the ones who didn't grow up in a theatregoing culture, who are more accustomed to getting their entertainment from computer and TV screens at home. No wonder, then, that theatre leaders worry especially about the lack of young audiences. Their absence forebodes a diminished future for the form itself, culturally irrelevant theatres playing to fewer and fewer people.

It's easy to see where this dark vision comes from. Theatre is shrinking at both ends. On one side, an aging audience can reinforce a theatre's caution in programming; on the other, without a stream of new, young theatregoers, it gets harder for a theatre to replenish itself. This double-whammy leaves the field itself, in the view of playwrights and observers as well, increasingly sapped. A veteran West Coast artistic director sums up this dilemma: "Audiences, as they get older, become a little more conservative." Meanwhile, he argues, the decades-long erosion of arts education is creating a preponderance of "cultural illiterates" who, unlike audiences of thirty years ago, are not predisposed to appreciate theatre.

This is not only a problem for regional theatre. One Off-Broadway artistic director minces few words in characterizing local theatregoers, including his own subscribers: "The traditional, mainstream, subscription-based audience in New York City is the most conservative, unyielding, and tough audience." The demographics of New York subscribers tend toward the elderly, he adds, and since he doesn't want to be the youngest person in the house—his experience when he sees plays at other Off-Broadway companies—he tries to keep subscribers "of the uptown, conservative-but-trying-to-be-open sensibility," to a third of his house. "I don't want a fully subscribed theatre."

Still, subscribers remain a key component of the majority of theatres' audiences.

FINDING: Of the theatres we studied, 78 percent reported having a subscription audience which, on average, accounted for 42 percent of a theatre's ticket sales. Subscriber ticket sales ranged from 10 percent to 85 percent of all ticket sales last season depending on the theatre.

Many artistic directors believe that the economic, political, and cultural climate of the past eight years has left audiences depressed and scared. In this environment, theatregoers have favored uplifting, happy endings and have ever-shorter attention spans. They "crave bolstering," as one artistic director puts it. "The audience's sense of concentration has been diminished by television, by the sound bite." Moreover, audiences are hesitant to see a play—and pay a great deal for tickets—unless they are sure they will enjoy it.

> Aren't we living in a moment in time where things are so binary, it's either a success or it's a failure? There's no gray anywhere. The only movies people want to see are the box-office successes for the weekend. The audience trends are to follow events, to go only to the place where you're perceived to be at the right place, where you're giving the right answer or you're seeing the right show.

As one associate artistic director, who directs across the country, puts it: "Audiences are much, much lazier than they were. The culture is lazy." Audiences are unwilling to "co-author the play….They are thrown by endings that have question marks. The audience thinks they didn't get it," even when, as becomes clear in post-performance discussions, they can clearly explain the very same character ambiguities and story elements they complain are confusing. This unwillingness to "co-author" plays seems paradoxical, given the prevalence of interactive media in the past decade in which the participant is asked to do just that. Again, generational divisions come into play: Older audiences are observed to be puzzled by plays from younger writers; younger audiences, meanwhile, are missing in action. "I'm not sure it's about laziness," another artistic director counters, "as much as it's about fear. Fear has gotten a lot bigger."

For all the anxiety about the present and future, many artistic leaders express emphatic admiration for their own season-ticket holders, even as they sometimes disparage other theatres' subscribers. "Our audiences are very sophisticated theatregoers," one declares. Another enthuses, "I just adore our audience. They get it. They're there because they know it's not going to be easy. It's going to be challenging and interesting." Likewise, from an Off-Broadway associate artistic director: "At least in New York, audiences are pretty adventurous, even the ones we think are conservative."

THE DISCONNECT (AS TOLD BY ARTISTIC DIRECTORS)

> *My own sense is of isolation from the playwrights and the broad-based community that are theatregoers. I don't feel like the playwrights are particularly writing about [the audience's] issues.*
> —ARTISTIC DIRECTOR

To many artistic leaders, playwrights are out of touch with, or not really interested in writing for, their theatres' audiences. They see a disconnect between the people writers hope or imagine will come to see their work, and the flesh-and-blood patrons in the lobby night after night. Several artistic directors lament that rather than writing for a broad, popular audience, too many playwrights speak narrowly to the audience in their heads, or to an insular group of their close peers.

One associate artistic director, who oversees her theatre's new-play development wing, was particularly concerned about younger writers, and whether their plays are relevant for her company.

> I wonder about the size and scope of what they are thinking about, and what they have to say, and how a different generation of audience, our mainstream subscribers, can find a way of embracing those ideas. There is a generational shift; the cultural concerns of one generation don't necessarily translate to the cultural concerns of another generation. I've been reading a lot of plays, and I don't know that they are going to speak to our audience.

A Minnesota-based artistic director agrees, also attributing this inability—or refusal—of younger writers to address broader audiences.

> Some artists can take a pulse on what speaks to an audience and create work of integrity for large audiences. Television does that. Rock 'n' roll does that. Bruce Springsteen says, "I can speak to a large audience and I can do it with integrity." Some artists can do that, and some artists chose not to do that, or can't do it. The disconnect occurs when an artists says, "I don't care if you don't look at my plays" and, simultaneously, "Why don't I have an audience?" or "Why don't my plays get produced?"

One artistic director, whose company brings theatre to populations well outside of mainstream theatregoers—prisons, women's shelters, nursing homes—levels a similar critique at contemporary playwrights: they don't know how to speak across class lines. Unlike Shakespeare and other classic writers, she argues, contemporary

> playwrights write with an upper-middle-class or middle-class audience in mind. Not that there's anything wrong with that, but what would happen if they shifted their perception of who they are writing for, and imagined *anyone* in their audience? What would that do to kinds of stories they would chose to tell? So often the plays are small, they are about people in a specific class, people in a specific world, and not that that's bad, but that's only going to speak to a certain audience. What happens if you broaden the audience you're writing for? Playwrights need a space to be nurtured and develop their vision and their voice, but then it comes to the test, and the test is: does the audience care? Are they engaged or involved?

Of course, the economics of theatrical production in America, specifically high ticket prices, may be responsible for this class gap or, at the very least, may exacerbate the situation. If the only theatres that can provide playwrights with meaningful income are institutions whose ticket prices effectively preclude low-income audiences, is it any wonder that plays are written with wealthier audiences in mind? Additionally, as a graduate degree becomes increasingly necessary for writers to get on the professional track, are writers of other economic backgrounds—with other experiences of class—being shut out of the system?

One artistic director, whose theatre is known both for classics and new work, challenges producers to create an environment that will enable new writers to speak to wider audiences, across social and economic divides, just as Shakespeare did. "What we're now doing is giving our writers the opportunity, but also demanding, that they speak to a broad populist audience." He takes playwrights to task for not thinking enough about audiences:

> Playwrights believe that the audience is willing to be
> challenged and rise to the level of their work if the audience
> is given that chance. That is essentially a mandarin notion
> of what an artist is—that an artist sees further, has a unique
> and difficult and complicated vision in which the job of the
> audience to either rise to that challenge or not. Part of the
> problem with that way of thinking is that it's also part of the
> job of the playwright to figure out, "How do I reach that
> audience, and how do I make sure that my work will speak to
> them?" As an artistic director, I am deeply concerned about
> what's being served to an audience. I am deeply concerned
> about our ability to excite our audience with the work, and
> it's very hard for me to get excited about saying the idea is to
> simply take an individual writer with their unique vision and
> hope that my audience will rise to the challenge of getting
> that, as opposed to saying we are all in this together and that
> the writer is trying to reach to the audience as much as the
> audience is trying to reach to the writer.

The militancy of this language—which makes populist demands on writers and, to a certain extent, casts them in the role of service-providers—is not everyone's language. More often, artistic directors speak of empowering writers to find their own voices, their own artistic necessities and modes of expression. Still, many artistic directors believe that writers have a deeper responsibility or obligation to audience than they currently exercise—especially when it comes to reaching a broader audience. It's a responsibility that artistic directors—for reasons of mission, personal values, fear of the red-stained balance sheet, or all of the above—feel acutely. They know their communities in ways that playwrights, rarely around for very long, can't. If this study is an indication, you'll never hear an artistic director say: "I really want to figure out how to do the work that I want to do and not worry about my audience."

A DELICATE BALANCE

> *Artistic directors are in their jobs because they are able to connect with audiences of enormous sizes, in the case of some of our theatres. They seem to be good at understanding what subscribers want to see.* —DRAMATURG

Artistic directors and their associates frame the work of programming seasons as a balancing act. On one side of the scale rests the personal taste of the artistic director; on the other side, the intuited interests of a community of hundreds or thousands. "You want to be aware of who the audience is, but not second-guess the audience too much." For some the balancing act sets up a creative tension, as they test the limits of their audiences with challenging fare, always gauging how far they can go. As one artistic director puts it: "I like to go out on thin ice and take as many people with me as possible before I start to see it crack, and then I move back and wait until the next time, see what it will take." In this way, artistic directors operate as Pied Pipers leading their willing adherents into a realm that they might not otherwise explore on their own.

Another approach might be described as a shared journey, an evolving negotiation of taste and interest. "I used to pick three for them and two for me, out of the five," an artistic director half-jokes. "Now it's probably flipped around, and next year I'm contemplating career suicide." This tongue-in-cheek depiction of play selection raises several questions: How do you program seasons that both challenge and please? How can artistic directors satisfy audiences and themselves? And (perhaps the central question) aren't there enough plays that do both? Clearly, as this same artistic director confesses, the process is two-way. It involves educating the audience and, also, being taught by it. "I'm opening my horizons a little bit and I'm listening more, too."

For some, this mutual education is the point. The theatre is a popular art form, so shouldn't it appeal to audience tastes? Larger companies may not have a choice, if they are to maintain their subscription base. "What's wrong with being market oriented?" a literary manager asks. "Shouldn't you be listening to your audiences?" Sometimes this listening tells you very specific things, she explains. For example, one southern theatre's audience doesn't like curse words or British accents.

Some institutional leaders are acutely aware of the dangers of this approach. "I can fall into the trap of trying to program to attract audiences, as opposed to program to speak to audiences," a Bay Area artistic director contends. Speaking to audiences entails developing a shared language that dovetails with the institution's values.

Sometimes an audience's expectations about outcome create problems. For instance, some theatregoers measure success by whether or not a production moves to New York. "We make sure our audience is excited about what we are doing, that we're birthing things to go into the national repertoire. Because so much of our work does go into New York and a lot of it has gone to Broadway, we have to be very careful that that is not how we lure them. That's not how we call something a success, or not a success."

"My Audience"
(The Playwright's Version)

*Theatres teach and raise their audiences. So when you get to
a particular place and people are not coming into the door for
the work that you are doing, it's because you've taught them to
expect to eat only bread, but not with real butter. There's this idea
now that the audience tells us what to do, and I don't think the
audience really tells us what to do. We've told ourselves that the
audience tells us what to do.* —PLAYWRIGHT

To hear playwrights tell it, the American theatre is suffering
an audience crisis. Especially at larger venues, playwrights
find audiences that they feel are too old, too conservative,
and too white to engage or enjoy the range of new writing for
the theatre. Or, to phrase it differently, young, adventurous,
multiracial audiences are hard to find. Many small theatres are
thriving, playwrights believe, and drawing more vital, albeit
tiny, audiences. Mid-sized theatres dedicated to new work
have dwindled to a handful of stalwarts. Playwrights believe
that these other audiences—their optimal audiences—are out
there. They just don't think theatres do a good enough job of
finding them.

Have audiences turned conservative because theatres don't
produce enough edgy work, or have theatres grown conservative because their audiences won't buy it? Writers and theatres
define "audience" differently; they value different things, weigh
these values on different scales. "Theatres are not interested in
producing for a writer's audiences," a leading experimental playwright asserts. "It's not that we're not interested in writing for
their audiences. Maybe they're defining audiences as ticket buyers, and that's the audience I can't write for. I have no idea who
that audience is." By this light, the theatres' mercantile relation-

ship with audience goes against the grain of the "collaborative engagement" sought by the playwright. Ticket buyers consume entertainment. The writer's more ideal audience accepts the challenge to enter into a dialogue.

Subscription is an ingrained system whose advantages and drawbacks most theatres wrestle with. On the positive side, subscription helps theatres build community. By committing to regular attendance, subscribers enter into a regular conversation with the theatre. They do what audiences increasingly hesitate to do: buy tickets to shows about which they know little or nothing. They support the theatre as a whole.

Subscription is more problematic for writers. In particular, writers worry that larger companies are too dependent on subscribers, a shrinking population that still makes up the patron base of institutional theatres. Writers single out subscribers, specifically, as that aging, conservative group resistant to plays that challenge notions of traditional dramatic form or that tell stories from outside their experience. Subscribers lack cultural diversity, writers observe, to an even greater extent than single-ticket buyers. Furthermore, subscribers by definition make a financial and emotional commitment to an institution rather than to individual plays. As a result, playwrights worry that theatres, aiming to strengthen that general commitment, do little to encourage these regulars to value individual plays on their own terms.

Most playwrights agree: because theatres depend on them for operating revenue and a large chunk of overall attendance, subscribers create a drag on both experimentation and diversity. Even those writers newest to the field share this diagnosis, as articulated by an early-career playwright in the Midwest.

> This whole subscription thing makes the artistic director
> wonder…can we do anything new, artistically? They're
> wondering if their subscribers are going to re-subscribe,
> and if there wasn't this big funding challenge then they

would be able to produce plays that are exciting and new artistically and attract a younger audience. You would have playwrights and plays that are actually speaking to [this audience's] experience, and they would actually want to come to a play.

Other writers take the analysis even further, asserting that theatres are beholden to a group that's even smaller than their subscription base. "Theatres think they're talking about their audience base, their 30,000 subscribers, but they're actually concerned about the ten or twenty people who give a lot of money," one explains. "They are dependent on private and corporate funding, so sometimes 'audience' is code for 'sponsorship,' which is very different than the larger group who could buy tickets to the plays." This handful of leading sponsors has a name, according to an artistic administrator with a long track record in new work development: "assets." Even his own theatre, he reveals, bends over backwards to avoid antagonizing its assets.

UPTOWN/DOWNTOWN

> *I would love to write for the Cort Theatre [on Broadway]. But how are the seats going to get filled?* —PLAYWRIGHT

Some playwrights confess to feeling most comfortable working in smaller, "downtown" spaces, such as Off-Off-Broadway theatres in New York City and similar venues in other cities, where they are closer to their audience, both literally and in terms of a shared aesthetic. These audiences tend to include few, if any, subscribers, and often a large contingent of colleagues and friends. A New York–based writer explains:

> There is the downtown tier of theatre spaces where the houses are under 100 seats and the run is not so long. There is a sense of actually writing for an audience. Most of the

audience is people you know or the cast knows. It's a theatre community that changes totally when you go into a larger house. It's very vigorous, in terms of an audience responding to experimentation and different kinds of acting and production. It's very alive. You get an audience in the smaller theatre that's actually up for the event. They're willing to roll up their sleeves and be there for it. It's not a consumable, which is what very often happens in a larger house.

In fact, many writers extol the pleasures of seeing their work in such intimate settings, among friends: "I'm happier doing a play in a living room than I am in a big theatre," one well-established playwright claims. "I do plays at big theatres to make a little extra money. I'm glad that all these people are seeing this play but it's not why I wrote it. For some, the eventual move uptown, if it happens at all, comes with anxiety.

I've had two plays produced Off Off Broadway, downtown, which then moved on to Off-Broadway contracts, with ticket prices much higher. Audiences came not because they knew of somebody, but because of reviews, or because they were subscribers. Both of those experiences have been incredibly educational and kind of horrifying. It's not as though these were impeccable plays that everyone downtown loved, but people understood the terms of the debate and responded to them in ways that were with the play or against the play—but against the play's own terms. Moving up a notch, audiences would be composed half of people who really adored it and half of people who just hated the experience and felt deeply bitter that they had been suckered into it—who I then feel terrible about because I feel like they spent all this money, and now they're in pain. Yet there are another 50 people out there who would be perfectly happy to be there. How do you get the wrong 50 out and the right 50 in so that nobody has to suffer?

If, as this playwright states, her plays "can't go Off Broadway in a way that's happy," then the question arises: how can she or playwrights like her hope to realize much meaningful income from playwriting? How do producers find a friendly audience for offbeat work in mainstream venues? One way, playwrights suggest, impractical as it may seem, it to run shows for months instead of weeks, to let satisfied theatregoers spread the word to others like them.

These writers may not be typical, but they are far from uncommon. Indeed, many of this generation of playwrights appear, for one reason or another, to have written off theatre as a form of mass entertainment. Are they staking out a new kind of theatrical intimacy? Have they given up on institutionalized theatre and its audience? Or are these writers, as some artistic directors contend, evading a challenge? Have they scaled back their ambitions, preferring to remain within the comfort zone of smaller, more intimate and welcoming audiences, rather than engaging in a larger conversation and a broader context?

For many in the theatre, as we'll see, the greatest concern is that the art form has fallen out of a larger cultural conversation. Are playwrights beating their own retreat from the culture at large?

If new plays have lost social and political currency, it's not clear where the blame lies. Is it a failure of will on the part of writers or producers? Is it a crisis of confidence or economics? Are writers writing for smaller spaces or are artistic directors steering their plays in that direction? It is distressing to hear playwrights who aspire to speak to large audiences doubt that there are places for such work on Broadway or Off Broadway, or in major regional houses. If there are, currently or on the horizon, writers whose ambition, power, and originality might put them in the company of the so-called great American playwrights, will we know them? Will there be houses capacious enough to accommodate their visions? Will anyone be able to fill those houses?

WHO ARE WE WRITING FOR?

> *I write for the perfect audience that is in my head, and I think*
> *it's [up to the artistic director] to decide if this piece of theatre*
> *will appeal to his audience. It's for the theatre to determine*
> *if the audience can be broadened. I don't think that's ever the*
> *playwright's responsibility.* —PLAYWRIGHT

For playwrights there are many audiences, real and imagined: the audience they imagine as they write, if they write for an audience at all; loyal fans of their work; colleagues and friends; the professional community that develops and produces new plays; and ticket buyers at the theatres they hope will stage their work, to name but a few. In the best of all possible worlds, these many audiences fuse into one.

The very word "audience" comes loaded with private meaning. For one widely produced writer, the ideal audience signs on for an extended conversation over a body of work. "I want continuity of an audience. I want my audience to have seen my last play and the play before that and the play before that." Some writers claim to know exactly whom they are writing for. Many admit the opposite. "I don't know what my audience is. I have no idea. I am interested to find out what people actually do like my work. It's always a little bit different than I think." Others avoid worrying about it. "I don't know how somebody in theatre administration anywhere, or an artistic director, can expect me to know about or be particularly interested in his audience. I don't think about these things much, to tell you the truth. I'm really focused on writing my plays." Still others, including this well-known writer, who teaches playwriting to college students from a range of disciplines, believe in an audience of one:

> The hardest thing is to encourage students to write for themselves. That's our ultimate responsibility, to have a writer write for themselves, to please themselves, to entertain themselves, to shock and move themselves. That's our job.

No one knows what the audience wants until it arrives. Production makes the audience real. Without it, or when productions are sporadic or infrequent, there can be no continuity, no specificity of address, no dialogue across the footlights.

One writer draws a contrast between the audience in her head and the one in the house. "When you're a writer, the audience is in some ways hypothetical, because of the way the system works...You're writing it for yourself, and your friends, your secret, dead partners, colleagues. The audience is in some ways imaginary." Once the play is accepted for production, the theoretical becomes actual. "The second stage is that part where you're actually thinking of a specific theatre company, or a group of people, artists that you want to work with and want to build something for." Only in production, she concludes, do you know whom you're writing for.

This process of gradual engagement with a specific audience happens differently, depending on the playwright and his or her relationship to the theatre and the community they're writing for. Some writers—by their particular genius or because they live and write within a particular community—tailor work to a specific audience, maximizing its appeal or relevance. The leader of a West Coast artists' lab describes one such playwright as "business-savvy." "He understands the demographics of what he's working with," she explains, and thinks about "the audience that's going to the theatre now." "'I'm going to write for those women,'" she quotes him as saying, "'I'm going to put those women in this play.'"

Likewise, artistic leaders tell of playwrights tooling plays to the theatre that commissioned them, and therefore, at least implicitly, to its audience. Many playwrights prize the opportunity to write for parts of the society with which they share affinity, including specific ethnic groups or the people of precise neighborhoods and communities. Many value the context provided by culturally-specific companies. Again and again, playwrights—even those who believe the process of writing a play is private and self-satisfying—clamor for connection with and knowledge of the audience. This connection, this knowledge, can only come over time, through production and/or consistent relationships with producing theatres.

If there is, as artistic directors suggest, a breakdown between playwrights and their audiences, the crux of the problem is this: **In the current system of new-play development, there are few opportunities for writers to get to know theatregoers over time—productions are too sporadic, and ongoing relationships with theatres (and, by extension, communities of ticket buyers) are rarely sustained.** With a few exceptions, most notably plays written on commission or within a residency, playwrights lack opportunities to write for a specific audience. They usually create without knowing which company will present their work, which subscribers will preview it, in which city, on what size stage. It is always, as one literary manager puts it, "a first date." Playwrights can hardly be expected to re-jigger each piece to maximize its appeal to the idiosyncrasies of a specific audience each time they submit a play.

Nor is it clear whether there is currently a national audience for new plays. Have audiences splintered into so many niche groups that a savvy playwright must tailor each play to the particular ethos of any given group? Will the specific translate to the universal?

Time factors in as well. Writers, especially those addressing political or social events, often work out of the fierce urgency of a moment. Ideally, they speak to the concerns of a specific audience at a specific time. In the real world of theatrical production, however, a lengthy gap exists between creating the play and getting it onstage—usually years. This passage of time waters down a play's immediacy and disrupts direct contact with its intended audience.

If a play's impact often depends on immediacy, its reach can grow over time. It is an article of faith among writers (and others) that a play will find its audience, given a long enough run. "A play finds its natural audience, and that audience also gets a chance to find that play," one writer insists. "Long runs are crucial." She offers a compelling, if unlikely, prescription to theatres: "If you have half a million or a quarter million appointed for a production, don't do a set. Run it for seventeen weeks longer than you would have otherwise." Artistic directors share this opinion. "The longer you can get the runs of your shows, the more possibility you have to make word of mouth work for you, and to figure out ways to foment it and use it." Of course, as the same artistic director points out, theatres don't have this flexibility.

> I could have extended [a certain show] for weeks and weeks,
> but our mission is not to tell the next production to go away
> into hibernation for a while. We care for each show, and
> the artists have committed to it, and [the next show] was
> in development for three years, so we only got a one-week
> extension.

Overall, writers express faith in audiences generally and believe that the heads of theatres need to trust their audiences more when it comes to challenging or unconventional work. Playwrights speak of what one writer calls "nervousness," from artistic directors. "Three times I had to calm them down and go, 'Actually the audience is going to like this.'" One playwright, whose name is, for many, synonymous with the unconventional, sums up the sentiments of most playwrights: "The people who underestimate the audience are the theatres themselves."

One playwright advocate agrees, insisting that playwrights are not the only ones who don't truly know the audience. Theatres are equally in the dark about the work they present.

> I don't think we can know what audiences want to see. That's
> a mythical notion. We think we know, but we don't. Every
> writer wants an audience, but the question is how do we
> perceive what audiences can handle? I have always believed
> that there should be a proliferation of work where some

make more sense and some make less sense. There's a pull to create art for something that we think we know, and that is really limiting to writers.

Marketing: One Size Fits All?

There is a wealth of audiences who are young and diverse who are dying to come to your doorstep. What are you doing about it?
—PLAYWRIGHT

For theatres, marketing is a layered process. In contrast to commercial producers, who promote single events, not-for-profits must sell individual plays and, at the same time, sell whole seasons. Both efforts are part of selling the theatre itself, promoting it to donors, funders, cultural decision-makers—specifically, the press—and other stakeholders (or potential supporters) within their local communities.

When playwrights talk about marketing, which they do a great deal, they describe something both singular and general. Effective marketing must sell plays. It must find or create the right audience for those plays, even if the audience is an uncommon one. It must generate excitement over new work in general.

On the whole, playwrights are quite critical of theatres' ability to market new work. Theatrical marketing, most believe, is beset by the same corporate-ness and homogenization that afflicts institutional theatres in general. Playwrights complain that theatres apply a "one-size-fits-all" approach to selling their work. "The loathsome side of corporate theatre is marketing," says one, "because it ultimately makes everything sound the same. You can't tell from any of the materials what the hell it is you're going to see, because it's written by the marketing people." Another writer concurs, pointing to a deficit in the exact area where playwrights excel—the ability of marketers to describe work. "They don't have the words, and they don't know about economy."

Playwrights find fault with marketing departments across the field, complaining that those who staff them possess neither the skills, the savvy, nor the knowledge to identify and communicate with the audiences for whom they are writing. "Sometimes the artistic director is very gung-ho about a show, the literary staff is very gung-ho," fumes one playwright, who is also a longtime arts administrator.

> It comes down to marketing. They say, "We love this play; we can't find the audience for it." It pisses me off, because a lot of people in marketing don't know how to find new audiences for these plays. They expect the audiences to be the same. So they don't do new work.

They are "out of touch," he continues; they do not know how to market newness in itself. By marketing to general audiences, a Minneapolis-based playwright reasons, theatres make it more difficult to connect individual writers with audiences of their own.

> The way we operate as a theatre community doesn't work well for the individual writer/artist to draw their own audience. Does what the playwrights want to say resonate with the audience of their generation? How do we relate to that particular frame in which that particular playwright lives, and the work lives? Or are we thinking constantly about the general audience and the general, you know, theatregoing public, whoever they are?

Another constant refrain is that marketing directors don't listen to writers, don't care to hear the things writers know about their audiences or about promoting their own work, which, in order to get productions and grants, playwrights constantly have to do. (As we'll discuss below, the situation is reversed for writers of color.) This especially frustrates writers aiming to reach a younger audience. One bicoastal writer with a track record of work about, and for, twenty-somethings, recounts one experience of many.

> I would say to the theatre, "I think this play is going to speak to audiences under thirty. What can you do to help me get those people in the theatre?" They would say, "Nothing." They weren't interested. I remember taking stacks of postcards and papering Chicago on my own. I thought, "Let's put them in cafés, bookstores, and record stores, places where people under thirty congregate, because I know that that's who this play will speak to.

One playwright-artistic director includes funders in the problem. Too often funding agencies inhibit innovation by frowning on nontraditional approaches to marketing.

"The expectation is that you have to market plays the same way all non-profit theatres market them or you're doing a bad job. People who are giving you money to put on these plays, if you don't market it exactly this way, are not going to give you any more grant money. At an established theatre there's no room for creativity."

Once again, playwrights look at the non profit theatre and yearn for some of the practices from the commercial theatre it, to a great extent, replaced. In the simplest terms, artistic directors of not-for-profit institutions must cultivate an audience for the theatre in general, for all their work, regardless of preferences for one kind of play or another. They benefit from the audience loyalty they engender, which for playwrights means a guaranteed audience. Commercial producers, on the other hand, must market each show on its own and, consequently, have to build an audience, a constituency, a brand, from scratch. With this risk, though, commercial producers gain the freedom to focus narrowly and intensely, to drum up one precise audience for one play at a time. The advantage for playwrights in this approach is the right audience for the play, an audience that knows what it is getting.

THE COLOR OF MARKETING

"Institutions are about a certain kind of system," a well-established playwright argues. "When plays come in, they want to systematically find a way to market them."

He mimics a marketing department in dialogue form:

> 'Black play!'
> 'No, black gay play, please!'
> 'That's hard; I don't know how to do that.'
> 'Oh, not too young, please.'
> 'No hip-hop; I don't get it.'
> 'Let's do August Wilson.'

One-size-fits-all marketing becomes especially problematic for writers of color. Again and again writers disparage the attempts of institutional theatres to reach specific ethnic or cultural groups beyond their usual subscribers. Theatres don't know what drives audiences that aren't part of their base, playwrights say. They don't know where to find them. They don't know how to address them when they do find them. And when they do get, for example, African-American or Hispanic audiences into the theatre for a show meant to appeal to them, theatres can't get them back. They fail to maintain anything like consistent contact, either through outreach or programming.

This situation profoundly impacts the playwright. Most white writers feel shut out of marketing discussions, unless they kick up a fuss. (Some make a point of demanding participation.) Writers of color face a different, twofold challenge. On one hand, marketing often becomes an obstacle to production. In other words, theatre leaders sometimes blame their marketing departments when rejecting a play, claiming that their staff does

not know how to find the play's audience. This may be true or
it may be a convenient excuse, code for "We don't want to do
your play." Many playwrights believe that theatres solicit work
by writers of color in new-play development programs in order
to fulfill funder-dictated obligations, but use marketing as a
rationale not to produce them.

On the other hand, once a theatre agrees to do a play
by a writer of color, playwrights claim, the responsibility of
identifying an audience and speaking to it is frequently deflected
onto the author, which is almost never the case with white
writers. "Every time I do a play, the first question they ask me is,
'How do we market to your audience?'" one African-American
writer marvels in exasperation. "So, I have to be a marketer?"
Yes, it seems. Like many other black, Asian-American, Latino,
Native American, and Arab-American playwrights, operating
in the field where theatre staffs are predominantly white, he
has learned the ropes of culturally-specific, niche marketing.
They know what to suggest and what they need to advocate for,
when the theatres turn to them—as they inevitably do—to help
reach potential patrons who share their cultural background.
And so, theatres that have no relationship to church groups,
for instance, or that rarely advertise on the radio, are led by
playwrights to African-American congregations or Spanish-
language music stations.

Writers usually acquiesce in this bring-your-own audience
approach, believing they have little choice at theatres big enough
to generate a decent income for them. No one else will do the
work for them. "Oftentimes I have to do the Spanish translations
for press releases," a Latino playwright adds.

This dynamic places an additional burden on writers
of color to generate new audiences for their own work. It
also sets up a system of failure. If the theatre does a play by a
writer of color and ticket sales are disappointing, it might be
less willing to produce other such plays, to stretch toward other
"nontraditional" audiences. One writer speaks for many:

We did a production, and they had problems filling the house. It really disheartened me in the end. I had to get audiences for them, calling the Asian-American community. What makes it frightening is they were going to finally say, "We did that play of color. See—no one came. Why should we do this other play?"

He goes on, connecting one kind of resistance to another: "It's the same thing, beyond plays of color, with new plays. 'We did a new play, but no one showed up.'"

SPEAKING TO AUDIENCES OF COLOR

You can't just invite a black audience for a black play and say good-bye to them. You have to make them part of the community. And invite them to see a white show, that Asian show. The same thing with other people. Every time a production becomes a specialty event, it becomes troublesome. —PLAYWRIGHT

When it comes to building more diverse audiences for the American theatre, outreach is on everybody's mind. Artistic directors of so-called "mainstream" theatres seek to develop audiences of color. Without a sustained approach, playwrights say, efforts to diversify can't succeed. Cities are not white, they point out, but the regional theatres big enough to generate reasonable income through production are—backstage, onstage, and in the house. A playwright describes what he sees:

Every time I go to the Goodman, that audience is over sixty and it's all white. It does not look at all like Chicago. At the Taper, the average audience does not look like Los Angeles. I found out that 47 percent of Hartford is Puerto Rican, 36 percent is black. That audience at Hartford Stage does not look at all like Hartford.

This disjunction leaves writers of color in a precarious relationship to the audiences they typically encounter. A Mexican-American writer elaborates:

> It's a kind of bravery that you have to do as a playwright in order to be in that space, because you're not going to address your audience specifically. This weird thing happens: You get thrown at these people, and they look at you, and I've never felt more un-American. I'm completely Chicano, born and raised here, but when I go to these theatres, I become an immigrant. That's a really interesting comment on the theatre in general, on the regional theatres that can pay you the kind of money to have a career. I'm definitely not speaking to my people any more. I speak to my people in books, in poetry, when I do community theatre projects, in classes, in the academy.

Many theatres pour their energy into marketing aimed at expanding their audience base to reflect the communities they serve. Writers maintain that marketing dollars and good intentions aren't enough. Until the number of productions by playwrights of color increases, until the stories told branch out, until the complexion of theatre leadership and staff changes, the audience of larger institutional theatres will remain monochromatic, out-of-sync with its time and place. Another Chicano writer relates:

> A lot of my projects have been dealing with companies who are trying to outreach to the Latino community. I want to bring in audiences that are not being represented in those institutions. I came from a theatre company where we developed plays by Latino writers, and I ended up coming to the conclusion that we were not going to bring those audiences in because we weren't producing enough work, being consistent and developing enough, and that the future was trying to reach young people and create a new population to eventually come and take those places over.

Calculating the Cost: Ticket Price

To change the audience, playwrights argue, you have to change ticket prices. They apply this truth to audiences of color, and they apply it to young audiences. "There's a lot of talk about how to get people age eighteen to thirty-five to the theatre," says a young playwright in Minneapolis,

> but they're not coming because they're paying $55 to see something that movies do a lot better. Make your tickets cheaper so that people who are younger can go see the work that appeals to them. I know how difficult that is in terms of expense, but it has to be a priority, or else there is going to be no audience in a generation.

"People have less money and everything is more expensive," another playwright says, with reference to the difficult economy. "They're looking at us as an extra. They don't think of the arts as part of their everyday life, so we're one of the things that's getting trimmed out." The answer is the same: charge less.

Some artistic directors make the identical argument, but from where they sit, the pressure to balance budgets, sustain institutions, adequately compensate artists, and demonstrate fiscal responsibility to funders (who may assess viability and success by the proportion of earned income) tends to counter the impulse to lower prices.

Theatre leaders wrestle with the value of their work in relation to its cost. One playwright, who doubles as a literary manager, quoted the warnings of her theatre's marketing consultant: "Value what you're producing, and if you've produced good stuff, the audience will buy your tickets."

In fact, calling for lower prices isn't easy for playwrights, either. They get paid (though, as we've seen, hardly anything) from royalties. Lower ticket prices would, therefore, subsidize audience development, in part, on the backs of playwrights.

Old Media and New

I don't think the audiences care about reviews. It's the people who
run the theatres who care. —ARTISTIC DIRECTOR

Along with marketing and ticket price, press is another part
of the audience development equation. As the environment of
journalism changes, theatres scramble to keep up. The days when
critics and arts journalists helped attract and cultivate the tastes
of theatregoers are gone. With the explosion of new media in
the past decade, print journalism itself, along with the brand of
cultural criticism it once published, has lost its currency. What's
more, as arts coverage shrinks, theatres find it more and more
difficult to generate feature coverage of their productions. New
work suffers uniquely from shrinking column inches, according
to artistic leaders. What's the story, especially if there is no
hook—a star, a familiar title, or the distinction of a regional/
national premiere? Declining newspaper readership renders the
measly coverage most papers muster that much less effective.

Criticism may have lost its depth, but it also seems to have
lost much of its power. Do critics still count? "Reviews just don't
matter," says a literary manager from the South. "There is a local
critic. He does not sell tickets. Good reviews or bad, his reviews
don't keep ticket-buyers away, and they don't sell tickets. It's
a little frustrating." A New England artistic director confirms
this view. "Regional theatre in general has everything to do with
word of mouth and very little to do with critics." Playwrights
agree: At least outside of New York, audiences don't respond to
reviews.

Still, critics continue to be seen, fairly universally, as a
hindrance to the kind of audience cultivation necessary for new-
play production to thrive. Instead of fostering useful dialogue
about plays, critics (hamstrung by dwindling word counts and
encouraged by editors eager to sell papers) have adopted a hit/

flop mentality, and shunned deeper engagement with the art form, turning reviews into consumer guides (see this, don't see that). "Critics see their role as of consumer reporters giving thumbs up or thumbs down to the future of something, instead of thinking critically about the strengths and weaknesses of a play, or the future of the particular writer, even in face of imperfection."

The good news: It may not matter in the long run, at least at the box office. Playwrights and some artistic directors agree that word of mouth remains the best marketing tool. "Audiences have stopped reading the paper," one celebrated playwright observes. "Excitement about cultural experience passes by word of mouth. What the audience buys tickets for is what somebody else told them they really loved." The head of an Off-Off-Broadway experimental theatre concurs: "Audiences will respond to the personal. If you do one-on-one solicitations that come from someone they know about something they saw, they really care about that." The challenge and opportunity for theatres, then, is to harness the power of new media to leverage that word of mouth.

Some writers and theatres are successfully using the Internet to promote their work, develop fan bases, create community, and stoke dialogue about productions. But while the accessibility of the Internet hurries the spread of individual voices, its speed has a downside, too. "People post reviews of readings, of dress rehearsals, of new plays at my theatre," an Off-Broadway artistic director complains. This affects "a lot of young playwrights, and not-so-young playwrights." The Internet may not make everyone a critic, but it gives every self-anointed critic a forum, exposing playwrights to the opinions of "anonymous fools" the minute their work sees the light of day. A literary agent strikes the same note. "The playwrights read them, and it affects them. A play's in previews and you call your clients and hear it in their voices. The playwrights don't listen to the subscribers, yet they'll listen to some little fifteen-year-old queen who doesn't know anything."

As print criticism loses its power, still, as we've seen, reviews published in New York, particularly in the *New York*

Times, can affect the whole field. A *Times* rave can set theatres across the country scrambling for rights to the same play. More problematically, a pan from that paper can, it is widely agreed, kill a play's chance for continued life outside of Manhattan. "Even among self-identified new-play producers who are into sharing and finding new work of emerging writers, several are just as influenced as anyone else by what the critics here in New York say," one playwright, speaking for most, contends.

Faced with hostile and diffuse criticism, theatres scramble to inoculate themselves, to reach and teach audiences otherwise. "I want, as much as possible, to have a critic-proof theatre," an Off-Broadway artistic director explains. "I never say, 'Come where the hits are.' I try to flatter my audience for having taste and being adventurous, reaching out to them, branding what we are, and then trying to get a little bit of a developmental and track record history."

Audience or Community

> *The fundamental artistic impulse is to express something to a body of people, to a community. And we are living in a moment where so much needs to be expressed.* —ARTISTIC DIRECTOR

The words "audience" and "community" echo, often interchangeably, in conversations throughout the theatre. In twenty-first-century parlance, "ticket buyers," "theatregoers," "patrons," "subscribers," and just plain "butts in seats" are all part of the grander "community" that artists crave and theatre leaders pride themselves in cultivating and speaking to. Communal activity lies at the heart of theatre. As one writer put it, a two-way, ongoing dialogue over time is the ideal. "Hopefully the theatre is where we can come together and have a dialogue and a relationship back and forth. It's not just sitting in the velvet chairs and watching something."

There are, of course, many overlapping definitions of

"community." The word is used to describe local audiences, civic affiliations, fellowships of artists, affinities of shared interest, the regional/national theatre scene, and specific cultural groups—to name just a few. When artistic leaders complain that playwrights don't write for their audiences, they are, to some extent, questioning those writers' idea of community. "Do playwrights have communities?" one artistic director inquires. "I mean, are they living in communities that they're writing about, from, to? Or are they into artistic enclaves, writing about each other?" How, she asks, along with many others, can theatres create deeper engagement between playwrights and particular communities?

Turned around—Do theatres have communities?—the question seems self-evident. The regional/resident theatre movement has traditionally emphasized ties to locally based audiences, artists, and cultural institutions. Many theatre towns take pride when productions are locally acted, directed, and designed. Furthermore, artistic directors are almost always immersed in their communities, and, in theory, become more deeply connected so over time. "I seem to have a feel for who they are," says one artistic director. "Many of them are my neighbors." For most artistic directors, this deep knowledge of the community is part of the job description.

> There are two things artistic directors have to know how
> to do. One is to read plays, and the other is, over time, to
> internalize their audiences in ways they like and don't like.
> Your audience gets inside your skin in ways you don't want
> them to, but in other ways that are good for you.

Playwrights in the regional theatre, however, are more akin to migrant laborers, traveling from city to city when their work is staged. How can you form communal bonds and a shared sense of place if you are always on the move? Some artistic directors complain that playwrights and their plays are "too New York"; playwrights, meanwhile, the large majority of whom live in New

York and, secondarily, Los Angeles, often regret that they do not get the opportunity to get to know specific theatres' audiences. Many long for true residencies that would allow them to develop the kind of familiarity with a community that staff artists feel they have.

Many theatres view this kind of community bonding as an important step in developing successful long-term relationships (and producible commissions). For some companies, fostering intimacy or, at least, acquaintance, between playwright and community is standard operating procedure. A West Coast artistic director begins his work with new writers by inviting them to experience the theatre's community first hand. "If there is a young writer that we've commissioned, often we'll bring them in to get the sense of the audience and network with other people. They will get to know what [our area] is like, what the building's like." Similarly, a literary manager from a large midwestern theatre calls for "more opportunities to engage playwrights in the community of the theatre, so they actually have some knowledge of who they're trying to talk to, particularly when we're building commissioning programs." The way to do this, she believes, is by "developing long-term relationships between playwrights and theatres, which is the only way you can get to know an audience. Over a period of time, sit with them and see how they respond to things."

Playwrights aren't the only ones who benefit from residencies. The equation works both ways. Nor are they the only ones who desire them. Many artistic directors believe in the value of true residencies. The playwright's exposure to the community, they believe, benefits the audience, and ultimately encourages the shared communal experience one artistic director likens to being "a family together."

> The closer the playwright can get to the audience, the more you can move away from selling just product and commodity, as opposed to a joint venture. The more we can talk to the audience, the more a playwright can talk to the audience, the

more successful the new work tends to be. I don't think that's any great piece of revolutionary observation. It has to do with people sharing the journey together.

This emphasis on community can even change the standards of play selection. For some a play's merit may have as much to do with how it communicates to a specific community as with other aesthetic concerns, as this artistic director says.

> I need to really engage the community. When I think
> about what we do, it's not always the plays that I admire
> the most that we do, but it's the plays that will speak to our
> community. Sometimes they're not necessarily the plays they
> want to see. Ultimately we do plays that sometimes are not
> necessarily the best, the plays that we most passionately want
> to do, but they're the plays that we feel most passionately our
> community needs to hear.

This shift of focus from the traditional assumption that plays are chosen for their artistic quality raises potent questions. To what extent is programming guided by artistic merit, by the needs of the community, or by the personal tastes of the artistic head? To what extent, in the theatre, should a play's merit be determined by an artistic director's perception of its ability to speak to, respond to, challenge, or anticipate the needs of a community? How do these community imperatives jive with the insistence of most artistic directors that they only pick plays they love?

Furthermore, to what extent is community portable? If a playwright feels a deep connection with the audience and place of a particular theatre, and if she or he writes a play informed by that affinity, will the play be of less interest to other theatres, or more? Undoubtedly, playwrights are in a bind. They are expected to speak to general audiences and specific communities at the same time, all with little sustained access to these very communities.

Audience Education

> *What we really haven't developed is our audience, on a long-term, fundamental and important basis—to celebrate, engage and collaborate in the ongoing growth of the indigenous American theatre. That's the most important step that we can take locally and internationally. Audience development is the next big movement that we're all ignoring. It has to do with an ongoing conversation with our audience base, our constituency, listening to what they find interesting and are compelled by, and then pushing them, bringing them close toward the artists. That's massive.* —ARTISTIC DIRECTOR

The development and production of new work generates real excitement within the field. Unfortunately, audiences don't, on the whole, share that enthusiasm. As a result, theatres struggle to fill houses when the plays and artists on their stages are unknown quantities. They struggle, too, with how to sell the *enterprise* itself, how to market the new. "Where is the audience for new work?" a literary manager asks. "How do we get them to come to all of the theatres to see new work *because* it's new work?"

Playwrights and artistic leaders advocate a proactive approach toward audience-building: creating more interest in new work by teaching audiences about the formal vocabulary writers employ; exploring the process of new-work development itself; and encouraging audience members investment in early stages of the process, so that they can serve as ambassadors or docents for the work within their communities.

Many theatres make some attempt to use the process of new-play development itself to educate their audiences about and generate interest in new plays and new work in general. "Invite the audience in. Make your work juicy. Get excited about getting dirty," a playwright advises. "Make an evening where the audience could come see a rehearsal. See how a play starts. Give them a taste not for the finished product, but for the excitement of how it gets there." Many writers echo this sentiment, urging theatres to open up the process. That way, audiences will be more interested in not only the finished play, but also the project of developing new work. Instead of conventional pre- or post-performance discussions, some suggest, use the time to invite the audience to understand what has happened. What changes did the writer make? How is the work evolving?

"The more people feel involved and part of the context," a literary manager explains, "the more enfranchised they'll be in the theatre and the more they'll come back." To that end, theatres invite selected patrons to a rehearsal or special presentation, or to readings and workshops of work under development. The motives for these invitations, though, are often mixed. Rewarding key donors with an insider's view or creating a perk for subscribers isn't the same as audience education. Such programs don't always serve the process, or the playwright.

Intertwining new-play development with audience development entails a careful negotiation of potential missteps. Giving audiences access to the process and also a voice in the development of a play are two very different things. Similarly, making the audience comfortable isn't always the best recipe for making the artist feel safe. While it may be in everyone's best interest to create active rather than passive audiences, playwrights need to be able to work on plays without being exposed to audience criticism before the work is ready.

Playwrights' concerns about tying audience development to new-play development are serious ones. Reading series, especially those featuring plays that have already been produced elsewhere, raise the most suspicion. They are seen, as one playwright puts it, as exercises "in compliance to the grant language of outreach." Again, clarity of purpose is key: who is the process for? While playwrights need audiences to test and understand their plays, they don't need audiences to tell them—in words—what's working or not and how to fix it. Audience development or cultivation passed off as artist-centered development harms both, alienating writers, showing audience "false" process, and training theatregoers that they somehow share in the authorship of the play, that their comments and feedback is part of the process. For playwrights, it is not.

> Theatres want the audiences to feel like they're participating in creating this work. It comes back to this idea that the playwright needs help, and the play is broken. That's the only avenue available to audiences to discuss the work, by telling you, "I did like this, but I didn't really understand why you did it this way," or, "They should make up at the end."

Some artistic directors understand this; most say they do. A frequent refrain: make sure the process fits the play. "To have these readings for audience development, that's very dangerous," an artistic director/playwright warns, adding the bottom line is whether the process helps the art. An Off-Broadway artistic director outlines the debate within his institution, and some pitfalls to avoid.

> We wanted to create more perks for patrons and special subscribers, and there's been this ongoing negotiation between literary and those departments. If a reading doesn't go well, if it's not cast right, I don't give a shit, I learned something about it. I've read the play and can reassure the writer that I heard it anyway, and it's instructive to know what the traps are. The unwashed or the unschooled, they may think, "Well, that was stinky." Or quite the opposite: You may do a reading of something that's pretty interesting; Marion Seldes is in it, and then they go ape shit and they ask if you're producing it. It's tricky.

A FORMAL EDUCATION

A common argument among playwrights goes like this: the conservatism of our contemporary theatre, in effect, moves the theatre backward by standing still. The more complacent or static the theatre, the wider the chasm between younger, pioneering voices and the theatrical expectations of audiences. Unless the field can collectively address the shrinking of audiences while at the same time expanding their palette for the untried and unconventional, the gulf will only widen.

There are many factors behind this gulf between audiences and adventuresome writers. The graying audience is one, and ticket prices that make theatre less accessible to audiences of the same generation as so many playwrights, is another. A third factor is a general decline of arts education, as one artistic director points out. "Now we're into a second generation where arts education in schools only happens when communities gather together and put special funds in place," to counteract abdication by the public sector. The consequences of this lack of access and orientation to the arts are profound, some argue, and may contribute to the still-birth of a future audience. One playwright, who also runs a small theatre in New York, blames the "poverty of dialogue about theatre" in this country.

> There's no one to say this is Harold Pinter, so you have to take it seriously whether you want to or not; or there isn't enough dialogue for that to be said about more than one playwright per decade—Tony Kushner ten years ago I suppose, today it could be Sarah Ruhl—for someone to say, this is the most important thing happening in our field, so you have to get serious even if you don't like it. There's no constant flow of dialogue between intelligent people, the way you can find in the *New York Times Book Review*.

This poverty of dialogue about the new is a rallying cry for numerous writers, several of whom cite an essay by playwright Jeffrey M. Jones that appeared in *American Theatre* magazine (October 2003) as showing a way forward. Jones's "Thinking About Writing About Thinking About New Plays," something of a touchstone text for many playwrights, came up in several meetings across the country. The crisis in new-play production is not a dearth of quality plays, Jones argues. "Playwriting, it turns out, is in fine shape," with both new plays and "theatrical experiment" thriving. The problem, he posits, is a failure of education: We do not equip audiences to embrace adventurous new work.

Jones takes the field as a whole to task for failing to create a context in which theatregoers understand and appreciate works that do not conform to a set of frozen formal assumptions that theatre practitioners have long since abandoned.

> You do a risky play...; you have a critic who understands and loves the play for what it is; and then your audience comes and hates it for the very thing it is. If this is what necessarily happens—and I believe most theatre practitioners in our country have this expectation, born alas of painful experience—then why bother?

He continues:

> Does this mean, then, that the great bold dream of the nonprofit movement—of revitalizing an art-form by expanding the definition of what's possible—stands now revealed, some forty years on, as a snare and a delusion? Is it in fact the case that theatre is so locked into a set of expectations—about what a play is, about what audiences want—that it is effectively paralyzed?

As in any art form, Jones writes, the theatre establishes normative conventions, "thresholds," beyond which only a few people are willing to be led. Because the field as a whole embraces the new "so incrementally as to make it imperceptible and marginal and irrelevant," he writes, the field as a whole is "profoundly and inherently conservative." As a result, we either abandon our audiences to their own tastes, and wonder why they come to feel hostile toward new work, or we disingenuously try to convince them that difficult work is "accessible," when it actually may not be. As a third option, theatres skip the challenging fare because they predict the audience will resist it—a self-fulfilling prophecy. Jones writes,

> . . . the problem of theatre isn't that audiences will only go so far; but that over time, and despite forty years of effort, they still seem unwilling to go anywhere except where they have gone before. And this, rightly, is recognized by theatres and artists as a paralyzing condition which is bad for all concerned, especially theatres and artists, even if a preponderance of those theatres and artists are—at any given time—quite happy in the mainstream.

Unless the field reframes the question, he concludes, we will remain paralyzed.

By contrast, twentieth-century painting has successfully brought along its audiences. Five or six decades ago, modern art was routinely the butt of jokes. Now, Jones writes, "Wander into any blockbuster modernist exhibit, and you will find little old gray-haired ladies going through the galleries, nattering on about 'the flatness of the picture-plane.'" This came about, he asserts, through a concerted effort on the part of the visual art community to educate their audiences, and to provide a context for the work. This shared vocabulary consists not just of the paintings themselves, but also of a "core set of terms and concepts by which the 'difficult' stuff could be discussed and understood." Museums issue massive catalogues associated with exhibitions, filled with accessible essays explaining the work.

> The catalogue does its essential work merely by existing. The catalogue stands as a sentinel; its mere existence demonstrating that the work-at-hand cannot simply be dismissed. The catalogue raises the bar of the discourse; it

sets the tone and chooses the weaponry. One cannot impugn (let alone dismiss) the art on the walls without going through the catalogue, and the catalogue gives no quarter. The catalogue does not even pretend to be easy or simple. The catalogue merely insists that you must respond, if you dare, on its own terms.

We do nothing similar in theatre, Jones argues. We need to provide the audience the tools to "get" the work. We need to equip our audiences not just to understand a spectrum of theatrical experimentation, but with the means to experience the "pleasure compounded both of enjoying the show on its own terms and feeling the self-congratulation which comes of 'getting' something you've been told is 'hard' and 'difficult.'"

Jones's prescription: Theatre institutions should act like art museums; they "must accept that the presentation of new plays is Smart Fun, and be prepared to promote it accordingly." Don't dumb down expectations. Audience members must be able to access the tools to give them enough confidence to face experimental work "with the expectation that they would understand and recognize what the artists were doing." It might take just a brief orientation beforehand. Or a more elaborate approach: Before spending money on production, he urges, "a theatre devoted to new work should spend enough to commission serious and substantive critical essays by smart, literate thinkers, and these essays should all be published in a big fat catalogue called the Program, and every effort should be made to get this fifty-page booklet into the hands of anyone who buys a ticket—if they don't, in fact, get the thing in the mail beforehand."

Will it work? Many playwrights think it can only help. "Can audiences actually be guided into enjoying something? How strenuous is the educational process? It probably isn't very, in a lot of cases," one writer muses. Another concurs, believing that a more open audience will lead to a more adventurous profession.

That's the level on which audiences need to be cultivated, not "I liked it, I didn't like it; I get it, I don't get it, what if you did this instead." Rather, to experience it more holistically, to experience it formally as well as what it's about. Form and style is something that audiences don't know how to look for. They could get a lot out of it if they knew how to look at a play on the level of form and style, as opposed to solely content. If audiences were willing and able and open to experiencing that way, theatres would be more willing, open and able to present work that is formally daring as well as content-daring.

Some companies have taken the bull by the horns. The *Lincoln Center Theater Review* in New York, which collects writing related to its plays by writers in and out of the theatre, is, for some, an exemplary tool for audiences. Steppenwolf Theatre Company in Chicago, too, has provoked admiration for the materials it offers theatregoers. An East Coast artistic director explains:

You see a show at Steppenwolf, there is a tome by [artistic director] Martha Lavey facing the title page. It's got a sense of academic substance to it, and then as you go to the back of the book there are two different articles about the playwright, interviews, layers and layers of dramaturgical material. Martha has built the image of Steppenwolf around their company members, but also around the sense of intellectual engagement, and that's what allows her to feel comfortable doing plays that are weird, strange, not necessarily that well formed.

In addition to these individual efforts, theatres may have to work together to make such "climate" changes happen. "How do we work together to build an audience," one literary manager asks, "as opposed to each trying to build it on our own, which is so frustrating?"

National Conversation

How do we become more relevant to audiences is the question I keep coming back to in one way, shape, or form or another. And I have no answer. —ARTISTIC DIRECTOR

This study grows out of concern for the future of new plays and fear that pathways to production are being blocked. These anxieties, though, cover a deeper one: That the theatre, specifically American plays and playwrights, has lost its voice within our ongoing cultural conversation. We've worried the economics, practices, and perceptions of production, but, under it all, we're thinking about *impact.*

In other words, the biggest challenge facing writers and theatres dedicated to producing new plays may be what one widely produced playwright calls "the place that theatre stands in the larger culture." It's rare to find a writer or artistic director who doesn't share his view. "We've been completely marginalized. We're out of the national conversation." As we scan the past for examples of playwrights connected to specific theatres and their communities, we remember, too, when playwrights graced the covers of *Time* and *Newsweek* or made regular appearances on op-ed pages or in articles about the state of the nation and beyond. There is little evidence today that dramatists are considered spokespeople for anything other than their own work. The entire field wrestles with its own irrelevance.

Is this a problem of plays, producing, or audience? Is there some larger cultural current waiting to be tapped? One director suggests the latter:

> We are, in fact, generating more arti
> of craft than we have been for a long
> theatres are producing new works tha
> in my consciousness. I think there is a
> The issue seems to be, how can that ti

consciousness in a way that people will no longer say, "Oh, well, there's a dearth of new plays."

Each play is one part of a larger conversation. Therefore, the question remains, how does the American theatre create the context for that conversation, for the dialogue in which each play and each audience takes part? This national conversation takes place between playwrights and theatres and audiences. It comprises thousands of simultaneous conversations at hundreds of theatres across the country. It is ongoing, and it begins now.

SIX

Positive Practices
and Novel Ideas

THERE IS no one solution to the issues raised in these pages. The divisions, economics, and obstacles are real, as is the loss of connection to audience and the general culture. These barriers tend to overwhelm another reality: an abundance of new-play activity nationwide. In this widespread, generative activity, playwrights and artistic directors alike find examples of people and theatres that "got it right." Admittedly, these encouraging examples carry less weight than the pervasive problems. Still, writers describe theatres from which they've received long-term support and commitment. They commend organizations and individuals who shepherd plays to production with creativity, sensitivity, and fervor. Artistic directors identify funders who, by regularly rethinking their grant-making assumptions, respond to the field, and influence it for the better. Artists, inside theatres and out, tell stories of deep community involvement, institutional collaborations—greater than the sum of their parts—and journeys to production that satisfied the writer, theatre, and audience alike.

If there is no single way over the many hurdles facing playwrights and new-play producers, there is also no magic bullet for the overarching problem: cost. The expenses associated with new-play development and production are out of control and growing. Without more extensive subsidy in this country, nonprofits will have to treat the symptoms of a basically untenable situation as creatively as they can, without being able to treat its source. As one economist, who served as an advisor to this study, puts it, "…surely it does not take an economist to recognize that lack of money is a good part of the root of the evils investigated."

In place of solutions, then, there are numerous ideas, practices, models, and attempts, instances of problems addressed with passion and imagination. We've gathered a handful of these examples here—some as case studies, brief or detailed, some as anecdotes or experiences remembered. These examples are in no way comprehensive. We don't presume that they are "best practices," in the sense of "the best." Inevitably, they would have different results in different settings. Rather, they represent practices that are working well or that epitomize productive thinking to colleagues throughout the field. They illustrate things done well at a certain place and time, with a certain cast of characters. Our hope, of course, is that these positive practices will point the way to others.

The ideas and practices discussed below fall into the following categories:

- theatres that forge strong relationships with playwrights, and how they do it;
- playwright residencies;
- community support for playwrights: local collaborations between theatres;
- community support for playwrights: collaboration between theatres and developmental labs across size, mission, and place;
- community support for playwrights: the power of multiple productions and the advantages of avoiding commercial production;
- combating "premiere-itis" through producing networks;
- successful audience education around new work.

These categories of attack are hardly exhaustive. For every obstacle described in this study, there are writers and theatres exploring ways to overcome it. Here are some of them.

Playwrights and Theatres: Relationships That Work

The heads of individual theatres tend to view large institutions as leaders in the field of new-play production. Playwrights, on the other hand, point more often to the support offered by smaller companies. In conversation, too, playwrights asked to recall positive experiences usually invoke the names of small theatres. The purpose of this chapter is to focus on the positive examples, but first, it may be informative to tease out the perceptual disparity about large and small, and the way leadership in the field is tallied.

We asked theatres to define their own place in the new-play ecosystem, and we asked them to list three theatres that have "the greatest impact on the development of new plays in this country." In a pool of theatres stacked toward those who focus on new work, of the ninety-four theatres surveyed, **79 percent rank themselves as "a major contributor" (21 percent) or "a leader" (58 percent) in new-play activity locally and 49 percent rank themselves as a major contributor (26 percent) or leader (23 percent) nationally.** Collectively, heads of theatres identified eighteen organizations as national leaders, those having the greatest impact on the field. Theatres were ranked by the frequency of their inclusion (see Figure 6.1).

With the notable exceptions of Woolly Mammoth Theatre, Victory Gardens Theater, and Childsplay, the organizations most frequently singled out by theatres as leaders are either larger theatres—twelve of eighteen are in the Theatre Communications Group's highest budget group (six) with annual budgets of $10 million or more, or they are based in New York City.

We posed a different question to playwrights to get at the notion of leadership among theatres that produce new plays. They were asked to list the five theatres that produced the most of their plays, starting with the theatre that had produced the greatest number. By this measure, their leadership tally—based

THEATRE	RANK (OF 9)	FREQUENCY
Actors Theatre of Louisville	1	34
South Coast Repertory	2	28
Playwrights Horizons	3	19
Manhattan Theatre Club	4	17
The Public Theater	5	15
Mark Taper Forum	6	8
New York Theatre Workshop	7	5
The Children's Theatre Company	7	5
Steppenwolf Theatre Company	7	5
The Goodman Theatre	7	5
Woolly Mammoth Theatre Company	8	4
Guthrie Theater	8	4
Childsplay	8	4
New Dramatists	8	4
Arena Stage	9	3
Primary Stages	9	3
Victory Gardens Theater	9	3
Seattle Children's Theatre	9	3

6.1 ORGANIZATIONS SINGLED OUT AS LEADERS (BY THEATRES)

on experience, not perception—both overlaps and diverges from the more subjective assessment of the theatres (see Figure 6.2). Actors Theatre of Louisville stands at the top of both lists. The Joseph Papp Public Theater/NYSF, South Coast Repertory, Playwrights Horizons, and the Mark Taper Forum also appear on both. But a whole other category of theatres appears, those important to the lives of playwrights, because of their accessibility and active dedication to producing new plays, but not deemed

THEATRE	RANK (TOP 5)	FREQ.	% OF TOTAL
Actors Theater of Louisville	1	22	2.6%
Ensemble Studio Theater	2	18	2.2%
The Joseph Papp Public Theater / NYSF	3	14	1.7%
South Coast Repertory	4	10	1.2%
New Georges	4	10	1.2%
Playwrights Horizons	4	10	1.2%
Mark Taper Forum	4	10	1.2%
Soho Rep	4	10	1.2%
Women's Project & Productions	5	9	1.1%
HERE Arts Theater	5	9	1.1%

6.2 THEATRES PRODUCING THE LARGEST NUMBER OF STUDY PLAYWRIGHTS' PLAYS

influential by other theatres. The theatres that are absent from the theatres' lists but appear most frequently on writers'—all New York–based, all small, with annual budgets well under $2 million—are the Ensemble Studio Theatre, New Georges, Soho Rep, Women's Project, and HERE Arts Center.

All told, playwrights named 454 different theatres. Outside of the leadership theatres named in the theatre survey, playwrights listed the following theatres as having produced most of their plays. (These companies were named more than once and as many as four times, in lists of theatres producing the second, third, fourth or fifth most of the writers' plays.) While there are large institutional theatres on the list (Yale Repertory Theatre, Seattle Repertory, Alliance Theatre, and CenterStage), the vast majority are companies with intimate staffs and undersized budgets.

Lonny Chapman Group Repertory Theatre (L.A.)

Flea Theater (NYC)

Yale Repertory Theatre (New Haven, CT)

Clubbed Thumb (NYC)

Vital Theatre Company (NYC)

Actor's Express Theatre Company (Atlanta)

7 Stages Theatre (Atlanta)

New Theatre (Coral Gables, FL)

Berkeley Repertory Theatre

Mill Mountain Theatre (Roanoke, VA)

Theater for the New City (NYC)

InterAct Theatre Company (Philadelphia)

78th Street Theatre Lab (NYC)

The American Place Theatre (NYC)

Love Creek Theatre (NYC)

Red Eye Collaboration (Minneapolis)

Theatre Limina (Minneapolis)

Theatre of NOTE (L.A.)

Magic Theatre (San Francisco)

Alliance Theatre (Atlanta)

Salvage Vanguard Theater (Austin, TX)

City Theatre (Pittsburgh)

Centerstage (Baltimore)

Mixed Blood Theatre (Minneapolis)

Borderlands Theatre (Tucson)

Northwest Asian American Theatre (Seattle)

Intersection for the Arts (San Francisco)

Kitchen Dog Theater (Dallas)

Curious Theatre Company (Denver)

Vineyard Theatre (NYC)

Blue Heron Arts Center (NYC)

The Road Theatre Company (L.A.)

6.3 OTHER THEATRES LISTED BY PLAYWRIGHTS AS PRODUCING LARGE NUMBERS OF THEIR PLAYS

This method of inquiry—theatres that produced the greatest number of a writer's plays—clearly favors theatres that produce playwrights more than once. In the context of our study, though, this is key. We are in search of deep and lasting support for writers and new plays, the kind of support that takes place over artistic careers and feeds bodies of work and, therefore, an evolving national canon.*

In conversation, as in our survey, playwrights single out scrappy theatres, including some that are defunct. Here are a few representative examples. One author hails certain small theatres for their unique ability and willingness to take risks on innovative work. She mentions the late and lamented **Frontera Theater** of Austin, Texas: "They would pick plays that had never been done before, experimental work, tiny little theatre, beautiful installation artists to do the sets, great people to come in and do lights.

---

*A few omissions are worth speculation. On the theatres' list of eighteen leaders, three devote themselves to work for young audiences: Children's Theatre Company in Minneapolis, Childsplay in Tempe, Arizona, and Seattle Children's Theatre. Is it possible that playwrights somehow define their work for children out of the category of serious playwriting, while theatres don't? Of the 250 playwrights surveyed many write for young audiences, but it could be that our outreach efforts missed some of those for whom this work makes up the heart of their efforts. A fourth omission, New York's New Dramatists, a playwright laboratory and service organization, while cited by theatres as a leader, does not produce and, so, along with other similar organizations frequently singled out by playwrights as important to their work and careers—the Playwrights' Center in Minneapolis, Sundance (with multiple homes in California, Utah, Wyoming, and Florida), and the Eugene O'Neill Memorial Theatre Center, Connecticut, among others—does not qualify for listing by playwrights. Other omissions are harder to account for. Among perceived leaders that fall off the playwrights' lists are the Manhattan Theatre Club, the Guthrie, Primary Stages, Victory Gardens, and Woolly Mammoth. The disappearance of two of these, Chicago's Victory Gardens and D.C.'s Woolly Mammoth, is particularly hard to explain: Victory Gardens has one of the only, if not *the* only, long-term playwright companies in the country and both theatres have actively committed to mounting second and third productions of works that premiered elsewhere, in addition to premiering several works each season.

Everyone was fearless, that's what made it fabulous." This same playwright also describes **Pillsbury House Theatre** in Minneapolis as "a place where people do really good work and take a lot of chances, they do new plays and they don't have an enormous budget, but they put in every single piece of sweat and tears."

Another playwright remembers her NEA/TCG Playwrights' Residency with **Infernal Bridegroom Productions** in Houston, underlining the extent of their commitment to her, and the speed at which they brought her work to the stage. She began a play in the summer, and it was scheduled for production in the fall. "I had written ten pages, and they're like, 'We're going to do the play.' Great! We kept writing and workshopping…. I wrote it specifically for their actors…. I was in the space." It was an "extraordinary and sometimes startling experience." Sadly, a year later, this struggling avant-garde company also closed its doors, due to insurmountable financial difficulties.

The New York City–based **13P (Thirteen Playwrights, Inc.)** is often cited. This collection of thirteen midcareer playwrights has come together for as long as it will take to produce one work by each of them. Each writer serves as artistic director for his or her own project, selects what will be produced, decides on the goals of the project, designs its process, and chooses the collaborators. Cited as a model for empowering playwrights, the company's log line is a cheeky retort to the field, "We don't develop plays. (We do them.)"

Local artists praise **Campo Santo** in San Francisco, which one writer calls "a little theatre I adore." "They don't do a play that they haven't initiated, that isn't written specifically for them," says a neighboring artistic director. "It's deeply community-centered and oriented. Their process is so open and caring and gentle, and their relationships with writers are so strong. They basically told [one writer] they'll do anything that he writes, and that's included something like five plays in seven years. He always knows he has a place to go."

Some theatres are lauded as much for the bonds they forge with audiences, as for their support of artists. The **Contemporary**

American Theater Festival in Shepherdstown, W.V., is one such organization. In separate discussions, a writer and an artistic director applaud the work of artistic director Ed Herendeen, for cultivating among his theatregoers a genuine interest in exploring dramatic form, especially in challenging work. The playwright marvels at the degree of investment this small theatre inspires from its semirural community. "He's a P. T. Barnum out in West Virginia. [Herendeen] has completely educated his audience. They're so excited that he is bringing in brand-new plays, and that they can now identify themselves as this breeding ground for new plays. He's also educated his board that he's going to pick something he loves. Don't question it. He would take a bullet for any of those four plays that he chooses. He believes in them so strongly and it's contagious. They may hate [his choices], but they love arguing them with him at the bakery, and saying, 'That was a piece of crap.'"

Several writers speak enthusiastically about the fusion of audience engagement and writer sensitivity at the Los Angeles–based **Cornerstone Theater Company**. This ensemble brings playwrights into specific communities or geographical areas (originally across the country and now primarily in greater Los Angeles), where they create work based on input from the local residents. The work is eventually performed with and for the community, in collaboration with a professional acting ensemble. As part of its mission, the company endeavors both to meet the needs of its audience/collaborators and to protect the integrity of the writer's vision. Many extol Cornerstone's success at creating direct connections between writers and their audiences, through deep and long engagement in the partner communities. Others emphasize the theatre's relationship with writers. This way of working can be extremely rewarding, one writer confesses, but it requires a great deal of discipline and self-confidence, as the theatre links up with a range of nontheatrical organizations, each with its own concerns, values, and vocabulary.

It helps to know from the beginning that though the play you are writing will be fully staged, one playwright acknowledges, even though the commission will only be produced once. It helps, too, to move swiftly toward production. "It was nine months from being hired to the opening night, starting from scratch," this writer notes. Elsewhere, another, more typical project, took nine years. "Everything that happened in those nine years actually happened in nine months" at Cornerstone. Because the company is an ensemble, he enthuses, "you're dealing with people who have been together for, I don't know, 15 years. They have a shorthand. That was amazing and beautiful for me."

Different contexts provide different artistic satisfactions. Several playwrights describe the experience of working in the **theatre for young audiences.** As one L.A.-based writer explains, "I have had a wonderful experience of being able to go from creation to production to publication that's been very smooth and has taken less than a year." For another writer her work with the Minneapolis-based Children's Theatre Company in a developmental partnership ("Playground") with New Dramatists in New York, enabled her to write for a size of theatre and level of technical accomplishment beyond her previous experience. "I had seen plays in their theatre; I knew the kind of production values they could handle. I wrote specifically for that situation." Still, she says, it took four years of development "and rewriting the play to very specific producer notes" to get the work onstage.

Developmental laboratories occupy a unique place in the new-play universe. They open up time for writers and, often, renew their sense of ownership over their own process and material. This praise for PlayLabs at the **Playwrights' Center** in Minneapolis is typical of the devotion inspired by such organizations:

> The Playwrights' Center doesn't produce plays, so there's none of that shopping aspect. You know what you're getting into. The mission is to develop plays, to help you achieve what you want, and really work on the play. I got to hear the play for the first time when I had readings of it. You get two weeks of rehearsal. It was the first reading I've ever had that did not feel under-rehearsed. There's a real audience in

Minneapolis that comes to Playwrights' Center events. It's
fiercely loyal, and they will come and see anything. That gives
[the Center] license to do things that are a little bit crazier.

Collaborations between these labs and producing theatres
also earn praise from writers and artistic leaders, as do opportunities
for mentorship. One playwright speaks admiringly of **Native
Voices** in Los Angeles, which provides avenues for Native American playwrights to enter the field without an Ivy League (or an
MFA) background, by pairing new writers with professionals in
the field who could become their mentors. Others mention the
Cherry Lane Theatre's Mentor Project in New York City, which
also pairs younger writers with experienced colleagues.

Among the heads of theatres, **South Coast Repertory**
in Costa Mesa, California, is held in particularly high esteem.
SCR has, over three decades, sustained an exemplary multiphase
new-play development and production process. SCR's enduring
commitment and its dedicated funding—a large endowment
specifically designed to support these efforts—is a field model,
though not one that has been emulated in any discernable way.
An artistic director colleague of that theatre explains the rare
"kind of commitment institutionally that is made by South
Coast Repertory to new writing."

> There's an endowment that funds commissions. There is
> money every year in the budget for play development. If
> they don't sell tickets, it's still there. There is an institutional
> commitment to play development that is twenty-five years
> old at that theatre, and an audience was built to support it.
> I don't think there's a six-month solution to this stuff. It is
> clear not every theatre does this. Most don't. If they're having
> marketing problems, one of the first things to go is money
> that was spent on play development. Money solves a lot of
> problems in play development. If you can commission a
> dozen plays every year, as South Coast has been doing, a lot
> of them are going to turn out.

IN RESIDENCE: JAMES STILL AND THE INDIANA REP

This study began with images of writers—Chekhov, Odets, Brecht—who became synonymous with the companies—the Moscow Art Theatre, the Group Theatre, the Berliner Ensemble—to which they gave voice. How can contemporary theatres deepen their artistic connection with playwrights? How can they foster stronger relationships between writers and audiences, between artist and community? Are such relationships still possible or desirable? Is it possible to make and keep a home for a playwright? Is there an ideal residency—one that matches writer to company, to audience, to place? These questions run under this report, so we were delighted when *American Theatre* published a portrait of a successful, sustained relationship between theatre and writer.

An article by Eric R. Pfeffinger in the magazine's October 2008 issue came shortly after Indiana Repertory Theatre (IRT) produced two plays by James Still (neither of them a premiere) in commemoration of the writer's tenth year as a playwright-in-residence at the company. IRT ended its 2008–09 season by premiering Still's *Interpreting William*, which was commissioned by the theatre. That marked the ninth production of Still's residency.

In Pfeffinger's telling, the secret to the success of this long-standing collaboration lies in several areas. First, Still "plunged deeply into the day-to-day concerns of the theatre" while avoiding the situation of other writers who never quite feel they belong in the theatre's workspace. Free of responsibilities, they find themselves without relevance. From artistic director Janet Allen's point of view, Still is a key member of the artistic staff. "I don't remember when it was that staff and board members started asking, 'What does James think of this?' but it happened." What makes this all the more surprising is that Still does not live in Indiana. He travels to the theatre each month from his home in California to attend board meetings, see all of IRT's productions, and participate in various IRT programs. He also directs other writers' plays at IRT once a season or so. The ideal insider-outsider, according to

Allen, "His biggest value, apart from his core artistic abilities, was that he had distance." As Pfeffinger points out, Still depends on the theatre for neither his income, nor even his health insurance.

Second, there is no "James Still slot" in the theatre's season. Instead there is clarity about what IRT expects from Still and vice versa. Says Allen, "We place commissions with other writers....There is no presumption that we're going to produce everything James writes, or that everything new we produce will be James's." In fact, he has continued to attract productions and receive commissions elsewhere. In our correspondence with Still after the article, he elaborates:

> I never expect Janet and the IRT to produce everything I write. However, and this is key to my own evolving artistic courage, I do expect Janet and the IRT to be interested in everything I write, to be curious about it, to want to consider it. I don't have to wonder whether or not Janet will read something I write.

Third, there was no pre-set model for the residency. It has evolved to suit the specific needs of both artist and institution, with both parties willing to adapt the residency as necessary. "From the beginning we've treated my residency like a living, breathing thing," he explains,

> capable of change, capable of surprise, and capable of challenges.... There is a definite commitment between us (and I feel that from Janet, Steven [Stolen, managing director], the staff, the Board, and the audience)—but there is also the understanding that we must be flexible, that both sides must be flexible. I sit down with myself on a regular basis and ask myself if this is still working—not because I fear it isn't, but because I never want to take it for granted or treat it like a habit or an obligation.

The residency began in 1998, and it came at a propitious moment for Still. At that time he had drifted primarily into writing for television and film. IRT had previously produced several of Still's plays, and so the theatre and Still applied for a two-year TCG National Theatre Artist Residency Program grant, funded by the Pew Charitable Trusts. The grant came through and was subsequently renewed. Since 2002, the theatre has funded Still's residency out of its budget. "The residency takes work on both sides," Still writes, but the payoff is invaluable.

> My relationship with the IRT works for many reasons I can speak to, and just as many reasons that remain a mystery to me. It's partly good fortune and timing….It's partly (largely?) the chemistry of the folks involved, and partly that sense of commitment….But for me, honestly, what keeps me making trips to Indianapolis, what keeps me still excited about the IRT? I believe it has something to do with the fact that I feel profoundly valued there—but always challenged. My work goes through enormous scrutiny—never more than when it's done at the IRT. There is such respect and I feel the commitment—and it only makes me want to dig deeper, take more chances, have harder conversations….All that is like having a secret weapon. It gives me more courage.

Even though his primary residence is 2,000 miles to the west, Still has achieved a remarkable connection to an institution and a community. Allen is quoted as saying, "Part of the value of the playwright-in-residence idea is that for our audiences, theatre is not just Shakespeare and Molière, but it's this guy, who you could run into at the grocery store." Pfeffinger observes that the author has become a "known quantity among Indianapolis theatregoers….[He] is not just a playwright here—he's also a brand." His long-term, multifaceted, if intermittent presence at the theatre solidifies this relationship. "I have a great interest in how a community interacts with a theatre," Still told *American Theatre*. "That's hard to do as a freelance artist….I really wanted to believe it was possible to work in a community where it didn't matter what my play was about, that people would come just because I was their playwright-in-residence." It took about five years, according to Allen, but that's exactly what happened.

IT TAKES A VILLAGE: SAN FRANCISCO

Sometimes it takes a village—or at least a region—to make a playwright a home. In the Bay Area, a fertile collegiality has created a rare instance of widespread support for writers Liz Duffy Adams and Adam Bock. According to Theatre Bay Area's executive director Brad Erickson, it took a number of theatres saying, "'We're not going to be able to do this show but you might be interested,' and passing things along. This seemed to be rare nationally and really common here."

Adams, a New York–based playwright, has been the beneficiary of this communal generosity more than once. As Kent Nicholson, who was running a small Bay Area theatre until recently, explains, "Liz got involved with multiple people at multiple times in the same city. We found ourselves sharing resources on a regular basis. As a result, she became the 'it' playwright in San Francisco for a year, because everybody was doing her work. It was really terrific for her. She felt wonderfully supported."

To hear Adams tell it is to enter an ever-unfolding pathway through a tangled web of connections ("…and that lead to another production, which is how I met…"). She had no connection to the Bay Area theatre community until her play *Dog Act* was selected for the 2002 Bay Area Playwrights Festival (BAPF), a program of a local laboratory organization, the Playwrights Foundation. A staged reading generated interest from several companies, and Shotgun Players in Berkeley eventually co-produced the play with the Playwrights Foundation in fall 2004. Meanwhile, a series of other opportunities radiated directly from the Festival. Another company, Crowded Fire Theater, was interested in *Dog Act*, but ended up producing Adams's *The Train Play* instead. Next came a Crowded Fire commission. "They had read another play of mine that was in early stages, and they wanted to commission that. I said,

'How about if I write something just for your company of actors? And why don't we actually talk about what you want?' They got very excited. It turned into this really fabulous collaboration."

The play was *One Big Lie*, and the Playwrights Foundation came on board to co-commission and later co-produce the work. "It was a very modest commission, financially," said Adams. "They kept bringing me out [to the West Coast]—it was a long process—to work with the actors, and go away and write, and come back and do a workshop of the first act." After multiple workshops, the play premiered in spring 2005.

Along the way came more activity that Adams links back to the BAPF. *Dog Act* received a second production at the Moxie Theatre in San Diego. The Cutting Ball Theater staged a workshop of Adams's *Wet, or Isabella the Pirate Queen Enters the Horse Latitudes*. More recently, Crowded Fire and the Playwrights Foundation joined forces yet again to co-produce the premiere of Adams's *The Listener*. She summed up the journey as a "rock ripple experience" that went on for five years, and counting.

Even if the dollar amounts and venue sizes were small, this is the kind of support Adams craves, because it involves long-term relationships with theatres. "The consistency was helpful for me, instead of being thrown from arm to arm like a drunken girl at a bachelor party." And, says Adams, it was always about putting the playwright at the center of the generative act. "In other places 'it's a collaborative art form' means 'rewrite it to please us.' Whereas in my experience in the Bay Area it means 'come on in, we're working on this together.' I love that."

Is this journey more than just a happy set of coincidences? Adams thinks so.

> There are a large number of small companies that do new work, and they very consciously link themselves. They pay attention to what's going on and they bounce off each other. Everyone comes to the Bay Area Playwrights Festival, so everybody saw the reading of *Dog Act*. There's a conscious

desire to be a fervent, fertile theatrical community. There
didn't seem to be a sense of territoriality. I've been wondering
whether that exists other places. I haven't quite found it yet.

Across the country, new-play labs and production
theatres are exploring innovative partnerships where different
kinds of organizations each bring something unique to the
table. The Playwrights Foundation's decision to team up with
producing organizations was one such partnership. Artistic
Director Amy Mueller explains, "We started thinking about
how we could foster productions on the West Coast, and
especially help smaller theatres produce a new play in a way
that made sense for the playwright: the playwright being there,
the playwright being in rehearsal, having a place to stay, having
some employment while they were here." With *Dog Act*, the
Foundation contributed elements it was well suited to deliver,
and which complemented, rather than duplicated, what Shotgun
offered. This included dramaturgical support, and more. "We
provided the playwright with housing and travel, and we gave
[Adams] employment at the New Play Institute where she
taught classes. So she was able to take time off work to be in the
city for six weeks and work on the play." Adams concurs that
support helped make her participation in the rehearsal period
economically feasible.

Playwright Adam Bock's case is somewhat different. For
one thing, he actually resided in San Francisco in the late 1990s,
for five years after completing graduate school at Brown. He
selected the Bay Area for very specific reasons. "I knew that at
some point I would be in New York or L.A., but I thought it
would be smarter for me to go to a mid-sized market. It was
a business-artistic decision. I needed a bigger theatre city than
Providence, but not as big a city as Chicago or New York, where
I thought I would get lost."

To illustrate the interconnectedness of Bay Area theatres,
Bock points out that his first production there was *Swimming*

in the Shallows, staged by Shotgun Players in the basement of Theatre Rhinoceros. It was directed by Kent Nicholson, who was then the literary manager at the Magic Theatre. In short order, he was embraced by multiple institutions in the community. "When I got to San Francisco, theatres started passing me around." Encore Theatre Company produced several of his works; he had workshops and readings at TheatreWorks in Palo Alto and at the Magic Theatre in San Francisco; and he taught at the Z Space Studio. Eventually he became an artistic associate at Berkeley's Shotgun Players and a playwright-in-residence at Encore. "People weren't jealous of your affiliations at all," he says. Bock had long since moved to New York, but his Bay Area relationships persist. Most recently, Shotgun and Encore co-produced his play *The Shaker Chair*, two years after its Humana Festival premiere at the Actors Theatre of Louisville.

These enduring relationships mean that Bock has a home for his work even though he no longer lives within the community. Lisa Steindler, Encore's artistic director, speaks of her history with Bock.

> After *Five Flights* I sat down and said, "This is your home. I will produce the next 20 plays of yours if you want me to." I've done four or five. Some have been more successful than others. But he knows he has a home with me, and whether it's a first production or a third or fourth production, I'm committed to him as a playwright for the rest of my career.

Bock, who is now being produced with increasing frequency by Off-Broadway companies, finds that support very important to him. "In New York you sometimes get the sense that you have to write to the theatres, that you have to sell them on a piece, rather than sell them on the writer. I really feel that Lisa, or Patrick [Dooley of Shotgun Players], if I went to them and said, 'I really want to do this,' they would more often than not take a chance on me." Small, nimble, and willing to roll the dice on him, these theatres provide havens for plays he does not want to open cold in New York, as well as for plays that need crucial second and third productions after their New York premieres.

Other writers too have made artistic homes in this community, notably Philip Kan Gotanda. "He has traversed all aspects of the Bay Area," says Nicholson. "Some plays that he writes are appropriate for the larger regionals, and some could only be done in a seventy-five-seat house. He's a Western playwright. He's done a lot here, relatively speaking, but he's almost never done on the East Coast."

Across the country, theatres join forces to produce new work, support the ongoing life of new plays, and share skills and resources in innovative, flexible ways. The Bay Area offers two examples, both funder-driven, arising out of conversations between theatre leaders about how to confront common challenges. Interestingly, the Bay Area's collegiality in support of playwrights extends to institutional and funding initiatives as well.

Northern California's Irvine Foundation funds a **New Works Initiative,** an inter-institutional collaboration that disseminates funds to commission and help develop and produce new works at Bay Area theatres and colleges. It provides a means by which mid-sized organizations, individually or in pairs, spread the resources down to smaller companies. A local artistic director explained that in addition to creating new work, the goal is to "foster a strengthened institutional sensibility and an institutional culture of sharing resources and sharing best practices so that we can learn from one another."

Similarly, the **Western Presenters Commissioning Initiative,** also funded by Irvine, involves ten to twelve companies that pool together their resources to commission new work. "If we commission a piece, our hope is to get that piece out to the ten different theatre companies. In that way, we get rid of 'premiere-itis,' and there is life after the first production. We're being supported by big foundations, and it's the only way we can do this. Without that support, the money's just not there."

The Journey a Play Makes

When it comes to moving a play toward production and ensuring its ongoing life, what is "success"? The unique trajectory of August Wilson's *Century Cycle* which we discuss in Chapter IV is never far from mind. Playwrights and artistic directors alike view it as a model for institutional collaboration, for giving plays the life they need before facing the New York critics. Sarah Ruhl's *The Clean House* is a more recent example, a play whose successful journey through numerous regional stages culminated in a major Off-Broadway production (at Lincoln Center Theater), but was not dependent on New York to give it life. Some question whether that journey would have happened without an out-of-town rave from the *New York Times*. Nevertheless *The Clean House* is the most commonly cited example we've heard of a play moving easily through the field, avoiding the "one and done" fate that befalls so many other works.

We heard several examples of successful journeys new plays have taken; we expect that there are many more we didn't hear. Two of these, described below, are representative of the fresh and collaborative thinking that spurs these plays along. In Los Angeles, collegiality between theatres of different size and mission helped *Taking Flight*, a one-woman show written and performed by Adriana Sevan, soar. Initially developed at Center Theatre Group's Latino Theatre Initiative, South Coast Repertory included the piece in its Pacific Playwrights Festival. Sevan subsequently brought the work to a Sundance retreat for further development. CTG produced it at the Kirk Douglas Theatre in Culver City as part of a solo performance festival, and, then, San Diego Rep mounted a full production. Eventually, L.A. Theatre Works presented several performances, which were taped and are now available for sale on an audio CD. The entire journey took about three years, and was made possible by the mutual excitement and cooperative push of these theatres' leaders.

In the Continuum by Danai Gurira and Nikkole Salter, a two-person show that began in the South Bronx, was developed

Off Broadway by Primary Stages and originally produced there on nights when its theatre was dark. These off-night performances helped generate word of mouth and, eventually, favorable press. Work on the play happened free from the pressure to sell tickets that accompanies mainstage productions. Primary Stages spread the word to other nonprofits and produced a national tour among like-minded theatres—beginning with Woolly Mammoth Theatre Company in Washington, D.C.—and, ultimately, overseas.

CALCULATING THE COST OF GOING COMMERCIAL, A CASE IN POINT

A playwright and her agent successfully shepherd a new play through a series of regional productions to an Off-Broadway premiere. They make a series of shrewd decisions to feed the life of the piece, turning down offers from Broadway producers, choosing to let the play be produced around the country before bringing it to New York. In this way they maximize the writer's income and solidify her ownership stake in the play. The play goes on to have a robust post–New York life, and continues to be produced with frequency. We heard the story of this successful, sustained journey many times—by an artistic director, a commercial producer, a literary manager, an agent, and, ultimately, by the playwright herself.

The facts: *The Beard of Avon*, a farce by Amy Freed, turns the "who-wrote-Shakespeare" debate on its head. South Coast Repertory in Coast Mesa, California, commissions the play and presents a staged reading in its 2000 Pacific Playwrights Festival. Several regional theatres immediately express interest. South Coast premieres the comedy the following year, productions at other major resident companies follow, and commercial producers begin to circle. By the time *The Beard of Avon* hits New York, though, a half-dozen high-profile theatres have staged the work. New York Theatre Workshop mounts an Off-Broadway production in November 2003. The reviews are positive, and the possibility of a Broadway transfer still looms and with it the possibility of a comfortable run, as happened for David Auburn's *Proof* and John Patrick Shanley's *Doubt*. Also: a reasonable shot a nabbing a Tony Award nomination for Best Play.

But questions loom, too. "How much [is a playwright] prepared to give away of their play in order to go after something Tony-eligible?" asks SCR's artistic director David Emmes. An early commercial move would have meant surrendering 40 percent of the author's subsidiary rights—a standard figure in Broadway contracts—to the commercial producers (the commissioning theatre would also retain a small percentage of the subsidiary rights). In other words, the playwright would have to give up nearly half of her income from subsequent stagings. Productions at the regional theatres that were interested in producing the play would have to be put on hold until the New York scenario played itself out. Of course, if the play is a hit, it will presumably generate enough future income to make this choice worthwhile.

By the time *Beard* opens in New York, though, commercial interest has waned, Freed says, in part because of cast size and the lack of a star. "As a sheer exercise in accounting, the show could not have recouped in a long Off-Broadway run with that size cast [eleven actors]. It would have to have gone to an 800-seat [Broadway] house to have made its money back, and run for a year and a half at over 80 percent capacity."

And then there are subsidiary rights calculations. "One of the arguments that the potential backers made," Freed explains, "was that they weren't that interested because too much of the sub rights had already been sucked out of the show by the regions." In other words, if *Beard of Avon* had gone straight to New York from South Coast, it would have been a more attractive property for the commercial producers. But the six out-of-town productions, essential to the development of the play, cut down the potential for profit. Without those regional productions the piece might not have been ready for New York. Says Freed, "That's kind of a catch-22, isn't it?"

The calculus is if the play goes to New York first, the chance is that it will be critically destroyed and not have an earning potential ever again in its life. So you're rolling the dice when you do that. In the equation is the argument that if the play becomes anointed in New York, it will have a life that it would have never had.

Size was another key factor in the life story of this play. With a cast of eleven, numerous locations, and lots of period costumes to build or rent, *Beard of Avon* is considered big by today's diminished reckoning—"huge," one artistic director labels it. Size was an obstacle "every step of the way," says Freed, who acknowledges that economics of a commercial transfer might well have been feasible if the cast were five or six.

Still, company after company found a way to produce what Emmes called a "relatively large play in terms of scope and ideas." Without successes like these, he said, more and more writers will gravitate toward television, never to return. The lesson to be drawn, he says, is that the community must come together to create "an incentive to want to write a play that has a big canvas, lots of characters, [and is] not concerned with being commercial."

Though Freed jokes that she would have sold her little brother for a chance to be produced on Broadway, she says she has no regrets about how the *Beard of Avon* scenario played out. For one thing, the commercial producers wanted to recast the lead role with a marquee name, but she didn't have the stomach or disposition to fire her leading man.

> I had one actor who had premiered the show with me in its first reading, performed at South Coast, reprised his role at the Goodman, and opened the show beautifully in New York. Actors like that were deeply part of the fabric not just of the show, but of its success Off Broadway. I don't think I could stand creating a show whose success is dependent on a group of people, and at that point having to replace those people.

Part of what situates this story squarely in the success column is that Freed has been able to realize a reasonable income from the piece. "Yes, the play did make me money," she confirms. "You can make six figures on a play in six [major regional] productions." As we've seen, though, the *Beard of Avon* is the exception.

The play's two-year odyssey from Costa Mesa to New York had its risks, both economic and artistic. "The difficulty was that I had to be present with that play for every major production before New York," Freed says. "I had great ambitions for the play. I very much wanted to see it open successfully in New York. When you have a play opening at the Goodman in Chicago or ACT in San Francisco, or at the Seattle Rep, as any playwright knows, you can't just turn your back on a new show and hope that it will come out all right." There was, says Freed, the worrisome possibility that a *New York Times* review would appear too soon, before the play was finished. A bad out-of-town review and the journey could have ended right there. Traveling around the country with the play had a cost. "There was an enormous disruption of my life, my teaching income, my ability to write another play. It was a lot of work, and I don't know how I could do that with every play I write."

In fact, Freed continued reordering and combining scenes, cutting and shaping material, right up until opening night Off Broadway.

> I learned from each new audience and each city's venue. By
> the time the play got to New York…I knew how it worked,
> I knew where its trouble [spots] were. I had a certain amount
> of deep confidence in its ability to communicate. I'm not sure
> the play would have opened successfully with no production
> history to refine, to learn itself, to grow. It could have been
> killed in the crib. Not because the critics were mean, but
> because the play was green.

Still, the opportunity to work in all these cities was "tremendously broadening," Freed admits. She saw "what the country has to offer in terms of acting and directing talent, and what the audiences' temperaments are from city to city." Freed adds, "I am still working with people that I met in that trip with that play."

Combating "Premiere-itis": The National New Play Network

I've had a great experience working with the National New Play Network theatres. What makes them so effective is that it's artistic directors talking to artistic directors, not a literary manager passing something on. It's the decision-makers coming together. Their mission specifically is about second productions. That's why they came together, to try and help new plays have a further life. —PLAYWRIGHT

The National New Play Network is one of the most promising forces to counter premiere-itis and to support the development of new plays through multiple productions. Founded in 1999, NNPN currently includes twenty-six-member theatres across the United States, mostly small to mid-sized institutions.*

....

* Current NNPN member theatres are: Actor's Express Theater (Atlanta); Actor's Theatre of Charlotte (North Carolina); Borderlands Theater (Tucson, AZ); Curious Theatre Company (Denver, CO); Florida Stage (Manalapan); Florida Studio Theatre (Sarasota); The Fountain Theatre (Los Angeles); Horizon Theatre Company (Atlanta); Interact Theatre Company (Philadelphia); Kitchen Dog Theater (Dallas); Magic Theatre (San Francisco); Marin Theatre Company (CA); Mixed Blood Theatre (Minneapolis); New Jersey Repertory Company (Long Branch); New Repertory Theatre (Watertown, MA); New Theatre (Coral Gables, FL); Orlando Shakespeare Theatre (FL); Performance Network Theatre (Ann Arbor, MI); Phoenix Theatre (Indianapolis, IN); Playwrights Theatre of New Jersey (Madison, NJ); Prop Thtr (Chicago); The Salt Lake Acting Company (UT); Southern Rep (New Orleans); Unicorn Theatre (Kansas City, MO); Victory Gardens Theater (Chicago); Woolly Mammoth Theatre Company (Washington, D.C.)

Among its programs, NNPN has pioneered the concept of the "rolling world premiere." Through its cooperative Continued Life of New Plays Fund, the Network helps fund three (or more) companies, each of which mounts a separate production of the same work. The playwright commits to being present at every Fund production, while the theatres share the right to call each production a "National New Play Network World Premiere."

This program is also designed to help the theatre community wean itself from a New York–down approach to circulating new plays throughout the country. "It's a very different way of thinking," Seth Rozin of Philadelphia's InterAct Theatre Company, one of the Network's founders, told us. "It's not that one big *New York Times* review and then you're set. The plays that we've done through this program have had anywhere from just three to sixteen or seventeen productions, without ever getting to New York."

This bold model for new-play production holds out a cure for the possessiveness premieres inspire; it re-draws a truly regional map, without reliance on New York's imprimatur; and it exemplifies institutional collaboration. It assumes the value of collective support for new-play production. Under the Fund, individual Network theatres receive a $5,000 grant to support the production. The dollar amount is not huge, but it represents a dollars-and-cents commitment to the program and institutionalizes the best kind of developmental process: That is, one leading to production.

The Continued Life of New Plays Fund also guarantees momentum by undercutting the power of critics over the life of a play. No matter what happens to the first production critically, it still has a certain life, as well as a chance to garner better reviews elsewhere. Most crucial, the play has a chance to evolve artistically, because the playwright can refine it at each successive theatre, until s/he decides it's done. Certainly, the rewards are artistic ones: the chance to see and hear the play enough—with different directors, designers, actors, and audiences—to get it right. Rewards can be financial as well; playwrights have earned as much as $100,000 from multiple NNPN productions of a single play, though they commonly earn much less. Thomas Gibbons's *Permanent Collection*, the Fund's pilot project in 2003, began its life with five NNPN "premieres" and was subsequently produced by at least twenty-two American theatres and two international ones—all without a New York production or *Times* review.

The Network has hitherto been limited to the regions. "We don't have a member in New York," Rozin explains. "Most New York theatres want to reserve the possibility of a commercial run, and they want to buy up the option of something. They want it to start in New York and go everywhere and make money, but that's not realistic for most plays." Once a play is established in the national repertoire, though, the hazards associated with New York production are diminished. "We would like to think that some of these plays would end up in New York, and at that point there's no risk if it gets killed by the *New York Times*," Rozin muses.

Within this extensive network of like-minded, if artistically varied, theatres, a great deal of script sharing occurs. Playwrights whose work has been produced under various NNPN programs speak encouragingly of them. Playwright John Walch had a play that ended up in the Network's Script Exchange, another program. "I got five other productions because all these people that were producing saw it." This happened without him having to sell his work; the system did that for him.

For all this groundbreaking, the Network remains invisible to some of the theatre community. Some prominent artistic directors, and at least one of the country's most powerful playwright agents, had never heard of the group. Rozin admits that "some agents have been pretty cool to it, for obvious reasons. They're always holding out for New York." Others, he reports, are more enthusiastic. In fact, one agent interviewed in the study considers NNPN one of the more visionary developments of recent years—"a depth charge."

Audience Education 101

Of all the challenges facing playwrights and new-play theatres, none appear as inexorable as the loss of connection with audiences. For this reason, innovative programs for engaging and educating theatregoers spark notice. Steppenwolf Theatre Company's First Look program is widely seen as a breakthrough.

The program takes place each summer in tandem with First Look Rep, a play development process that culminates in limited-run full productions of three new plays staged in rotating repertory. The audience-education component, First Look 101, invites theatregoers into the artistic process at key moments that usually take place far from public view. Participants attend first read-throughs and various rehearsals. They sit in on design presentations, technical rehearsals, and production meetings. They meet regularly as a group to talk about what they are seeing.

For Steppenwolf's director of new-play development, Ed Sobel, the two defining terms behind First Look 101 are "access" and "transparency." The program's goal, says Sobel, is to "create a group of people who have a strong understanding of the context of what we're doing, of why we make certain choices, of what the ingredients are, of what the investment is on the part of Steppenwolf in terms of creating new work." Participants' fly-on-the-wall status gives them both a sense of ownership of the work, and also a deeper education into the process of making new plays.

In the words of the Arena Stage's David Dower, First Look 101 succeeds because it invests the audience in the venture of new-play production, and underscores the role of the new play in the health of an institution. Participants then become ambassadors for the theatre. "They really are inspired by new work and what it takes to create new work—Not re-writing anybody's play, or thumbs up or thumbs down. All the conversations are about process."

In its first year (2005), the theatre signed up thirty "101ers," most of whom were donors and board members who had expressed interest in new work. The program was so successful that each year since, Steppenwolf has opened it to include more participants—101 per summer, to be exact.

First Look Rep came about as a direct response to critiques of play development programs that end in workshops and staged readings, casting them as dead-end exercises. "Steppenwolf's operating philosophy is that you don't really fully develop a play until it's in production," says Sobel. Under this initiative, the theatre selects three new plays for development each summer, ultimately producing them in rep, for nine performances each. They receive limited but full design support. Most of the First Look Rep plays have gone on to receive world premiere productions at other theatres. "We don't claim the world premieres for those plays," says Sobel.

Neither the Rep, nor First Look 101 takes place in a vacuum at Steppenwolf. "It's been on the vanguard for us, but it's all happening in the context of a strong institutional force to increase this kind of transparency and access," Sobel says. He cites the theatre's tradition of post-show discussions after every single performance; as well as a blog on which there are fresh postings two or three times a week from artists involved in a project.

Although the initial participant group was largely made up of donors to the theatre, Steppenwolf's Sobel asserts that First Look 101 is not intended as a fundraising mechanism, at least not in a direct way. "Of course we're hoping that as people become more invested in Steppenwolf because of the program, that they're going to be more inclined to support us," he says. "But that support can be financial, or there can be other ways that support manifests itself," like creating a sense of ownership for the theatre in the community at large. The $75 fee per participant (including tickets to three shows) does not cover the program's expenses, which are absorbed by Steppenwolf's general budget.

This new dynamic must be negotiated carefully. The

needs of the audience must be balanced with those of the artist. "We try to make sure that the needs of people to have access to the artists are being met, but also to respect the need for a safe environment, and the need for artists to be able to take risks," Sobel says. "We don't alter what we are doing because of the presence of those people. If a director and playwright are working on five pages of a play for two hours during the open rehearsal day, that's what that group of people sees." And while participants are encouraged to speak about their responses to what they experience, the artists are in no way obligated to hear their specific feedback. Furthermore, transparency about the process extends not just to audiences, but also to the artists involved. "When we select the artists, they are fully informed of what the program involves, and the degree of transparency required. I have not had anyone say, 'I don't want to participate.'"

"What's been interesting is that the 101ers have actually served an artistic purpose in a way that I didn't anticipate," says Sobel.

> It is very easy in an intense development process, for the work to turn and look very inward, and what the 101ers have helped provide is a constant reminder that this work has to go outward, that at some point this play is going to be performed. So the conversation around the development of the work does consider how this is being communicated to an audience. What is it that we are trying to communicate? Those kinds of questions are being brought to mind more frequently than they might be without the 101ers present.

In many ways this program signals a re-thinking of the conventional relationship between theatres and their audiences, says Sobel. "We are moving away from a transactional model into deeper engagement." He makes an analogy to the visual arts: "You can go to an art museum, and if you have no background at all in art history and the visual arts, you can still appreciate what you're seeing. But if you have had an art history course or a drawing class, that gives you an added depth of experience and a deeper level of engagement with what you are seeing, and provides for a richer experience."

———————

THE HISTORY of theatre is marked by adaptation. The present moment, as the list above shows, is no exception. The seemingly boundless activity of new-play writing, development, and production can't be denied. Nor can the very real divisions between playwright and institution, the impossible economics of playwriting, the obstacles to production and access, the competitive emphasis on premieres that too-often stops plays in their tracks, the diminished expectations for new work, or the dwindling of our audiences. These are all real—the vitality of the scene and its palpable conflicts.

The examples listed above represent openings, cracks in what has hardened, movement where things have become stuck. After several years of study, and hundreds of hours of listening to the field, we have become aware of powerful commonalities that run through even the smallest ideas and innovations. Our intention is description, not prescription. The following list, too, is a description—of common threads among these examples. These practices share principles, many of which are so basic to the theatre as to seem self-evident, even cliché. Still, they run through the examples above and many others we've heard. So here they are.

The things that are currently working well for new plays, production, and playwrights

- stress the depth and duration of relationship—between artists and institutions;
- favor communication that is clear and authentic; explore the potential of resource sharing and collaboration, organizational cooperation and, even, institutional humility;

- stay flexible, suiting the process to the project;
- alter scale—little theatres dream big and large ones progress intimately—and redraw maps;
- re-think assumptions about how money is made, paid and granted (e.g., that Broadway is the only way to make big money, that sub rights are a "right," that writers make their living from royalties, etc.);
- bring audiences into the work early (and often), giving them better tools to appreciate new plays, while keeping artistic development distinct from audience development;
- acknowledge that context alters perception, that playwrights and artistic directors, funders and audiences look at the same picture and see very different things;
- admit, and, wherever possible, *embrace* risk, ambition, the untried.

This study sets out to take a snapshot of the field of new-play production. It aims at opening doors for playwrights and paths for plays, to bring new ideas, new talent, and new voices into the stream of American theatre production. But even as we've tried to capture the field as it is, the picture has changed. What felt like an end in itself—a comprehensive view of the field of new-play production and the lives and livelihoods of playwrights—now feels like a tentative beginning: the start of a conversation.

Study Participants: Playwrights

Liz Duffy Adams
David Adjmi
Keith Josef Adkins
Edward Albee
Luis Alfaro
Janet Allard
Laura Axelrod
Jenny Lyn Bader
Trista Baldwin
Andrew Barrett
Frank Basloe
Mike Batistick
Joan Beber
Hilary Bell
Glen Berger
Alan Berks
Brooke Berman
Susan Bernfield
Greg Beuthin
Lee Blessing
Adam Bock
Eric Bogosian
Timothy Braun
Deborah Brevoort
Hindi Brooks

Mary Burkin
Sheila Callaghan
Bridget Carpenter
Lonnie Carter
Jonathan Ceniceroz
Julia Cho
Eric Coble
Constance Congdon
Kara Lee Corthron
Kia Corthron
Jeannine Coulombe
Aida Croal
Migdalia Cruz
Alexandra Cunningham
Gordon Dahlquist
Lisa D'Amour
Lucia Del Vecchio
Kristoffer Diaz
Steven Dietz
Tom Donaghy
Noelle Donfeld
Steven Drukman
Tom Dudzick
Jillian Dykhouse
Erik Ehn

Dennis Escobedo
Christine Evans
Joann Farias
Joe Feinstein
Kitty Felde
Michael D. Fels
Robert Fieldsteel
Catherine Filloux
Kenneth Finkle
Hugh Fitzgerald
Ron Fitzgerald
Stephanie Fleischmann
Mike Folie
Richard Foreman
Sam Forman
Amy Fox
Hikaru Freeman
Tanis Galik
Michael John Garcés
Anne Garcia-Romero
Marcus Gardley
Greg Gasawski
Stephan Gaydos
Michael Geither
Madeleine George
Alexandra Gersten-Vassilaros
Thomas Gibbons
Graeme Gillis
Marie Giorda
Keith Glover
Sandi Goff
Megan Gogerty
Jorge Gonzalez
José Cruz González
Idris Goodwin
Kirsten Greenidge

David Greenspan
David Valdes Greenwood
David Grimm
Garret Jon Groenveld
Rinne Groff
John Guare
Jessica Hagedorn
Christina Ham
Sarah Hammond
Wendy Hammond
Ken Hanes
Chris Hare
Karen Hartman
Julie Hébert
Mark Hein
Jules Hil
Rachel Hoeffel
Michael Hollinger
Ron Holsey
J. Holtham
Olga Humphrey
George Hunka
Arlene Hutton
David Henry Hwang
Yehuda Hyman
Julie Jensen
Susan Johnston
Mrinalini Kamath
Michael Kassin
Victor Kaufold
Jeremy Kehoe
Elizabeth Keiser
Nambi Kelley
Robert Kerr
Chip Keyes
Stanton Korey

Carson Kreitzer
Lisa Kron
Larry Kunofsky
Sunil Kuruvilla
Deborah Zoe Laufer
Kristen Lazarian
Diane Lefer
Tracy Letts
Mark Harvey Levine
EM Lewis
David Lindsay-Abaire
Victor Lodato
Larry Loebell
Craig Lucas
Stacey Luftig
Kirk Lynn
Jim MacNerland
Jennifer Maisel
Barry A. Manhcimer
Ruth Margraff
Donald Margulies
Mia McCullough
Marlane Meyer
Frances Mizrahi
Allison Moore
Steve Moore
Alejandro Morales
John Morogiello
Gregg Mozgala
Julie Marie Myatt
Peter Sin Nachtrieb
Nancy Nevarez
Qui Nguyen
Lynn Nottage
Dominic Orlando
Sally Oswald

OyamO
Jaime Pachino
A. Rey Pamatmat
Nathan Parker
Maggie Patton
Catherine Pelonero
Christopher Piehler
Christina Pippa
Larry Pontius
J. Paul Porter
Spence Porter
Kathleen Potts
Robert Earl Price
Jerry Quickley
David Rambo
Jack Raymond
Jay Reiss
Daniel Reitz
Jonathan Reynolds
Elizabeth Scales Rheinfrank
Kate Robin
J. T. Rogers
Elaine Romero
Sarah Ruhl
Edwin Sánchez
Said Sayrafiezadeh
Laura Schellhardt
Lisa Schlesinger
Phillip Egan Schmiedl
Sarah Schulman
Buffy Sedlachek
Betty Shamieh
Julian Sheppard
Art Shulman
Mat Smart
Tommy Smith

Adam Sobsey
Bernardo Solano
Octavio Solis
Diana Son
Lois Spangler
Rosanna Staffa
Jennie Staniloff-Redling
Deborah Isobel Stein
Linda Felton Steinbaum
Victoria Stewart
Kelly Stuart
Valerie Stulman
Lloyd Suh
Gary Sunshine
Caridad Svich
Matthew Swan
C. Denby Swanson
Staci Swedeen
Jeffrey Sweet
Adam Szymkowicz
Jeff Teitler
Eugenie Trow
Brian Tucker

Enrique Urueta
Karen Smith Vastola
Paula Vogel
Francine Volpe
Stacie Vourakis
Kathryn Walat
John Walch
Malachy Walsh
Lucy Wang
Anne Washburn
Jennie Webb
Annie Weisman
Mac Wellman
Barbara Wiechmann
David Wiener
Elyzabth Gregory Wilder
Sheri Wilner
Lee Wochner
Marc Wolf
Karen Zacarias
Nancy Zaman
Jenna Zark
David Zellnik

Study Participants: Theatres

7 Stages
About Face Theatre
Academy Theatre
ACT Theater
Act II Playhouse
Actors' Gang Theatre
American Theater Company
Arena Stage
Arizona Jewish Theatre Company
Arkansas Repertory Theatre
Aspen Theatre in the Park
Atlantic Theater Company
Bay Street Theatre
Boarshead Theater
Book-It Repertory Theatre
Bristol Riverside Theatre
B Street Theatre
Center Theatre Group/Mark Taper Forum and Ahmanson Theatre
Childsplay
Cincinnati Playhouse in the Park
Detroit Repertory Theatre
Ensemble Theatre
Florida Repertory Theatre
George Street Playhouse
Goodman Theatre
Guthrie Theater
Hartford Stage Company

Hippodrome State Theatre
Horse Cave Theatre
Illusion Theater
INTAR Hispanic American Arts Center
Intiman Theatre
La Jolla Playhouse
Lincoln Center Theater
Long Wharf Theatre
Lookingglass Theatre Co.
Mabou Mines
Magic Theatre, Inc.
Manhattan Theatre Club
Maryland Ensemble Theatre
McCarter Theatre
Melting Pot Theatre Co.
Metro Theater Co.
Milwaukee Repertory Theater
Miracle Theatre Group
Mum Puppet Theatre
Nautilus Music-Theater
Nebraska Theatre Caravan
New Dramatists
New Freedom Theatre
New Georges
New Jersey Repertory Company
New York State Theatre Institute
New York Theatre Workshop
Northlight Theatre
Open Stage of Harrisburg
Orlando-UCF Shakespeare Festival
Penumbra Theatre Company
Pittsburgh Irish & Classical Theatre
Pittsburgh Public Theater
Playwrights Horizons
Plowshares Theatre Company
Primary Stages

Roadside Theater
Roadworks Productions
Round House Theatre
Seattle Children's Theatre
Seattle Repertory Theatre
Seven Angels Theatre
Signature Theatre
Signature Theatre Company
South Coast Repertory
Stages Theatre Co.
Ten Thousand Things
The Acting Company
The Children's Theatre Company
The Cleveland Play House
The Dell'Arte Co.
The Empty Space Theater
The Foothill Theatre Company
The Playwrights' Center
The Puerto Rican Traveling Theatre
The Repertory Theatre of St. Louis
The Súgán Theatre Company
The Theater at Monmouth
Theater J
Theater Mu
Theatre West (Los Angeles)
Tribeca Performing Arts Center
Unicorn Theatre (Kansas City)
Victory Gardens Theater
Vineyard Playhouse
Virginia Stage Company
Weissberger Theater Group

APPENDIX C

Study Participants: Roundtables

(Affiliations listed were current at time of roundtable)

Elissa Adams, The Children's Theatre Company
Liz Duffy Adams, playwright
Doug Aibel, Vineyard Theatre
Luis Alfaro, playwright
Sarah Bellamy, Penumbra Theatre Company
Brooke Berman, playwright
Susan Bernfield, New Georges
Mark Bly, Arena Stage
Chris Burney, Second Stage Theatre
Steve Busa, Red Eye Theater
Polly Carl, The Playwrights' Center
Laurie Carlos, playwright
Bridget Carpenter, playwright
David Catlin, Lookingglass Theatre Company
Anne Cattanco, Lincoln Center Theater
Gordon Dahlquist, playwright
Lisa D'Amour, playwright
Gordon Edelstein, Long Wharf Theatre
Erik Ehn, playwright
David Emmes, South Coast Repertory
Brad Erickson, Theatre Bay Area
Paige Evans, Manhattan Theatre Club
Shirley Fishman, La Jolla Playhouse

Michael John Garcés, Cornerstone Theater Company
Marcus Gardley, playwright
José Cruz González, playwright
Jessica Hagedorn, playwright
Rob Handel, 13 P (Thirteen Playwrights, Inc.)
Karen Hartman, playwright
Michelle Hensley, Ten Thousand Things
Philip Himberg, Sundance Institute Theatre Program
Tina Howe, playwriting program, Hunter College
David Henry Hwang, playwright
Yehuda Hyman, playwright
Susan Johnston, playwright
B. J. Jones, Northlight Theatre
Celise Kalke, Alliance Theatre
Damon Kiely, American Theater Company
Jennifer Kiger, Yale Repertory Theatre
Ben Krywosz, Nautilus Music-Theater
Andrew Leynse, Primary Stages
Jeff Liu, East-West Players (and Lodestone Theatre Ensemble)
Jason Loewith, Next Theatre Company
Quincy Long, playwright
Craig Lucas, playwright
Eduardo Machado, playwriting program, Columbia University;
    INTAR Theatre
Emily Mann, McCarter Theatre Center
Kristin Marting, HERE Arts Center
Allison Moore, playwright
Emily Morse, New Dramatists
Amy Mueller, Playwrights Foundation
Julie Marie Myatt, playwright
Timothy Near, San Jose Repertory Theatre
Kent Nicholson, TheatreWorks
Tanya Palmer, The Goodman Theatre
Christian Parker, Atlantic Theater Company
Jerry Patch, The Old Globe
Michael Robins, Illusion Theater & School

Diane Rodriguez, Center Theatre Group
Seth Rozin, InterAct Theatre Company
Tim Sanford, Playwrights Horizons
Buffy Sedlachek, playwright
Howard Shalwitz, Woolly Mammoth Theatre
Chris Smith, Magic Theatre
Ed Sobel, Steppenwolf Theatre Company
Rosanna Staffa, playwright
Deborah Stein, playwright
Lisa Steindler, The Z Space Studio
Maria Striar, Clubbed Thumb
Lloyd Suh, playwright
Caridad Svich, playwright
Adam Szymkowicz, playwright
Russ Tutterow, Chicago Dramatists
John Walch, playwright
Lucy Wang, playwright
Anne Washburn, playwright
Les Waters, Berkeley Repertory Theatre
Amy Wegener, Guthrie Theater
Mac Wellman, playwriting program, Brooklyn College
Sheri Wilner, playwright
Sam Woodhouse, San Diego Repertory Theatre
Rhiana Yazzie, playwright
Chay Yew, playwright
Dennis Zacek, Victory Gardens Theater

Individuals here may have more than one affiliation (e.g., institutional affiliation and playwright). We have listed individuals in the context of the roundtable in which they participated.

Study Participants: Individuals Interviewed

(Affiliations listed were current at the time of the interviews.)

Adam Bock, playwright
John Breglio, Paul, Weiss, Rifkind, Wharton, and Garrison Law Firm
John Buzzetti, The Gersh Agency
David Dower, The Z Space Studio
John Clinton Eisner, Lark Play Development Center
Oskar Eustis, The Public Theater
Peter Franklin, William Morris Agency
Amy Freed, playwright
Morgan Jenness, Abrams Artists Agency
George Lane, Creative Artists Agency
Marc Masterson, Actors Theatre of Louisville
Elizabeth I. McCann, producer
Marsha Norman, playwright
Bill Rauch, Oregon Shakespeare Festival
Molly Smith, Arena Stage
Stuart Thompson, producer
John Weidman, playwright (President, Dramatists Guild of America)

About the Authors

TODD LONDON is in his fourteenth season as the artistic director of New Dramatists, the nation's oldest center for the support and development of playwrights, where he has worked closely with more than a hundred of America's finest playwrights, and advocated nationally and internationally for hundreds more. In 2009, he was the first recipient of Theatre Communications Group's Visionary Leadership Award "for his work to advance the theatre field." A former managing editor of *American Theatre* magazine and the author of *The Artistic Home*, he has written, edited, and/or contributed to eleven books. London won the George Jean Nathan Award for Dramatic Criticism for his essays in *American Theatre*, and a Milestone Award for his first novel, *The World's Room*. Under his leadership, New Dramatists received both a special Tony Honor and the Ross Wetzsteon Award from the Village Voice Obies. He currently serves on the faculty of Yale University School of Drama.

BEN PESNER has been writing about the theatre since 1987. Currently the manager of creative services at The Broadway League, he is also content producer of TonyAwards.com. For the Tonys, he has scripted numerous special events, and edited the *Tony Awards Songbook*. A former editor of the *Dramatists Guild Quarterly*, and literary manager of Young Playwrights Inc., his extensive involvement in the not-for-profit theatre community has included associations with Playwrights Horizons, New York Theatre Workshop, Circle Rep, and Lincoln Center Theater, among others. He has authored and edited numerous publications for theatres, service organizations, and charitable foundations, and has written for *American Theatre*, *Playbill*, and other magazines.

ZANNIE GIRAUD VOSS (Ph.D., IAE, Aix-en-Provence) is Chair and Professor of Arts Administration in the Meadows School of the Arts and the Cox School of Business at Southern Methodist University, and an affiliate professor at Euromed Management in Marseille, France. She also served on the faculty at UNC–Chapel Hill and was Managing Director of PlayMakers Repertory Company; subsequently she was a professor at Duke University, where she was Producing Director of Theater Previews at Duke. Voss is a consultant for Theatre Communications Group, co-authoring their *Theatre Facts* since 1998. She has published articles in numerous marketing journals, and serves on the editorial board of the *International Journal of Arts Management*.